the loyal republic

CIVIL WAR AMERICA

Peter S. Carmichael, Caroline E. Janney, and Aaron Sheehan-Dean, *editors*

This landmark series interprets broadly the history and culture of the Civil War era through the long nineteenth century and beyond. Drawing on diverse approaches and methods, the series publishes historical works that explore all aspects of the war, biographies of leading commanders, and tactical and campaign studies, along with select editions of primary sources. Together, these books shed new light on an era that remains central to our understanding of American and world history.

the loyal republic

TRAITORS, SLAVES, AND
THE REMAKING OF CITIZENSHIP
IN CIVIL WAR AMERICA

Erik Mathisen

The University of North Carolina Press   Chapel Hill

This book was published with the assistance of the Authors Fund of the University of North Carolina Press.

Set in Minion by codeMantra
Manufactured in the United States of America.
The University of North Carolina Press has been a member of the
Green Press Initiative since 2003.

Portions of Chapter 6 appeared previously in Erik Mathisen, "'It Looks Much
Like Abandoned Land': Property and the Politics of Loyalty in Reconstruction
Mississippi," in *After Slavery: Race, Labor, and Citizenship in the Reconstruction
South*, ed. Bruce E. Baker and Brian Kelly (Gainesville: University Press of Florida,
2013), 77–97. Reprinted with permission of the University Press of Florida.

Cover photos: District of Columbia, Company E, 4th U.S. Colored Infantry, at
Fort Lincoln, ca. 1863–66 (Library of Congress Prints and Photographs Division);
Confederate POWs taking an oath of loyalty to the United States at the Rock Island
Prison Barracks, ca. 1865 (Abraham Lincoln Presidential Library & Museum)

Library of Congress Cataloging-in-Publication Data
Names: Mathisen, Erik, author.
Title: The loyal republic : traitors, slaves, and the remaking of citizenship in
Civil War America / by Erik Mathisen.
Other titles: Civil War America (Series)
Description: Chapel Hill : University of North Carolina Press, [2018] |
Series: Civil War America | Includes bibliographical references and index.
Identifiers: LCCN 2017026943 | ISBN 9781469636320 (cloth : alk. paper) |
ISBN 9781469636337 (ebook)
Subjects: LCSH: Citizenship—United States—History—19th century. |
Citizenship—Confederate States of America—History. | United States—
History—Civil War, 1861–1865. | Allegiance. | Nation-state. | Freedmen—
Civil rights—United States—History—19th century.
Classification: LCC JK1759 .M39 2018 | DDC 973.7/1—dc23
LC record available at https://lccn.loc.gov/2017026943

For my parents and Joanna Cohen

contents

illustrations

acknowledgments

It is a humbling thing to put into words my thanks to all those who have helped to put this project between two covers. I have been bucked up, sustained, encouraged, and inspired by so many friends and family who have offered help at every stage. Each page of this book bears the fingerprint of some wise comment or act of kindness, and though a hat tip is a small gesture, it must do, at least for the time being.

I have had the great fortune to have been taught by inspiring scholars. At Northwestern University, Dylan Penningroth pushed me to think in the broadest possible terms about slavery and emancipation. At the University of Pennsylvania, Kathleen Brown, Phoebe Young, Walter Licht, Barbara Savage, Steven Hahn, Kathy Peiss, Daniel Richter, Rogers Smith, and the late Robert Engs all taught me how to ask good questions, seek complex answers, and do both with humility. The dearly departed Sheldon Hackney taught me more about collegiality and the art of the carefully posed question than any other teacher I have ever had the pleasure to know. His gentle words of encouragement still ring in my ears. And though I started this project after I had finished my time at Western University, so much of how I think about the past was shaped by the devoted teaching of Ian K. Steele, Margaret Kellow, and my old friend Craig M. Simpson, whose imprint on me remains indelible.

To begin the project, I benefited from the assistance of a variety of institutions. The University of Pennsylvania gave me the means to do much of the research. A fellowship from the Penn Humanities Forum proved a lifesaver, where Wendy Steiner, Jennifer Conway, Sara Varney, and Gary Tomlinson made me feel incredibly welcome. The Centre for European and International Studies

Research at the University of Portsmouth provided a term's worth of leave to start writing the early chapters and additional funds to finish research in Washington. My thanks to director Tony Chafer for seeing his way clear to scraping the funds together to help when it was sorely needed.

Archivists, librarians, and county court clerks also helped in all kinds of ways to crack open boxes of correspondence and point me in unforeseen directions. At the Mississippi Department of Archives and History, Joyce Dixon-Lawson, Grady Howell, Anne Webster, and Clinton Bagley answered all my questions with patience and grace. Gordon Cotton at the Old County Courthouse in Vicksburg lived up to his status as a gracious host par excellence. Rosie Simmons all but gave me the keys to the archive of the Bolivar County Courthouse, and Jill Abraham persevered through my countless questions at the National Archive in Washington. To all of them I owe my heartfelt thanks.

None of this help would have amounted to much had it not been for a family who took me in when I was knee-deep in Mississippi archives. I had the pleasure to be all but adopted by Ben and Dorothy Puckett, who opened their home to a stranger and made much of this book possible with their incredible kindness and unmatched hospitality. By making a home for me in Mississippi, they made the lonely work of research a joy. My one regret about this book is that I did not finish it in time so that Ben could see it in print. My thanks to him and to Dero, as well as their daughter Carol, who introduced me to the Delta in style.

I tested out most of the ideas in this book at all manner of colloquia, conferences, and seminars. My thanks to participants at Queen Mary University of London, Keele University, the British Association for Nineteenth Century History conference, the University of Portsmouth, the Institute of Historical Research, King's College London, the British Library, the University of Sheffield, the University of Sussex, the University of Cambridge, the British Association for American Studies, Temple University, the McNeil Center for Early American Studies, and the Richards Civil War Era Center at Pennsylvania State University for their interest and all of their advice. A wonderful opportunity to present work as part of the After Slavery Project in Belfast in 2008 led to close readings of my work from a fantastic group of scholars that included Brian Kelly, Bruce Baker, Michael Fitzgerald, Richard Follett, Thomas Holt, Moon-Ho Jung, and Susan O'Donovan. The meeting of the After Slavery working group also led me to Eric Foner, who has since offered the kind of support for a young colleague that more than eclipses his reputation as one of the class acts of the profession.

Doing American history outside the United States comes with its challenges, but it has been my great good fortune to have worked with and learned from so many fantastic British academics. To name them all here would be difficult, but my thanks go to Kendrick Oliver, Daniel Matlin, Patrick Doyle, Max Edling, Lydia Plath, Iwan Morgan, Adam Smith, Emily West, Uta Balbier, Alex Goodall, Martin Crawford, and David Sim, who have all, at one time or another, offered help and intellectual companionship. Though my time at the University of Sussex was brief, Robert Cook, Richard Follett, and Jarod Roll listened to early ideas and steered me clear of potholes. At the University of Portsmouth, Lee Sartain was a true brother-in-arms, and both Ann Matear and Emmanuel Godin helped me in ways only they can say. Finally, I had the pleasure of completing this book as a member of the School of History at Queen Mary University of London, where Miri Rubin, Colin Jones, and Julian Jackson were judicious with my schedule to allow me to complete the manuscript, and where so many colleagues have made my time there a wonderful experience and made this book better too. My thanks particularly to Katrina Forrester, James Ellison, Mark Glancy, Reuben Loffman, Mark White, Daniel Peart, Chris Moffat, and Patrick Higgins. And though they probably didn't realize it, I tried out many of the ideas in this book on captive audiences of students, who took my classes over the years and pushed me to clarify so much of my thinking. My thanks to them for their interest and their passion. They have improved this book, and it has been a joy to learn with them.

It is a real honor that this project found a home with UNC Press, where Mark Simpson-Vos and Lucas Church patiently guided me through every stage of the publication process and made this book better at every point along the way. This book also joins the incredible collection of titles in the Civil War America series and has benefited from the editorial eye of Aaron Sheehan-Dean, who read every chapter with a careful eye and thoughtful encouragement. Stephanie Wenzel edited the manuscript with the utmost skill, and anonymous readers for the press helped me to clarify a lot of my thinking and saved me from several dead ends. Their thoroughness improved every part of this book. Portions of the sixth chapter of this book were drawn from a piece I wrote in *After Slavery: Race, Labor, and Citizenship in the Reconstruction South*, published with the University Press of Florida. My thanks to the press for permission to include some of that chapter here.

At every point, I also learned from the many friends who listened attentively to weird ideas and offered sage advice all the same. Rene Alvarez, Dan Amsterdam, Erin Park Cohn, John Kenney, Clem Harris, Andrew Lipman, Kyle Roberts, Brian Rouleau, Nicole Maurantonio, Eric Taylor, Sarah Van Beurden, Julie Davidow, Will Kuby, Julia Gunn, Nicole Myers Turner, Jack Dwiggins, Adrian O'Connor, Larisa Kopytoff, Justin Behrend, David Sellers Smith, Aaron Astor, and Zara Anishanslin have all contributed to this book in ways large and small. My quasi-roommate in Philadelphia, Sarah Manekin, listened patiently and read a lot of what became this book. Both she and her husband, Ari Abramson, remain testaments to transatlantic friendship. David Brown, Adam Smith, Andrew Heath, James Ellison, Colin Jones, Frank Towers, and Bruce Baker read drafts of manuscript chapters and pushed me to hone some key ideas. Two graduate school friends went above and beyond the call of duty. Matthew Karp read several chapters and made each one better with his humor and panache. Gregory Downs read the entire project, pushed me to clarify my argument, and keep a tight grip on what was important. I owe them both a great deal.

My family have supported my every move with love and good humor, and this endeavor would have meant nothing without them. My mother, Gloria, my father, Brian, my stepfather, Doug, and my sister, Ashley, have encouraged me with countless conversations, and my extended family have taught me more than they know about what it means to keep at it and never give up. My in-laws, Micky and Jonathan, my brother in-law Richard and his wife, Karin, as well as Natasha and Simon Ruben and Miri Sigler, also helped in all sorts of ways, never tiring of asking about "the book," even if they found my answers perplexing to say the least. And though they did not live to see it on a shelf, this book and my interest in history was stoked by my grandparents, whose life stories inspired me to be a historian and whose experiences taught me the value of hard work, perseverance, and laughter.

One of my biggest debts is to the mentor who encouraged me to think big and never settle. Stephanie McCurry's passion, her counsel, and her sharp reading of my work never failed to amaze me. As anyone who has ever had the pleasure of being her student knows, seminars with Stephanie are feverish, intense experiences. They rearrange your mental furniture in the best way possible. She urged me to get lost in the archives and encouraged me to follow my own path. Her laser-beam focus refined so many of my ideas, and her friendship has remained steadfast. Through all the roadblocks along the way, she has truly been a champion. Her wit, wisdom, and honesty, the depth of her knowledge, and the arresting way that she views the past have influenced me in ways that are hard to calculate.

Finally, mere words do not do justice to all that I owe Joanna Cohen, the indomitable, loyal, side-splittingly funny, passionate, brilliant woman I share my life with. Her sharp eye improved every page of this book. Her creativity as a historian challenged me to think longer and harder about what I was doing and why I was doing it. Over the course of this project we have moved across an ocean, made a life together and a family as well. And even if Olivia and Jacob show no interest in what lies between these pages—beyond their potential for crayon scribblings—I hope that when they are grown they might read this one small part and know how much their mother has improved their father's life, in all the ways that matter.

the loyal republic

introduction

Late in February 1864, almost three years into the Civil War, five planters from the Mississippi Delta county of Bolivar were forced from their homes by a detachment of Confederate militia. Handcuffed, the men were made to watch as militia set to "insulting the ladies, taking all the clothing and dry goods they could lay their hands on" and any scant currency the soldiers found tucked away for safekeeping. The scene of armed men pillaging homes was hardly new in the Delta by the middle of the war. But this was no act of undisciplined looting. The militia had arrived that morning to dispense wartime justice. All five planters had been caught trading with the enemy. The raid was their punishment.

In the wake of the raid, the planters had few options and even fewer friends. Desperate, they drafted a petition to the governor of the beleaguered state government of Mississippi, begging him for his help. They claimed that the American occupation of their county had made it impossible for them to obtain "the absolute necessaries of life from any portion of the Southern Confederacy not occupied & held by the Enemy." Without assistance, the planters doubted that they could survive the rest of the winter, let alone plant a crop that might sustain them for the year to follow. While they underscored their devotion to the Confederate cause, the petitioners stated that to keep their families from ruin and their slaves from running away, they had been forced to trade with American merchants in nearby Memphis. Exchanging cotton for sundries was a transaction that would have been interpreted by many, if not most, as an act of treason. They argued, however, that their hands had been tied. "Necessity," they wrote, "is said to have no law." Publicly shamed, they sought the personal protection of Mississippi's governor, Charles Clark, a fellow planter from the county who they believed would "not suffer his fellow citizens to be thus trampled upon." Suspect in the eyes of American occupying forces, suspicious to Confederate officials, and fingered as traitors by the neighbors in their occupied community, the petitioners had gambled with their loyalty and lost, perhaps more than they could appreciate. They had wagered not only their property but potentially their right to the protection of a state in a time of war. Their decision to cross lines and trade with the enemy had won them the derision of friends and the ire of their enemies. For dry goods, the planters from Bolivar had been left stateless, stripped of their rights as citizens in a war-torn South.[1]

That desperate people might wrestle with their loyalties in a civil war will not come as a surprise.[2] What is interesting about these claims, however, are the broader questions they reveal about why two nation-states made such unsparing demands of loyalty from people living within their borders and how those demands redefined what it meant to be a citizen in a divided United States. This is a book about these questions. It is about how the Civil War encouraged the creation of two modern states and how that transformation changed how Americans understood their relationship to those modern structures of bureaucratic power. It is about how secession and a cataclysmic conflict of arms forced people to confront the rapid expansion of two national governments in their lives, and how that expansion and the obligations that those governments placed on people to be loyal created opportunities for some and foreclosed opportunities for others to lay claim to a place in two rapidly shifting body politics. It is a book that is at once about the everyday reality of making do in a time of war and about the abstract and often contradictory ways in which people reckon with the power of government. And it is a book that helps to explain why the United States fell apart and the materials that people used to knit it back together again, however imperfectly.

The study of loyalty has long been of interest to scholars of the Civil War. What has animated much of this literature is the question of whether certain people in particular places remained loyal to the United States or the Confederacy during the war, as part of the internecine fighting during the conflict that convulsed so many communities. This study builds on this work. It focuses more attention, however, on the ways in which loyalty—as a political act, a language, and a bundle of state policies—became part of a larger attempt to redefine citizenship and reckon with the power of nation-states, all at once.[3] The story that this book tells, then, is of how loyalty became fused with ideas about what citizenship meant on both sides of the battlefield, at the same time as both American and Confederate nation-states grew in dramatic fashion. To survey these twinned developments, this book tracks how the experience of the Civil War altered the terms of citizenship by making loyalty the key to membership in two shifting body politics.

Moving from high politics to conflicts over loyalty that emerged in one of the most important battlegrounds of the war, Mississippi, this book examines how people in and out of power, as well as two nation-states, clarified the obligations at the heart of modern citizenship. At the same time, this book also focuses on the actions of bureaucrats, military officials, secessionists, and slaves, all of whom attempted to reckon with the power of states by using a politicized language of loyalty. If the war altered the terms of the relationship between individuals and the nation-state, it also widened the terrain on which a postwar struggle over the shape of a new republic would be fought. Between the start of the Civil War and the tumultuous years that followed, Americans attempted to rebuild their nation on new foundations. To achieve this, they had to confront not only those who had severed the republic but also those who had been counted as human property when the war began. While it would not serve as the most durable of political tools, loyalty during and immediately following the Civil War would become an implement that sorted the patriots from the traitors and gave former slaves their most important means to secure a lasting bond with a postwar United States.

In taking up this history, this book makes several interventions. First, by focusing less on the rights of citizens and more on the obligations bound up with the title, this book charts a different course in the literature. It shows how nation-states and individuals attempted to clarify what it meant to be a citizen at a moment of profound change and why, over time, this concern slowly ebbed from debate. Second, in contrast to the story so often told about the Civil War as a conflict between Americans who merely disagreed about the future direction of the republic, this study shows just how much white southerners were counted as traitors by many in and out of government in the years that followed the war. Peeling back the layers of the Lost Cause that continue to obscure popular understandings of the Civil War and its aftermath, this book reveals an alternate narrative of national reconciliation that nearly sent the republic down a very different path. Third, by looking more closely at the possibilities that professions of loyalty presented to African Americans, who were not yet citizens when the war ended, this project highlights the canny ways in which freedpeople used loyalty (and the disloyalty of their former masters) to pry open the body politic to demand their place as citizens in a reconstituted republic. Though their efforts did not come without hazard or sacrifice, African Americans augmented a legal claim to citizenship with a powerful argument that their wartime loyalty to a republic that faced the greatest of challenges ought to win them a place in the nation's body politic when the dust had settled. And finally, by connecting the history of loyalty to the various attempts made by people to understand the long shadow that two warring states would cast in their lives, this book reveals how state formation looked through the eyes of those who were witness to its development, and how ordinary people played a part in that process.

To make sense of how ideas and practices of loyalty and citizenship intertwined during the Civil War requires that we think in new ways about what it meant to be an American citizen or, at least, to think again about why Americans had such trouble coming to agreement about what the title entailed by the middle of the nineteenth century. Prior to the Civil War, Americans lacked a clear, national definition of citizenship and, by extension, had an equally unclear understanding of what connected them to the nation-state. While the national government possessed the potential to expand and cast a long shadow over many on the geographical and jurisdictional edges of American society before the war, citizens, individual states, and local communities enjoyed a closer connection to one another as part of a constitutional bargain that made the American federal system possible.[4]

It was not that Americans had no idea of what the nation meant to them. The rhetoric of revolution that suffused the early national period, the public demonstrations of national memorialization, and the swirling energy of a party system all connected Americans to a common taproot of republican belonging by the middle decades of the century. Moreover, at points throughout the republic's early history, Americans had expressed their love and devotion to the nation, as something to be saved when threatened or as a bundle of ideas worth protecting. Times of war had called forth pledges of allegiance to ideals, if not to the government that had distilled some of them. But the obligations bound up with citizenship—the hard expectations that states could demand of people and what people could demand of states—lay buried beneath inchoate constitutional language and hazy case law. Americans were clear about what rights they enjoyed but less so about what tied them to the national state or what obligations the state could demand of them in return.[5]

The Civil War marked a sharp break in the relationship between citizens and the national government. In its wake, both American and Confederate nations demanded loyalty from persons living within their borders and extended the reach of the state into every corner of civic life and in unprecedented ways to secure it. Moreover, as the war bore down on people on both sides, demands for loyalty generated a politics of allegiance, a politics that allowed a variety of people to prove their value, lay claim to protections, and bolster their bid for a new kind of citizenship that they would help to fashion by the war's end. By the time American forces began to make inroads into Confederate territory and certainly as Union policy sharpened its focus on emancipation as the price white southerners were to pay for their treason, loyalty emerged as the animating principle of wartime citizenship. The disloyalty of white southerners who had cast their lot with the Confederacy left them on the outside looking in, as Unionists on the ground and in Congress demanded retribution for the hundreds of thousands of dead soldiers strewn on battlefields all over the country. Plans for a unified postwar future became infused with serious discussion about whether the disloyal Confederacy ought to be tied to the republic as a colonial possession and not as a collection of states equal in law with the rest of the nation. And as the war turned in earnest into a battle over emancipation, African Americans amplified their devotion to the United States to make the claim that their loyalty in war ought to secure for them the rights of citizens and the possessions of their former, disloyal owners. Over the span of only a few short, tumultuous years, Unionists, Confederates, and African Americans would come to terms with the chaos of war and the rapid development of warring nation-states by using loyalty as the lens through which they made sense of such dramatic, historic change. They and their governments would fashion new definitions of what it meant to be a citizen in a modern republic, one in which the obligations of loyalty that individuals owed the nation-state loomed particularly large.

The study of citizenship has long been the narrative thread that has bound the whole of the republic's history: a story of struggle, disappointment, adversity, and perseverance that gives the nation's past much of its propulsive force. In that narrative, the Civil War remains a major plot point, but the broad sweep of the literature has focused on the question of who did or who did not enjoy the constitutional rights of citizens. Envisioning the history of citizenship as a series of concentric circles in constant motion—expanding at some points, contracting at others—scholars track various groups into and out of the orbit of the body politic. Whether it was women who pressed to be counted, immigrants who struggled for inclusion, or African Americans who pushed for rights after the Civil War—or who marched for equal protection in the decades that followed—a focus on rights remains central to the study of citizenship.[6]

What has not been as well studied are the obligations at the heart of modern citizenship, and the reasons for this have a lot to do with how we conceive of citizenship in the modern era.[7] As political theorist Carole Pateman observed decades ago, the contradiction at the core of modern liberal citizenship is such that the obligations that citizens owe modern liberal states are assumed. Liberal democracies focus on rights—to hold property or to elect representatives in government—rather than on the harder commitments that are bound up with living in a modern state. This focus clouds the study of citizenship, pushing the rights that citizens enjoy to the forefront, obscuring citizenship as an often fraught compact between individuals and nation-states. As a result, the relationship between citizens and states remains opaque, made manifest only at times of conflict, when the obligations of citizenship take precedence to safeguard the nation. If the organizing principle and animating power of the modern state is that it is both everywhere and nowhere in the day-to-day lives of citizens, wars crack open that paradox, allowing historians to trace more carefully the struggle for rights and the expectations that governments demand of those who live within their borders.[8]

While the study of citizenship remains one of the strongest undercurrents in American history, the history of the American state has only more recently received sustained scholarly attention. Part of the reason for this stems from the way that historians and political scientists have traditionally approached the topic: a doggedly comparative model of study against which scholars have set the American state alongside European ones and found the former wanting. More recent work has avoided this interpretive dead end. Scholars now resist measuring the formation of states against an ideal type and have examined the history of the American state on its own terms. With this reorientation, they have pushed back the rise to power of the American government from the early twentieth to the first decades of the nineteenth century. At the same time, more recent work has also focused on the potential capacity of the American state: its constitutional power, its reach across the continent, and its ability to knit the republic together. We now have a clearer picture of American statecraft, a more contextualized understanding of the point at which the nation-state expanded and a deeper appreciation of the economic, legal, and military apparatus that allowed the national government to grow.[9]

But scholarly work that has measured how and when the American state grew reveals very little about how Americans understood this change. Work that has focused due attention on the relationship between the growth of the national government and the protections it provided to the nation's slave system has offered some important insights that make it clear that African Americans certainly understood all too well what state power meant. So too has work on Native Americans documented a long, intimate, brutal experience with the panoply of coercive powers at the disposal of government officials on the nation's shifting frontier. Yet the reactions of people to the development of state power stand in the literature more as a set of inferences than a subject of focus. The result is a call without a response, an often-one-sided attempt to see like a state without paying closer attention to how people watched the state grow. What a focus on the Civil War reveals is the opportunity not only to examine the rise of not one but two nation-states but also to see how a variety of people made sense of this development. Moreover, examining this history in contested territories that both the United States and the Confederacy coveted lays bare a tumultuous story of state formation and its lasting effects.[10]

One of the best places to examine these transformations can be found in the Mississippi Valley. Few parts of the American South had a more bruising experience with civil war and state formation. Before the conflict, the region was the beating heart of the American plantation complex. By 1860, Mississippi's plantations alone produced the lion's share of the nation's cotton crop, with only 11 percent of the nation's slave population. Unsparing, ruthlessly efficient, and profoundly powerful, slavery in Mississippi was the institution that secessionists dreamed of when they closed their eyes: a system of black bondage guaranteed by white supremacy and a system of local, state, and federal governance that protected the institution and insulated slaveholders. By the middle of the Civil War, however, Mississippians collectively experienced the collapse of the state government, the hollowing out of the local power that had propped up the plantation system, the ebbing of Confederate authority, and the rapid development of the American state, bent on destroying slavery, that would come to occupy some of the region's most precious plantation lands. The jewel in the crown of King Cotton when the war started, Mississippi would become one of the Western world's largest laboratories of emancipation by the war's end.[11]

Within this chaotic, state-sponsored experiment of free labor and African American emancipation, Mississippi also became the site of a brutal clarification of both citizenship and state power. And loyalty would become the thin thread that tied the state's wartime experience together. The hot-house firing of public support for secession in the region quickly spilled over into the equally public naming and shaming of individuals who offered anything less than their full-throated support for southern independence. The sweeping call to raise a Confederate army threw white Mississippians into a nation-building project where an increasingly centralizing state strengthened its grip over its citizens by fashioning a new kind of citizenship that dispensed with state allegiances and called for citizens to be wedded to the national government alone. When the war's western theater engulfed Mississippi and its government, those who found themselves in the line of fire were made to feel the brute force of two states, through the seizure of property and the separation of the loyal from the disloyal. And when the state lay divided—its government in ruin and the underpinning of Mississippi's slave system left exposed—African Americans seized the opportunity to stake a claim to their freedom by using their loyalty to the United States as the wedge that opened the door to emancipation. Fully aware of what loyalty meant, many free slaves made the powerful argument that in a region of the South where white loyalty was anything but certain, black loyalty to the Union was made of harder stuff. In offering their allegiance, African Americans who made this case were anything but naive. They fully appreciated the risks and were quick to object to the many inconsistencies in American policy, which at best assumed black loyalty and at worst demanded it, while at the same time subjecting black soldiers and black laborers to second-class status. By the end of the conflict, however, freedpeople understood that in the postwar South, their loyalty was a key ingredient in any postwar republic. When the Civil War reached its inconclusive end, African Americans stood as the most loyal group in the emancipating South, and freedpeople were quick to use that status to its fullest effect whenever the opportunity arose.[12]

Loyal blacks and treasonous whites in Mississippi—locked as they were in a struggle for access to an expanding American state by the war's end—joined a broader, national discussion about citizenship in a changing republic. The sectional politics of the previous decades had thwarted any consensus about what a definition of national citizenship might look like, but by the middle of the war, discussion within and outside Congress had given the debate added urgency. Talk of constitutional amendments to cement emancipation in the republic provided the opportunity that freedpeople needed to press for change. However, what emerged from this debate was a paradox: on one hand, a belief that loyalty ought to be the benchmark for any citizen to enjoy rights and freedoms in the republic, and on the other hand, a growing acceptance of the idea that professions of loyalty were too difficult to measure and, ultimately, too hard to trust. For all the ink spilled on the subject during the war, the result of the angst over secession, civil war, and the collective act of treason that the conflict represented to many was an uncomfortable silence when the time came to etch a national definition of citizenship into the nation's founding document. Inasmuch as loyalty remained important in American politics in the decades that followed the war, it became part of a collective stepping back from more radical action that so many Americans had called for only a few years before. Despite the Fourteenth Amendment's protections of the "privileges and immunities" of all persons born in the United States and the setting out of a minimum requirement of loyalty to all aspirants who might seek federal office, the force and effect of constitutional change looked nothing like the more radical debate over loyalty that had convulsed the republic only a few years before.[13]

And for African Americans, who stood at the center of so many of the constitutional changes wrought by Reconstruction, emptying national citizenship of loyalty removed one of the sharpest weapons in their political arsenal. Without that claim of national loyalty, African Americans were left to fend off white opponents with little more than a legal claim to citizenship—a principled argument for civic equality rather than a more historically grounded accounting of who had stood with the republic and who had not—at a moment when white supremacy was on the march. As quickly as they had erupted, ideas about loyalty receded from national discussion. By the 1880s and '90s, black Americans would experience the growing terror of coordinated campaigns devised to divest them of their newfound citizenship all over the country, and with that effort, the harder obligations of citizens to the state became, once again and for all Americans, difficult to see with any clarity.

This book examines the debate over citizenship that the Civil War set in motion, by both tracking back to the national level and zooming in on the conflicts that helped to shape the debate over loyalty in Mississippi. The first chapter takes the longer view, by focusing on the many ways Americans defined and redefined citizenship in the early to mid-nineteenth century, right up to the secession crisis. Examining the problems and peculiarities of American definitions of citizenship, the chapter argues that as the sectional controversy gathered steam, Americans on both sides of a growing divide found that they could not distinguish their relation as citizens to the national government from their growing anxieties about whom that government served. While even loyal Americans found it difficult to separate their devotion to the United States from their worries about the protections the federal state guaranteed to slaveholders, slaveholders in turn used older arguments about state's rights to justify a vision of government in which southern states, and not the nation, enjoyed true loyalty of citizens. As the chapter suggests, it was this argument, as much as anything else, that led to the fraying of the American nation in the wake of Abraham Lincoln's election in 1860, as the conflict over slavery emptied the idea of American citizenship of any real meaning.

A conflict of arms would force Unionists and Confederates alike to confront not only the ambiguities of their relationship to their national governments but also the rapid expansion of both states in ways that were unimaginable when the Civil War began. The second chapter of this book considers the development of citizenship and state formation in Mississippi and examines the rise and precipitous fall of Mississippi's own state government. The chapter revolves around the state's first wartime governor, John Pettus, a stalwart secessionist who attempted to build a strong state government but ultimately failed as American incursions into Mississippi, as well as the growing power of the Confederacy, swallowed his government whole. By focusing less on how states grew during the war and more on why some failed, this chapter makes it clear that the ambiguities of citizenship created a vacuum in which national interest trumped state loyalties and that rendered the Republic of Mississippi a failed state by the end of the war.

If Mississippi's state government collapsed as two national states expanded, a closer look at the way the Confederacy grew shows how the experience of war and the collective experience of being a soldier created a new kind of citizenship in the national army. A third chapter examines the military as a space within which the Confederate government turned its army into a school of citizenship, a site where faith in the national cause melded effortlessly with religion and where white southern men were schooled in how to become soldiers and citizens, all at once. A focus on the military makes clear that a collective experience of fighting for a state that would fail, ultimately created a lasting bond between white southerners and the Confederacy, long after the Civil War ended. In the religious sermons they listened to or in the public punishments they watched being meted out to deserters, loyal Confederate soldiers learned all they needed to about citizenship and the power of the state that secured their service and their allegiance at all costs.

The fourth chapter shifts focus and turns back to the wartime United States. In particular, this chapter looks at the debates over loyalty both at the highest levels of government and in the embryonic American occupation of Mississippi. Beginning at the start of the war, the growth of the American state worked in tandem with a concern about the threats to that state's survival from disloyal persons, all of which generated a rapid expansion of state power. By the middle of the Civil War, ideas about loyalty had coalesced around a new plan for the occupied South, a plan in which white southerners, shorn of their citizenship, would become colonial subjects of the American state. At the same time, the doctrine of emancipation created opportunities and challenges for African Americans, who grabbed the idea of loyalty as a key to their inclusion in the republic. Looking at how freedpeople both encouraged and challenged U.S. policy—as soldiers and laborers—the chapter examines how officials came to realize that any future for the United States in the Confederate South lay in providing some measure of protection for loyal African Americans, in contrast to white southerners, whose loyalty was suspect.

The wartime focus on national loyalty brought all kinds of people out of the woodwork, not least members of Congress and the U.S. government, who made names for themselves as paragons of civic virtue. Few were more successful in this regard than Andrew Johnson, a longtime member of Congress and two-time governor of Tennessee who emerged from the war as Lincoln's vice president and, later, his replacement. Johnson styled himself as the symbol of wartime loyalty in the American South. As governor of his home state, he turned his own unsparing ideas about loyalty into equally unsparing public policies. By the time he ascended to the White House, however, Johnson had made his ideas about loyalty the foundation for national reunification, with the president acting as loyalty's arbiter. A fifth chapter examines Johnson's short-lived career at the helm of Reconstruction, focusing on the kind of loyalty Johnson imagined as the key to postwar citizenship and on the pleas of whites in Mississippi for pardon.

As the chapter argues, one of the by-products of Johnson's tumultuous reign in the White House was the slow debasement of both him and his ideas about loyalty. Ultimately, it would be his profound belief in the healing power of loyalty oaths and personal acts of contrition on the part of former Confederate citizens that would spell the slow end of loyalty as the key to citizenship.

Moving from the halls of Congress to the struggle between white and black in emancipating Mississippi, the final chapter examines the many ways in which loyalty became part of a struggle for property, a struggle that would have profound consequences for the shape of Reconstruction in the Mississippi Valley. The chapter examines how state-sponsored emancipation worked in lockstep with the wartime seizure of property to create an environment within which loyalty to the United States gave worthy individuals claim to their possessions and left disloyal traitors with the flimsiest of holds over their land, their homes, and the black laborers many once owned. In this environment, African Americans seized on the language of loyalty to claim a meaningful freedom for themselves and knit their families together again. Struggles over loyalty and property traversed all parts of state, local, and national government. The twinned power of allegiance and property nearly proved the undoing of white supremacy in the state. In the claims and counterclaims of black and white alike, what emerged was potentially the most radical edge of American emancipation: a bold attempt to give to former slaves the property of their disloyal former owners. In this, the collective stepping back from the most revolutionary of Reconstruction measures also spelled the slow erosion of loyalty, leaving former slaves without the means to claim anything more than political rights.

Though the fusion of loyalty and citizenship in Civil War America proved short lived, the mark that it left on the republic would endure. While former Confederates would benefit from the uncoupling of loyalty from citizenship by the later decades of the nineteenth century, the treason at the heart of the Civil War and the collective memory of that conflict would live on every time a politician waved the memory of the war before the electorate in a bid for votes. The national state would experience a hollowing out of its wartime powers in the decades that followed the Civil War, but the experience of Reconstruction would set the nation against individual states. And for more than a century after the war, former slaves and their descendants bore the hardship and galling discrimination in the nation's military, to prove and prove again their allegiance to the United States through their service as soldiers in war. The deep division that had brought the war about would be stitched together without ever being fully healed, leaving the obligations that citizens owed the state submerged once again, along with the potential power of the state itself.

Even as the loyalty of Americans became more the stuff of cultural politics than the policy of the national government by the end of the nineteenth century, the complicated ways in which citizens understood their relationship to the national government would persist, its echoes informing the present as well as our collective understanding of the past. Crystal clear at some moments, opaque in others, the problem of obligation would become part of the inconsistencies and peculiarities of what it meant and means to be a citizen of the United States. What the Civil War era forced Americans to confront was a chaotic moment of state formation. In that moment of national rupture, the language of loyalty laid bare the basic obligations and the profound problems at the heart of modern citizenship. The war tested the limits of Americans' political imaginations. It forced people to come to grips with what being a citizen entailed. The reverberations of this change shaped the history of the republic as it emerged from civil war and assumed a greater power in the world. It can still be felt today.

CHAPTER ONE

A Government without Citizens

Imagine the United States as a government without citizens. The notion might sound like nonsense, but between the early nineteenth century and the Civil War, this was how many Americans envisaged their republic. It was not that the notion of a citizen lay beyond their understanding. Many could recite a worn list of rights that were bound up with the title. But to create their nation in the first place, Americans searched for loose, almost boundless definitions of what connected people to the republic, and in an Age of Revolution, a kinship with national ideals and a relation to individual states mattered most. By the early nineteenth century, when Americans thought at all about their political identities, it was their connection to the smaller republics that made up the Union that commanded their most immediate attention. For many if not most, the nation-state was a far-off thing. And this hazy relationship between Americans and their national government presented some clear and present problems.

The ambiguity of national citizenship was due, at least in part, to the intricacies of American statecraft. With power spread across a layered political system of incredible complexity and with jurisdictional authority invested in competing pieces of government, Americans in the early decades of the nineteenth century built a state of massive potential capacity. But the American nation-state was a bundle of contradictions, and over the early decades of the nineteenth century, Americans had become persuaded by the idea that the best government was the one that governed the least. As a result, Americans wrapped up their nation's leviathan and tucked it away.[1] The act of rendering the power of the national state invisible when in fact it was not was a feat of political fiction. But it was a useful one. When Americans settled the West, built new businesses, expanded their farms, or traveled abroad to sell their products in international markets, the national government that helped to make these things possible remained tightly controlled and in the background.[2]

The fiction of a small national state also went part and parcel with ideas Americans held about their citizenship, for it was in the act of explaining away their connection to the national government that Americans could best correlate their ideas about personal liberty with their desire to hide the state in plain sight. Between the founding of the country and the Civil War, in courtrooms and state legislatures, and in newspapers, constitutional conventions, and countless political debates as the century wore on, Americans hammered away at these questions, attempting to define and refine their status as citizens in the republic. Their efforts, however, resulted in more failures than successes.[3] The recent literature on the history of American citizenship has focused due attention on the important question of who did and who did not count as members of the body politic.[4] The issue in the early to mid-nineteenth century, however, was not simply that American citizenship excluded many more than it included. Rather, what Americans lacked was a clear understanding of who an American citizen was. In the absence of clarity, the multiple ways in which Americans defined and redefined their citizenship and their relation to the national government only added to the confusion. And as sectional tension and the development of regional identities increased, confusing ideas about what connected Americans to their national government were easily shredded in the debate over the future of the republic. Though citizenship was spoken of in political speeches on the stump, pointed to in the halls of Congress, venerated at moments of conflict, and referred to with reverence in popular culture, by 1860 the United States really was a government without citizens. It would take secession, the formation of a rival state, and a civil war to bring the problem to a head.

IN THE EARLY SPRING OF 1834, South Carolina's High Court of Appeals decided a case involving two officers in the state militia, Edward McCready and James McDonald, who had refused to swear a new oath of allegiance that had become law in the state a few months before. In a standoff with the national government over the rights of individual states to nullify laws passed by Congress, South Carolina's legislature had argued that citizens owed their most basic loyalty to their states first, the nation second. To that end, in December 1833, the legislature demanded that every officer in the state militia and every representative elected to government pledge to bear true allegiance to the state of South Carolina alone.

The demand that representatives of the state government—armed or not—swear their full and public loyalty to the cause of nullification was an artful bit of political theater. However, it did carry consequences for those who were forced to choose sides. Only weeks after the passage of the act, when the newly elected Lieutenant McCready and Colonel McDonald refused to take the new oath—believing that it amounted to a treasonous act against the United States—they were stripped of their positions.[5]

McCready and McDonald brought suit, though it was not long before their brush with nullification became burdened with broader concerns. At the heart of the case was the question of whether states or the federal government possessed the closest connection to the people. The issue was hardly semantic. At its root was an abiding question in American politics about legitimacy and sovereignty, the question of who best expressed the popular will of "the people."[6] Almost immediately, the ties between states, the national government, and citizens became key to the McCready and McDonald case.[7] Supporters of the two men argued that the connection between individuals and the nation trumped all other ties. As Thomas Grimké argued it, the answer was simple: "South Carolina *cannot* make a citizen of the United States. The United States *can* make a citizen of South Carolina." Other arguments, however, pointed to a larger universe of personal loyalty and allegiance that locked citizens to localities in a warmer embrace. As one lawyer in support of nullification had it, the most lasting tie of allegiance between citizens and government flowed naturally between persons and the states of their birth. A citizen's most important loyalty connected individuals to their native states, "the State which has protected him from birth, in the enjoyment of his rights, and which still stretches over and around him, the ample aegis of its sovereignty." Thus, when a state obliges a citizen to respect this bond before all others, including to the nation, it is a "homage he is proud to render—it is the homage of his heart." This was a kind of citizenship honored only at times when the interests of the citizen's state were not in question. In the breach, however, the tie between a South Carolinian and his home state was more lasting. Even when they traveled farther afield or when they settled in a western territory of the nation, Americans were not, strictly speaking, Americans. South Carolinians "owe *allegiance* to their native sovereigns—the states from which they emigrated—and *obedience* to the Territorial authorities, in whom no sovereignty exists." If the connection between citizens and their state was bred in the bone, national citizenship was only skin deep.[8]

Perhaps the clearest argument was issued by lawyer William McWillie. An opponent of nullification who had stood against the measure in the state legislature, McWillie raised the stakes by simply asking why the legislature's oath of allegiance was not treason, as McCready and McDonald claimed. Having agreed to join the Union, citizens in South Carolina and all other states were bound in a federal compact. Ties of loyalty that connected citizens to the nation in a time of war hardly dissolved in moments of peace. The national government, reminded McWillie, "has the power of binding us by its legislation. . . . It has the right to require our property and our blood, in its defence. Is this not the duty of citizens, and citizens only? and is not the fact that the Government relies on our military services in time of war, for its preservation and defence—the strongest evidence that we owe it allegiance?—is not this the tie of our fidelity?" Reaching for the reductio ad absurdum, McWillie wondered, "WHO ever heard of a government without citizens? The supposition is a monstrous anomoly!"[9]

In the end, nullifiers would not get the legal decision they longed for. South Carolina's highest court accepted McCready and McDonald's writ of mandamus, reversing the lower court decision by a 2-to-1 vote. All the same, the question that grew out of the case—the idea of an American government without citizens—unleashed a whole new debate. Even before the McCready and McDonald case had been decided, John C. Calhoun took aim at the very idea of national citizenship on the floor of the U.S. Senate. In answer to a speech by John M. Clayton of Delaware, who had argued that the Union was indivisible and that nullification was little more than treason, Calhoun shot back that for all the talk of Americans being citizens of the United States, there was little meaning in the title. Calhoun argued that the very idea of an individual claiming national citizenship without a tie to a state or a territory was ludicrous. Every citizen, Calhoun argued, "is a citizen of some State or Territory, and, as such, under an express provision of the constitution, is entitled to all privileges and immunities of citizens in the several states." It was in this sense and in no other "that we are citizens of the United States." Coming at a dramatic moment, Calhoun's comments should not be stripped of the politically charged context in which his argument was offered. For a man who claimed the title of war-hawk nationalist only two decades before, Calhoun, the consummate debater and political strategist, was out to make an explosive point. What remains intriguing about his comments, however, is that his idea about national citizenship as little more than a chimera reflected a growing consensus about the concept, in and out of Congress.[10]

By the 1830s, ideas about national citizenship and ideas about the powers of the national government became connected in the popular imagination, just as both became harder to define. The result was a question without a clear answer: if the United States was to be a nation of small republics, what common purpose or personal bond of loyalty connected people to the national government? No matter how hard they tried, even supporters of the idea of a nation of citizens could not escape the constitutional bindings that kept the notion in its diminished place.

Though nullification pushed citizenship to the center of national debate, it had been the subject of discussion before. Only a few years after the Revolution had ended, David Ramsay published a tract making it clear that after a decade of struggle, American citizenship was the opposite of the subjecthood colonists had thrown off in their war against Great Britain. "Dukes and earls are the creatures of kings," declared Ramsay, "but citizens possess in their own right original sovereignty." Having made it clear that the sovereignty of individuals gave the people ultimate power over government, Ramsay still felt it necessary to delineate several classes of persons, including denizens and slaves, who proved the exception to the rule. Writing as he did at a moment of deep worry about the loyalties of persons living in the new country, Ramsay was also at pains to make clear that citizenship in the American republic was "daily required by tacit consent of acquiescence." Service to the country in war was the most lasting surety of a citizen's allegiance. Citizenship was also a title that conferred membership in the body politic only after persons satisfied the litmus test of serious personal sacrifice. "Those who died before the revolution could leave no political character to their children, but that of subjects which they themselves possessed." Had they survived the war, Ramsay reasoned, they would have taught their children of the sacrifices necessary to ensuring that they would become loyal citizens. Without that education, however, even the sons of fallen patriot soldiers should be found wanting. They "may claim by inheritance the rights of *British subjects*, but not of *American citizens*."[11]

For Ramsay, the crucible of revolution dissolved older political ties and fired new ones, rigid and unequivocal. But the idea of a strictly volitional citizenship would be tested in the messier process of lawmaking. The result was an idea of citizenship far different. The Constitution, ratified the same year that Ramsay published his endorsement of national citizenship, offered little guidance as to what tied citizens to the new republic. The document used phrases like "the people" and "citizen" interchangeably, creating a loose language that in no way crystallized such a vital point of law. In only three stipulations—the qualifications to hold office, the power to naturalize the foreign-born, and the demand that citizenship rights bestowed to persons in one state be respected by all others—was citizenship mentioned. Whether citizenship was left ambiguous because it reflected the difficulty of the many compromises that went into the construction of the republic or because it reflected a broader understanding among the Revolutionary-era populace that citizenship ought rightly to be tethered to localities, jurists who searched for constitutional clarity found only hazy allusions or outright silences. Within the structure of American federalism, the national government was to be the arbiter of citizenship, with powers left to individual states to make that title meaningful.[12]

The development of federal law turned an opaque constitutional definition into a disquieting problem. The first naturalization law, which Congress passed in March 1790, defined citizenship as birthright and nothing more. According to the law, a citizen was any "free white person" who had lived in a state for at least five years and who could swear to uphold the Constitution and renounce "all allegiance and fidelity to every foreign prince, potentate, state or sovereignty whatever." Foreign-born persons already in the country were offered a shorter, two-year path to citizenship, while later iterations of the law stipulated that the hereditary privileges of the title were bestowed upon children from fathers alone. While the application of this important federal power seems clear enough on the surface, what naturalization laws betrayed were the chaotic ways in which such laws were policed, and the ambiguity of what power newly minted citizens should pledge to respect once older allegiances were swept away. The 1802 amended naturalization law went to great lengths to stipulate precisely which courts in the country could judge the veracity of a claimant's application for citizenship, in the face of stiff criticism from those who complained of local courts doing less than they should in judging applications. At the same time, the law made every effort to specify the many kinds of allegiances would-be citizens would be required to abjure, without specifying what would or should replace them. The practical effect of such capacious language was to obscure the very relationship between citizen and nation-state that many had deemed self-evident. Birthright citizenship tied individuals to states, leaving the federal government at an arm's length. Later amendments to the nation's naturalization laws invested more energy in stipulating the racial background of applicants than in clarifying the ties that connected newly minted citizens to their adopted home.[13]

Perhaps because citizenship was so difficult to define, the legal confusion over it required that Americans take an inchoate title and mix it with their feelings for the nation to give it meaning. The battles over revolutionary memory and the fight over the future character of the country dominated the early decades of the nineteenth century. But the pamphlets and the street theatrics left room for Americans to define their attachment to the nation through acts of national veneration. It also allowed people to define and redefine citizenship in all kinds of contradictory ways. Given the intellectual heritage of the Revolutionary generation, this was hardly surprising. Ideas about nationalism in the late eighteenth and early nineteenth centuries were rooted in a desire to collapse ethnic, religious, and class distinctions and replace them with a common, romantic civic identity, even if the effort did more to obscure differences than to erase them. Yet even though Americans expressed their affection and even love for the republic in public demonstrations that connected them ever more closely to the nation, the sharpest divisions of opinion over what the country stood for or what it should be were as muddled as citizenship itself. Even a hardened nationalist like Noah Webster, whose *American Dictionary of the English Language* sought to connect all citizens in a common lingua franca, could not bring clarity to a common definition of national citizenship. The entry for "citizen" in the first edition of his dictionary directed readers to define the word primarily as "the native of a city, or an inhabitant who enjoys the freedom and privileges of the city in which he resides."[14]

Capacious, overlapping understandings of citizenship were hardly limited to the experiences of white Americans like Webster in the first decades of the nineteenth century. As the slow dissolution of slavery in northern states created small but growing populations of free African Americans, several state legislatures offered opportunities for free black men to vote. Moreover, the nature of the organizational effort that went into the Revolution created a civil society of incredible depth and variety for white and black alike, a public sphere into which people at the top and bottom of the American social hierarchy vied for control, or at the very least the last word, in public affairs. More broadly, the demand for individual rights and the renegotiation of colonial power produced broad, sweeping calls for inclusion and political participation all over the Atlantic World. The French Revolution and its more radical twin in Haiti showed just how malleable and potentially radical an expansive definition of citizenship could be. Former slaves on that Caribbean island, who used the language of the era to demand their rights in a manner that French revolutionaries of the Third Estate had never accounted for, proved that in an age of upheaval, the base alloy of political membership was not the iron of monarchical duty but the slippery mercury of a new kind of political membership.[15]

Only at moments of national threat did citizenship become easier to define. Having set a very high bar for membership in the republic, writers like Ramsay made a common Revolutionary experience the litmus test for citizenship. For later generations, however, conflicts like the War of 1812 sharpened vague political relationships only at the point of conflict with a common enemy. The British refusal to accept that American citizenship trumped British subjecthood proved a particularly powerful trial by fire for American sailors on the high seas and for American communities on the border between a new republic and a familiar empire.[16] Yet as war with Britain abated, old patriots died, and as new immigrants flocked to the republic, the Revolutionary ideas about what tied individuals to the nation-state frayed and, in some cases, disintegrated altogether. In the decades that followed, supporters of national citizenship would still trot out the older Revolutionary arguments about a common past and a common experience of adversity, though by then it had become a worn call for unity. In 1832, lawyer

Benjamin Oliver published an extended rebuttal to nullifiers like John Calhoun. Deploying the considerable skills of a seasoned jurist, Oliver argued that venerable ties, forged in the nation's founding, fused Americans to the nation-state in a manner that would outdistance any talk of state's rights. As Oliver had been born during the Revolution, his conception of citizenship still placed the collective memory of that conflict at the center of the debate. For him, the United States was a social compact, forged in war, that bound individual members to a national political power capable of withstanding the attacks of enemies. This power, Oliver argued, was bestowed upon the national government not by individual states but by the people themselves. "It would seem to be a great mistake," he wrote, "to suppose that this general constitution was made by the *state governments*, for, they had no authority from the people of their respective states to do any such act." If sovereignty lay with the people, individual states had no part to play in this political relationship. Whereas nullifiers like Calhoun explained national citizenship away, Oliver argued that this connection superseded all other ties. So long as the American people voted for their representatives in national government, it was that government and not states that held ultimate authority.[17]

The only thing that nationalists like Oliver and nullifiers like Calhoun agreed on was that in the absence of a clear constitutional definition of what made citizenship meaningful, its primary right lay in the right to vote. By the early decades of the nineteenth century, suffrage had become the sine qua non of American citizenship. Between the 1790s and the 1850s, loosened restrictions on the right to vote had made the franchise a symbol of civic membership as never before. By the middle of the 1840s, as one writer would argue, the vote had become less a privilege than a right, as "common law considers every adult man as the equal of every other, in regard of his rights . . . and will not suffer another to control him in the use of them."[18]

Yet at the same time as it ascended to the top of the imagined list of rights that Americans took to be their birthright, the act of voting increasingly became divorced from national citizenship. As suffrage was a power reserved for individual states, the connection between citizens and the national government became even more tangled as states began to assert themselves to define who could vote and what the right entailed. The issue cropped up often in Congress. In the 1836 debate over whether to admit Michigan as a state, Ohio congressman Thomas L. Hamer answered those who argued that the new state's constitution— which allowed persons to vote who were not citizens of the United States—was in violation of federal power. Michigan's expansive imagining of the body politic was clearly in opposition to the Constitution, though the idea of states trumping the national government had its supporters, Hamer among them. He argued that despite possessing the power to naturalize individuals as citizens in the face of a state wielding sovereign authority, the federal government's hands were tied. Hamer reiterated the point that suffrage and citizenship were constitutionally distinct. Though the national government maintained the right to *make* citizens, the power most closely associated with the title fell within the purview of states, and as far as Hamer was concerned, this was only right. "Look at the constitutions of Ohio and other new States," argued Hamer, "and you will find that they require *residence* only, and not *citizenship*, to enable a man to vote. It gives them no rights beyond the limits of the State. It cannot make them citizens, for that would violate the naturalization laws; or rather, it would render them nugatory." Hamer's argument was clear. Even if states permitted unnaturalized persons to vote, Congress had no right to stop them. "The General Government is not based on the masses of the people throughout the Union, without connection with the States," claimed Illinois Democrat John Reynolds in 1841. "The people of each State, separate and apart from the others, vote for the President of the United States; and the Legislatures of the respective states elect Senators to the Senate of the United States." Though the nullifiers in South Carolina had lost their bid for state supremacy, theirs was an interpretation of federal power and citizenship that carried the day. While suffrage was becoming ever more closely associated with citizenship, the relationship between citizens and the national government was becoming looser.[19]

Broad changes to definitions of citizenship were driven not only by the fusion of national belonging with the franchise. They were also driven by territorial expansion and the emergent rhetorical power of manifest destiny. Just as in the debate over the rights bound up with citizenship, the malleable nature of citizenship provided opportunities for all manner of interpretations. Though his party was cool to the idea of territorial expansion, Whig congressman Ebenezer Shields presented a resolution to the House from the Tennessee legislature in April 1838 that expressed the hope that "the ties of a kindred and common ancestry" would bring citizens of the new Republic of Texas into the Union, having expressed the "anxious desire . . . to become citizens of these United States." The idea of American settlers in Texas giving up their rights as citizens only to claim them again in a bid for statehood added ambiguity to an already complex issue. It was not that politicians like Shields expressed a view out of step with the electorate. It would have come as a surprise to those Texan pioneers who lit out with Stephen Austin to found a new settlement that their citizenship was not a birthright to be claimed, no matter where they put down roots. Though the terms of the Texas settlement required American pioneers to abide by Mexican law and become Mexican citizens, did citizenship in another nation require Americans to disavow their rights as citizens of the United States? On this point, Congress and the nation's governing documents fell into an uncomfortable silence, and legal semantics quickly gave way to deeper concerns. Did Americans who ventured out onto the frontier of the continent retain their rights as citizens? Was the title and the rights bound up in it as portable as the ideology of manifest destiny that lured people to the edges of the continent in ever greater numbers? Moreover, if citizenship was as portable as the belongings Americans carried with them to parts unknown, what obligation lay with the federal government to protect these rights? It was at the edges of the republic that the problems of national citizenship demanded clarification, and the answers of the national government and Americans themselves would complicate the project of national state power and citizenship, all at once.[20]

To say that definitions of citizenship and clarifications of federal power were refined on the edges of the republic is not to add a new dimension to the debate over its history. Much of the recent work on the history of both the American state and American citizenship is united in its focus on measurements and margins, accounting for the size of the national government over time and focusing due attention on the outer edges of the body politic, to those groups who called loudly for their inclusion throughout the nation's history. In their effort to secure a lasting equality, free blacks and women from across the social spectrum used the malleability of national citizenship to claim the title for themselves. They argued that their standing as American-born persons gave them a constitutional right to citizenship, and that in a nation of migrants, they surely possessed a stronger claim to the title than those born in other parts of the world. In addition, as the fusion of citizenship and suffrage shifted the terms of the debate, securing the right to vote became the primary object of concern and has since attracted the lion's share of attention by historians. By the 1840s, women's groups called loudly and often for the vote as the means of securing female civic independence, and as the African American editors of *Freedom's Journal* remarked in their first editorial in 1827, the power of the vote compelled free blacks around the country to do nothing less than use their right to suffrage, when it was permitted, to represent their race, or risk becoming "the tools of party." One of the most famous voices in the emergent abolitionist movement belonged to David Walker, who called on "coloured citizens of the world" to unite in common cause against slavery. Though the explosive idea at the heart of his pamphlet's title was tantalizing, Walker never expounded more fully on it. All the same, the bid for citizenship would become the center around which abolitionist agitation would revolve.[21]

The social margins of American society were not the only locations where citizenship in the 1830s and '40s was being refined. Just as nullifiers and politicians in Congress were uncoupling citizenship from the federal state, Americans on the geographical edges of the republic also sought difficult answers to the same complex question. The constitutional convention in California, called to order in 1849, made the complex nature of citizenship on the territorial edges of the republic abundantly clear. For Californians, the circumstance was unusual. The Treaty of Guadeloupe Hidalgo that ended the Mexican War included the provision that Mexican citizens who called California home could enjoy rights as citizens, provided that they could demonstrate their wartime loyalty to the United States. This provision presented the constitutional convention with a sticky problem. At a moment in the republic's history when state after state expanded the suffrage to men while limiting access to the vote based on race, accepting Mexicans as citizens with voting rights worked against white supremacy. Moreover, as Texas congressman V. E. Howard made plain in the House debate on the subject, the terms of the federal treaty that gave loyal Mexicans citizenship by fiat ironically abrogated federal power over naturalization. For these reasons, the territorial government made it clear in their instructions for the convention vote that special "care should be taken by the Inspectors" in southern California to ensure that "votes are received only from bona fide citizens actually resident in the country."[22]

Once the state constitutional convention met, it did not take long for citizenship to emerge as an explosive issue. W. M. Gwin, delegate from San Francisco, made it clear that it "was not for the native Californians we were making this Constitution; it was for the great American population, comprising four-fifths of the population of the country." To this, Californio delegate J. A. Carrillo replied that if support for the United States in a time of war was all that was required to cement one's claim to citizenship, he considered himself "as much an American citizen as the gentleman who made the assertion" that Carrillo's rights were in question. What lay behind the debate in the state's convention was not only the racially charged question of whether Mexicans should be counted as true citizens. There was also the issue of whether American citizenship was a portable thing and whether the title of citizen conveyed a bundle of rights so loose that a variety of people could rightly lay claim to them. If all residents of California could be counted as citizens, what ultimately did citizenship mean, particularly if contemporary understandings of the title relied on defining a citizen as someone who possessed rights that other people in the republic did not? From the moment delegates began to craft a constitution, the convention was hamstrung. The shotgun marriage of former Mexican citizens with American-born citizens threw all definitions up in the air.[23]

Rather than deal with the nuts and bolts questions of government structure and the division of powers, constitutional delegates in California chose to attack the question of citizenship, with predictable results. A Declaration of Rights, with a third clause stipulating, "No member of this State shall be disfranchised, or deprived of any of the rights or privileges secured to any citizen thereof, unless by the law of the land, or the judgement of his peers," complicated more than it clarified. The clause caused immediate consternation, with one delegate seeking to strike the word "member" from the document. It was a measure of the difficulty of defining just who was a citizen of California that the convention chose instead to use the word "inhabitant" rather than "citizen," though even this half-measure opened the door to a debate about whether not only Mexicans but African Americans and Native Americans could also seek protection in the declaration. "If you provide that no member of this State shall be deprived of the rights and immunities of a citizen, it is to be presumed that such member enjoys those privileges and immunities," charged L. W. Hastings. "Indians are inhabitants, but they do not enjoy those privileges [of citizenship] in any portion of the United States; they are disfranchised. Yet we declare here, that they shall not be disfranchised without the due process of law."[24] Other delegates saw the virtue of protecting the rights of all while restricting the power of certain groups to control government. "We cannot deprive the Indian, or even the free negro of the right to hold property," offered Sacramento delegate W. S. Sherwood, though white Californians should reserve the right to "say who shall and who shall not elect the officers of the government. We have a right to govern the state."[25] For delegates like Sherwood, the racial hierarchy and the portability of citizenship gave Americans the justification to limit access to rights in whatever way they wished.

The arguments surrounding the California constitution rested upon a vision of citizenship that was capacious and portable. The practicalities of this vision for the government obliged to protect the rights of citizens, however, were unclear at best. Though the Constitution's "privileges and immunities" clause made certain aspects of citizenship uniform across the states of the Union, that provision made no allowance for citizenship as a meaningful political title in territories that were not yet states, and even within states, the privileges of citizenship were not protected. Free African Americans retained rights in some states by the 1840s that were not respected across the country, and while some white Californians appeared confident of their rights in a newly won territory, members of Congress expressed some doubts as to the status of white Americans on the edges of the nation. For House members like Maryland Democrat William Hamilton, the rights and duties of people living in American territories, no matter their background, were anomalous. While Hamilton allowed that persons living in territories fell within the corporate limits of the republic and were thus bound to the Constitution, by living in a region without representation in Congress, settlers in the territories did not possess the voting privileges of citizens that would allow them to take active part in national government. Even with these caveats, however, the lure of manifest destiny resulted in the nation's political leaders stretching the terms of citizenship beyond reason. Texas's Sam Houston argued that so long as migrants to the West were undertaking to extend the influence, power, and wealth of the republic, it hardly mattered whether their movements stretched constitutional or legal definitions. Those who wished to make a home on the western frontier did so in the interests of the nation. It was incumbent upon the nation to protect them. Pioneers "are still American citizens, and the Republic should encourage the enterprise which takes them thither. It is not a benefit conferred upon strangers; it is one which tends to the developing of our vast resources, and the opening of new markets to our enterprise and liberty."[26]

The portability of citizenship and the variety of ways in which it was being defined by the late 1840s suited a generation of Americans who had territorial ambitions. However, the focus on the rights bound up with citizenship—rather than on the political relationship between the citizen and the government that protected these rights—only allowed the arguments of nullifiers and the agenda of southern slaveholders to calcify into received wisdom. Particularly as the political debate over what to do with slavery in the territories swept Congress into a period of profound sectional gridlock, ideas about the loyalties and true allegiances of Americans emerged in ways that presaged disaster. At the same time, the ambiguity of national citizenship also created a vacuum for proslavery advocates to fill. In the late summer debate over slavery in the territories in 1850, North Carolina Democrat Abraham W. Venable offered a speech that showed just how much all the talk of a capacious citizenship was damaging the republic's foundations. Venable argued that while it had become custom on the House floor to appeal to the paramount allegiance of all citizens to the Union, he begged to differ. "My allegiance is not due to this Government, but to the sovereign state of North Carolina. She commands me to obey this Government—I cheerfully acquiesce in her commands. . . . I was not born a citizen of the United States," nor had he ever considered himself one, apart from his connection to his home state. It would be, Venable argued, "asserting the absurdity of two citizenships in one. . . . I am an American citizen because I am a citizen of North Carolina. That gives me equal rights and immunities by compact." So long as North Carolina deemed the Union worth the membership, Venable would obey. However, Venable's loyalty and the loyalty of those he spoke for had limits. If the rights of North Carolina were to be infringed, nature and the venerable ties that connected citizens to their states would demand action and the dissolution of the republic.[27]

By the time Venable joined the rest of Congress in the verbal marathon that resulted in the Compromise of 1850, talk of ties dissolved and bonds torn asunder were everywhere. While aged political leaders like John Calhoun conjured dark predictions of the cords of Union that had already snapped, the most profound connection, between individuals and the nation, had all but dissolved some time before.[28] Calls for national unity met hardened sectional difference head-on, with a healthy dose of cynicism that the federal government could do anything to heal the rift. "We have yielded our opinions too easily to the arguments of faction," allowed an editorialist for the *American Whig Review*; "we allow men to lead and represent us, and to exercise public authority, whom in private we would scorn to trust or meet with respect." The republic could survive only by doing away with a generation of discredited leaders and investing authority in a strong, stentorian leader, able to unite the disparate elements of a tattered party system. Ominous talk of strong leadership and appeals for unity were hardly surprising, particularly from a paper that represented a party that confronted oblivion. But the pleas for a more authoritarian politics stemmed in large part from an anxiety that the national government was powerless to stop the sectional drift that, according to some, could only be countered with force. Not to be outdone, J. B. D. DeBow offered his own assessment of what ailed the republic. His solution, however, was the opposite of strong-armed leadership. Instead, DeBow, the self-styled southern rights champion, blamed the national government for all that ailed the nation. "To say that the world has been too much governed, is to say that it has been badly governed, since each additional restraint, beyond what is absolutely necessary, constitutes an additional link in the chain of oppression. . . . Call it democracy or despotism, that government is a tyranny which delights in weaving the legislative web to entangle its subjects." In ways large and small, talk of a flailing national government and the obligations of individual citizens to it became ever more closely linked.[29]

The one link in the chain between individuals and the nation-state that had yet to be broken was the implied ellipsis at the end of DeBow's argument. If a national government proves tyrannical—if it is no longer fit for purpose—what obligation does a citizen owe that government to sustain it and remain loyal? For many northerners, this issue became clear with the passage of a new Fugitive Slave Act, which placed federal power behind a slaveholder's right to seize escaped slaves from any part of the nation.[30] From the moment the act was put before Congress for debate, the legislation bent the idea of citizenship and federalism to the breaking point. George Ashmun, Massachusetts House member, made the case that if authorities seized an African American man from a state that made him a citizen, because a citizen from a slave state claimed him as property, "is it to be said he may be summarily sent away by the decree of any one magistrate, without the privilege of vindicating his title to his citizenship before a jury of the country?" Ashmun allowed that individual states retained the right to define citizenship in whichever way their legislatures deemed proper, but the Fugitive Slave Act effectively threw this inviolate right into question. To make his case, Ashmun hit on the inconsistency of American sailors being protected by national citizenship abroad, even if their status at home was under threat. Black sailors, Ashmun charged, "can go from our ports armed with the rights of an American citizen, around the world. . . . Everywhere the flag of our nation heralds him, and guards him. But if his voyage brings him into the harbor of the republican slave States of this Union, what becomes of his boasted right of citizenship[?] . . . He is instantly seized upon a charge of being 'guilty of a skin not colored like our own.'" For many northerners, the presumption that the rights of slaveholders trumped the sovereign right of states to define citizenship within their borders, and of the place of the federal government in ensuring slaveholder rights to property, brought forth a searching debate about citizenship, the national government, and the remaining ties of loyalty that connected them.[31]

For some abolitionists, it was the immorality of slavery that compelled citizens to disobey the government on the fugitive slave question. For them, citizens owed their most basic allegiance not to the nation-state but to God, and no government was deserving of loyalty if it demanded citizens act in a manner contrary to their religion or their conscience. In an 1852 pamphlet titled *The Higher Law*, William Hosmer argued that while an imperfect civil government ought to command the authority of those who lived under its protection, the citizens of an imperfect government as well as the government itself were all subject to a higher power. In this regard, Hosmer made plain that those who stood against slavery should, rightfully, act to undermine civil authority when it insisted upon an unjust law. Though never mentioned in the text, Hosmer's Hobbesian understanding of the state permeated his sense of the "tremendous engine" of public authority that needed to be held in check if guided by persons bent on contravening Christian morality. If a national government became twisted and was made to serve the favor of a particular group in society at the expense of the others, "either society, as a whole, becomes the victim of its own institution, or the injury falls upon some particular class of persons, who are thereby stripped of their rights, and ruined by what should have been their inviolable protection." If the national government instituted an unjust law and demanded obedience to it at the expense of God's will, Hosmer argued that this act of state-driven immorality absolved moral citizens of any responsibility to the national government, while making "the state, or its officers, answerable for the guilt of obedience to wicked laws."[32]

Citizenship ties were not always cut so simply, even for those who looked to the heavens for answers. John Krebs, a Presbyterian minister from New York, made no attempt to downplay the immorality of the Fugitive Slave Act, but he did stop short of calling for a divinely inspired national disintegration. If, Krebs argued, "an enlightened conscience discerns that human law is in flagrant opposition to the divine law, there is surely no obligation to approve it or even to obey it," particularly if that law ran counter to the sympathies of a growing number of northern abolitionists. At the same time, righteous opposition to any law ought to be channeled through the political process, rather than being left to fester without meaningful solution and do greater damage to the country as a result. The ballot box was the "only field where the Christian American Citizen should ever strive to revolutionize his government." Notwithstanding Krebs's plea for dispassionate reason, some religious leaders saw no easy way out of the spiritual corner into which sectionalism had painted them. Episcopalian bishop John Henry Hopkins, a leader of his church in Vermont, felt compelled to write an 1857 treatise on citizenship that echoed many of the same sentiments and straddled a fine line between opposition and nationalism. Hopkins, born in the immediate aftermath of the Revolution, was undoubtedly old enough to remember when republican nationalism held a clearer, more ringing definition of citizenship at the center of national culture. By the 1850s, however, circumstances had changed, and for Hopkins, the democratic spirit of the age was to blame for damaging the principles that the country was founded upon. "The power of voting is vested in the multitude," Hopkins wrote, "but the power of *governing the votes* is really exercised by a comparative few. Hence, the democratic element, of which we boast, sinks into oligarchy of the worst kind, because it is altogether irresponsible." Though Hopkins clearly intended his book as a primer for the growing number of European immigrants who populated northern cities, even religious leaders like him who venerated the country no longer looked with optimism on the nation's future. So long as political leaders lacked the religious fortitude and migrants diluted the republican virtue forged in the Revolution, there was little but gossamer keeping the nation together.[33]

While sectionalism and federal compromise weakened support for the national government among many northerners at the same time that it further weakened the idea of national citizenship, southerners who dreamed of a slaveholder's nation adopted a more strident pose. "The nature of our Government is such as to render it short-lived," wrote one writer in *DeBow's Review* in 1858. "Our political organization in its operation is cumbersome and unwielding; and, therefore, calculated to weary its constituents with its useless machinery." It was not only the architecture of the national government that lacked strength. Southern sectional leaders and opinion makers reached back to an earlier decade to resurrect the older problem of sovereignty as well. The "distrust of government is rapidly growing in our community," and given that federal power lay in the hands of such a motley collection of democratically elected members, political factions "composed of the dregs of our inhabitants" made it impossible to see what good there was in sustaining a tired government that was no longer fit for the times. Given the circumstances—with a Republican Party that could potentially take the White House and with Democrats losing their grip on power—it was perhaps natural that southerners looked to the only federal branch that had yet to step into the sectional controversy. Just as nullifiers had done more than two decades before, southern supporters looked again to a court that might provide them with the means to halt the abolitionist advance.[34]

The case involving Dred Scott, the Virginia-born slave who sued for his freedom in 1846 and whose case was decided by the Supreme Court in 1857, remains one of the most infamous judicial decisions in the nation's history.[35] By upholding the rights of slaveholders to take their human property wherever they chose, Chief Justice Roger B. Taney's majority opinion damaged a decade's worth of federal compromises over slavery and the place of the institution in the territories. Few now doubt that Taney overextended himself by ruling that African Americans possessed "no rights which the white man was bound to respect," given that the Constitution provided Taney with little direction on this ambiguous point of law. For this reason, students of the case have focused on Taney's effort to make law and have looked to the impact of the ruling as a catalyst of the sectional controversy. After all, it was the Dred Scott case that forced candidates for national office to defend their positions regarding the constitutionality of slavery, providing sharp jurists like Abraham Lincoln with the means to address a nation that was listening more attentively than ever before.[36]

Yet, in the opinions rendered by both Taney and his fellow justices, there is much more to puzzle over. Scott's defense was, in many respects, predicated upon a reading of citizenship that exposed the constitutional ambiguities of the title, not to mention the legal and political ambiguities on the question that had built up over the decades. Scott's counsel, who claimed Scott's freedom on the grounds that he had lived in parts of the country where slavery was forbidden, relied on a reading of the Constitution that made an individual's birthright as an "inhabitant" of a state coequal with citizenship.[37] To this Taney attempted an end-run around the prevailing consensus, by actually making a bold case for national citizenship from which African Americans were forbidden to lay claim. While Taney did not deny that a state "had the undoubted right to confer on whomever it pleased the character of citizen, and to endow him with all its rights," the constitutional right of naturalization reserved power to make citizens in the federal government alone. No individual state, according to Taney, possessed the power to "introduce a new member into the political community" created by the Constitution, and that document was drafted and ratified by men, Taney reasoned, who clearly did not count African Americans (slave or free) as equal members of the body politic with them. As part of an attempt to insulate slavery behind a firewall of federal protections—by claiming that regardless of whether states admitted African Americans into the body politic, federal protections could not protect their status—Taney staked his opinion on a rather broad understanding of national citizenship and belonging. It beggared belief, according to Taney, that a republic bound up with slavery would have ever provided the possibility for the inclusion of slaves as equal members of the republic. In his mind, this fact alone suggested that the nature of American federalism made the federal government the powerful steward of a racially delimited definition of citizenship.[38]

Even among the other justices of the Court who concurred or dissented from the majority opinion, few went as far as the chief justice in making such a sweeping attempt to resuscitate national citizenship. In their opinions, however, the place of the national state and the relationship between it and Americans were no less complex. The *Dred Scott* decision showed just how little had been resolved since the early decades of the century, while also showing just how much questions of citizenship and the power of the national state were connected. Though he concurred with Taney, Justice John A. Campbell distanced himself from the reasoning of the majority opinion by emphasizing the relative powerlessness of the federal state. For Campbell, the essence of the case in support of Dred Scott lay in the idea that federal laws banning slavery in territories in which he lived trumped his owner's rights to his person as a slaveholder. To this, Campbell slapped Scott's claim down with a clever bit of misdirection. Campbell argued that the idea of Congress possessing supreme power over territories like Wisconsin or Illinois had no legal or historical basis in fact. The distinguishing features of the American system of government, he argued, "consist in the exclusion of the Federal Government from the local and internal concerns of, and in the establishment of an independent internal Government within, the States." Campbell suggested that despite this structure of government, "those controversies which . . . have occasioned most peril to the peace of the Union, have had their origin in the well sustained opinion of a minority among the people that the Federal Government had overstepped its constitutional limits to grant some exclusive privilege, or to disturb the legitimate distribution of property or power among the States or individuals."[39] This, for Campbell, was the key to the sectional controversy, and though he concurred with Taney, his opinion could not have been more different. Whereas Taney saw the federal government and the Constitution as a bulwark in the defense of slaveholder interests, Campbell envisioned a national state kept not only in check by the power of individual states, but emaciated and enfeebled for the good of the republic.

It was an indication of just how incendiary the *Dred Scott* decision was that in its wake, members of an increasingly divided Congress found ample ammunition to assail one another. What had changed was that the fusion of a diminished notion of national citizenship with an equally diminished national government was so complete in the political talk that swirled around Washington in the run-up to a presidential election that every issue, no matter how germane to the sectional conflict, became wrapped up in it. As part of a debate over the organization of Oregon—which allowed foreign persons who were not yet citizens of the United States to vote on the new state's constitution—both Democrats and Republicans used the state's inclusion in the Union as a weapon to beat one another. Whereas Democrats pointed to the Constitution as an example of popular sovereignty, which was not respected by northern members of Congress in the case of Kansas's admission as a slaveholding state, several Republicans used Oregon's constitution as an opportunity to raise the problem of citizenship and its relationship to personal loyalty. Ohio Republican John Bingham cleared this particular path by questioning the legality of a constitution that permitted persons to vote who possessed no clear allegiance to the republic to which they sought membership. "By declaring his intention to become a citizen of the United States, an alien does not renounce his allegiance to the Government of his native country, nor does he acknowledge any allegiance to ours." To sharpen the point, Bingham went on to question just what defined a citizen of the republic: "Who are citizens of the United States? Sir, they are those, and those only, who owe allegiance to the Government of the United States; not the base allegiance imposed upon the Saxon by the Conqueror . . . but the allegiance which requires the citizen not only to obey, but to support and defend, if need be with his life, the Constitution of his country." By taking this stand, Bingham offered a rather blunt appeal to the nativist minority of the Republican Party. Yet while his argument may have been intended in part as a broad call to anti-immigrant voters, it was also a sly attack on those who stressed the primacy of state-level allegiance. By implying that allegiance to one's home state negated one's claim to loyalty to the United States, Republicans like Bingham were out to frame state's rights opponents as potentially treasonous noncitizens.[40]

As the 1860 election loomed, even the most ardent supporters of secession walked a very fine line between conciliation and confrontation. Between the extremists on either side of the sectional controversy lay a broad spectrum of Americans who would not be cajoled easily into radicalism. Particularly in the southern states, where sectional identities and protections for slavery were inextricably linked, convincing those who did not possess an economic interest in slavery represented one of the most vital challenges for secessionists. It was left, then, to canny leaders and moderate opinion makers to make the case that even if the currents of sectionalism strained them, venerable ties of Union remained. "We do not know an individual," claimed an editorial in Mississippi's *Oxford Intelligencer*, in the immediate aftermath of Abraham Lincoln's election to the presidency, "who, if the rights and honor of the South could be secured in the Union, would be in favor of secession even now. There is, in the heart of our people, a deep and abiding love for the Union; but that love is not stronger than their sense of justice and self-respect." Reaching back to the Revolution, in what would become a ubiquitous rhetorical move for secessionists, the editorial argued that Mississippi's moderates were the "same men who were as true and loyal subjects as any who were born within the allegiance of the British crown," but whose loyalty was not then blinded by devotion at the expense of their rights.[41] Where even moderates fell silent, however, was on the very issue that Republicans, now to assume power, pressed with even more urgency. If southerners left the Union, what rights did they possess as citizens, particularly if their bid for independence brought about armed conflict? It became the circle secessionists could never square. Though they appealed to a shared revolutionary past and claimed that their secession proved their devotion to the spirit and ideals of the nation's founding, they could never bring themselves to fully give over to the idea that southern independence required that they renounce their status as Americans.[42]

Moreover, given their intellectual lineage, which dated back to nullification, ideas about citizenship in a potentially independent South were tethered to a state's rights argument that left little room for a nation-state to claim pride of place. Between the winter of 1860 and the spring of 1861, a discussion of loyalty erupted in American politics as it had not done since the nation had been founded. Particularly in the southern conventions called to debate the question of secession, the issue pressed upon supporters of southern independence in several states. South Carolinians who, more than two decades before, had attempted to fuse the loyalty of the populace with the state rather than the national government wasted no time in achieving exactly that. Twenty-four hours after issuing their declaration of secession, the state convention amended the oath of office to ensure that all members of government and the state militia swore their loyalty to South Carolina alone. In addition, once South Carolina was made part of an independent republic of southern states, its legislature embedded state's rights into the fabric of the new republic's laws in April 1861. The legislature drafted a new constitution that ensured that even if the anticipated national government reserved the right to naturalize citizens (as the Union government had done), this process could only take place "provided that such laws shall require the foreigner to swear allegiance to that Confederate State in which he is naturalized," and not an imagined southern nation. In many respects, it was the nature of the conflict that Americans confronted that loyalty became of a paramount importance. Particularly in parts of the country on the border between the Union and a growing Confederacy, it was natural that politicians gave voice to the worry of whether the loyalty of the average person could be trusted. Concerns about the loyalty of friends and neighbors grew much more quickly, however, as rival governments began to harden the lines separating two nations, while at the same time governments armed themselves with sharper weapons to compel the loyalty of those who did not offer it up willingly.[43]

Early in the secession conflict, talk of loyalty and its political opposite, treason, became part of the debate over southern independence, particularly once secessionists realized that their dreams of a nation-state might well die at the hands of their own people. In Alabama—where an energetic state government under the direction of Governor Andrew Moore used state militia to seize a federal armory three days before the state's secession convention met to discuss the question— delegates to that convention made it plain just what independence entailed. "I am no believer in peaceable secession," Lowndes County delegate and Unionist J. F. Clemens claimed on the first day of deliberations. "I know it to be impossible. No liquid but blood has ever filled the baptismal fount of nations." Given the dark prognostication about what the future might hold, secessionists thought little of their tie to the United States, even before secession was brought to a vote. Delegates resolved to ask the governor to come to the aid of the state government of Florida by sending troops to help it defend the state from federal forces, even though the resolution (coming before a vote on secession) amounted to treason. By turns, when it became apparent that the secessionist cause would not receive unanimous approval, supporters used their most divisive weapon to make clear just what standing against secession entailed. On the attack at the same time as he conceded ground, arch fire-eater William Lowndes Yancey argued that even if secession passed by a bare majority, it still had the full force and effect as if it had been unanimously adopted. What's more, a new independent state of Alabama "will expect and demand, and secure unlimited and unquestioned obedience," of all who lived within its borders. Should any oppose the measure, they would be dealt with harshly, divested of their rights as citizens and made to feel the full weight of the state's power. "There is a law of Treason, defining treason against the State," Yancey warned, "and, those who shall dare oppose the action of Alabama, when she assumes her independence of the Union, will become traitors—rebels against its authority, and will be dealt with as such."[44]

Yancey was attacked by many in the convention as little more than a fanatic who sought bloody retribution against all who voiced principled opposition to secession. Yet the picture painted by his threat—of secession creating a power-ful state that invited the loyalty of the populace but extracted it from the people if need be—would become a common theme that cut across secession debates across the South. What lay at the center of the secessionist dream was a collection of independent states united in common cause but possessing individually the deepest loyalty of the populace. Buoyed perhaps by histories of nullification and the arguments born of that era, secessionists argued that while white southerners ought to wave a national flag and pay due service to a national cause, with poten-tially their lives, the tie that mattered most would be the link between individual states and their people. Even though Florida's secession from the Union on 10 January 1861 took place only weeks before the creation of the Confederacy, the secession delegation's effort to specify the ties of loyalty that connected citizens to the state reflected a will to cement the sovereignty of states at the expense of any national government. Florida's secession convention passed an ordinance stipulating that the state's general assembly alone "shall have power to declare who are citizens of this State," and to cede the right of determining citizenship to the state legislature alone.[45]

The desire to tether individuals to localities rather than to an embryonic Con-federacy worked at cross-purposes with a desire to pitch the actual definition of citizenship as broadly as possible. The need, for one, to erect a stable, white supremacist and male body politic meant dissolving as many of the divisions in that group as possible, while at the same time building high walls that would keep others out. James Dowdell, delegate to Alabama's convention, offered his objec-tion to an amendment of the new state constitution that would have extended the right of citizen to all persons who were residents, rather than born citizens of the state. To cement the loyalty of all white men, Dowdell argued that the divide between black and white was the only division that mattered. "I am perfectly willing to throw around citizenship all proper safe-guards to elevate and dignify the privilege, but not at the expense of equality between white men." Delegates also cast a wide net to invite sympathetic persons into the southern fold. "Our policy now should be to invite men to live with us who are willing to fight with us," claimed George Shortridge. "Wherever a white man can be found—it mat-ters little where born—who will enlist under our flag and march to the field to defend our independence and our homes, he should be honored with the rights of citizenship." The result of this broad understanding of citizenship often tied secessionists in knots. In drawing up a new constitution for Georgia, secession delegates in that state defined citizens as persons who were born or naturalized citizens at the moment of secession, while also offering the status to those who moved to the state within twelve months following secession and volunteered to serve in the state militia or, significantly, to any woman who was the wife of a citizen.[46]

For many northerners, the southern reaction to Lincoln's election brought a fractured nation out of a collective stupor. National prosperity, wrote a writer in the *Atlantic Monthly*, had lulled Americans into thinking that the republic could withstand any crisis. As a result, the prospect of secession encouraged citizens to reexamine their connection to government as they had not done in decades. Mixing singular and plural into a complex whole, the writer argued, "The United States are not a German Confederation, but a unitary and indivisible nation," and in the midst of secession, it was time that "the traitors of the South should know that the Free States are becoming every day more united in sentiment and more earnest in resolve." Once southerners saw through the secessionist argument as little more than "empty bluster, a public spirit will be aroused that will be content with no half-measures, and which no Executive, however unwilling, can resist." Talk of emboldened citizens and emboldened nation-states went hand in hand. The article made light of the state's rights argument of secessionists by claiming that the notion of states possessing sovereignty equal to that of the national government was ludicrous: "The legitimate consequence of secession is, not that a State becomes sovereign, but that, so far as the General Government is concerned, she has outlawed herself, nullified her own existence as a State, and become an aggregate of riotous men who resist the execution of the laws." The editorial stopped short of advocating armed violence to put down the secessionist cause, but it did call for "responsible force prudently exerted," to compel the allegiance of those Americans in the southern states who had forgotten their loyalty.[47]

What had started in the 1830s and gathered pace as the sectional conflict grew was not simply the emergence of regional identity but the dissolution of the few, fragile ties that connected Americans to the national government. Though they disagreed over the specifics, often vehemently, Americans on either side of the yawning gap between the United States and a newly minted Confederacy seemed resigned to the idea that William McWillie had posed as an absurdity only three decades before. There was, in fact, no such thing as a citizen of the United States, and even if the notion had merit, it was only in the relationship between an individual and his state that citizenship carried any explanatory power. Having bent, stretched, and damaged a political relationship that was never clearly defined in the first place, Americans clutched what was left of their republic, while secessionists concerned themselves with erecting a new kind of citizenship: rooted in race, governed by gender, policed by individual states, and driven by a broad, nationalist call to arms. Americans in and out of government began to build a new understanding of citizenship, though it was slower to crystallize: driven by a common cause of defending the republic from disaster and riven to the basic obligation of all to defend the American republic, with persons who sought to demolish it deemed nothing less than traitors. The Civil War would bring about a revolution of citizenship, fired in war and animated by the massive expansion of two rival nation-states, while at the same time encouraging the development of two leviathans that demanded loyalty at all costs.

BY THE TIME DEEP SOUTH STATES left the Union, talk of loyalty was everywhere. It was an understandable reaction. Given the possibility of military action, people expressed loyalty to their section or the nation in ways that were at once wounded, bellicose, and nervous. It would not take long, however, for expressions of loyalty to meet a determination on the part of governments to extract loyalty at all costs. Policing the boundary between the loyal and the disloyal would, in time, become almost as important as defending the border between the two nations. Yet the overwhelming sentiment expressed by southerners across the social spectrum during secession was of the most powerful, most tender tie of affection connecting people not to the United States but to the individual states that held their truest allegiance. Perhaps the most eloquent example of this was expressed in the speech that Mississippi senator Jefferson Davis offered to the Senate as his state took its leave from the Union. Having served the nation as a soldier, a representative of government, a secretary of war, and a senator, the future president of the Confederacy had spent a lifetime pledging his devotion to the United States. For this reason, Davis was a quiet, reluctant advocate of Mississippi's independence. But when it became clear that the state would go, Davis rose before the Senate on 21 January 1861 and delivered a long-considered speech in which he explained his reasons for leaving and his sadness at the circumstances that compelled him to take such a course.[48]

Caught between home and nation, Davis was in a bind. His remarks balanced regret at the dissolution of the Union with a determination to burnish his credentials as a state's rights champion. Ever the politician, Davis could not help but imagine a place for himself in a new Confederacy, even if his prospects in his new career as a citizen of a new nation were at best unclear. Davis claimed that his philosophy of American government rested upon his belief in the right of a state to secede. As it had become clear that Mississippi would remove itself from the republic, he was bound by honor and his "allegiance to the State of which I am a citizen" to do the same. For Davis, loyalty to his state trumped all other ties. As John C. Calhoun had argued three decades before, it was the essence of American citizenship that the allegiance to locality superseded any bond of loyalty that Americans might have felt toward the nation, even if a man like Davis had fought for that nation as a soldier in war. Davis then called on the memory of Calhoun and nullification as a peaceful, reasonable, constitutional doctrine, more reasonable now that southerners, Davis claimed, were left with little option than to follow the radical course of secession. Embedded in his remarks were all the hallmarks of three decades of debate over the terms of American citizenship. Davis defined the Union as little more than a compact, with individual states given the right to shape their future in whatever way they wished, independent from the national government. He also claimed that so long as abolitionists and northern members of Congress insisted on interpreting the Declaration of Independence as a broad, sweeping document of liberty and equality for all, regardless of race, Davis and white southerners generally would beg to differ.[49]

The day after he delivered his remarks, Davis and his wife, Varina, boarded a train bound for Mississippi. Reaching Vicksburg at the end of the month, he immediately made his way to Davis Bend and his plantation, Brierfield. By the time he arrived home, his state was in the midst of a dramatic transformation. After having severed ties to the Union, secessionists encouraged whites all over Mississippi to devote themselves to the new cause of independence. Yet even with the wind at their backs, secessionists proudly proclaimed their new nation-state, their new Republic of Mississippi, all the while harboring worries about what it was taking to bring that republic into being. "We presume that ere this reaches our readers' eyes," wrote the editor of the *Natchez Daily Courier* three weeks before Jefferson Davis returned home, "a majority of the Convention of ninety-nine gentlemen now assembled at Jackson, will have proclaimed Mississippi out of the Union. If it has been done irrespective of any vote of the people sanctioning it, it is worth only the paper upon which the ordinance has been written, unless the people, by sufferance and tacit consent hereafter, approve it. A peaceful revolution (and secession but claims to have that peaceful character) must have the assent of the people." In the wake of secession, the architects of an independent Mississippi would wrestle with this, the same question that had bedeviled Americans since the nation had been created. For a new republic built on the bedrock of the nullification argument, the notion that individual states held citizens in a closer compact than that of a nation would pose a profound challenge for every secessionist who dreamed of a slaveholding republic. The issue of sovereignty would organize the terrain of a whole new struggle in the Confederacy, as secessionists put their convictions about citizenship to the test of sustaining their cause in war.[50]

CHAPTER TWO

The Rise and Fall of a Slaveholder's Republic

Mississippi governor John Pettus had been in office for only nine days when, in November 1859, he received a letter that threatened disaster. It detailed an abolitionist attack, "much better planned than the Harpers Ferry affair," filled with the foreboding mention of determined whites, revolutionary slaves, a cache of rifles, and wooden pikes. Though rumors of servile insurrection in the slaveholding South were hardly news by the late 1850s, vivid imaginings of scheming abolitionists and plotting slaves still touched the rawest of white southern nerves. Many slaveholders confided this very nightmare to their diaries. Masters believed that unless they remained forever vigilant, the Cotton South would follow Haiti and Jamaica down the same sinkhole of black freedom and white ruin. What made the letter Pettus received an unusual one, however, was that the primary target was not a cotton store or a master's cherished abode. It was Pettus's own state government. The letter disclosed that once abolitionists had joined slaves and disaffected whites, the state capitol building in Jackson would be taken and legislators would be held captive until they passed "an act emancipating all the Black people in the State." With banks robbed and public records set alight, the indiscriminate massacre of slaveholders would follow, leaving no doubt that the state of Mississippi lived on borrowed time. Unless armed abolitionists and slaves were stopped, "they will succeed in revolutionizing the government."[1]

Threats of black revolution were ironic, given that what John Pettus and secessionists all over the South were planning was a revolution of their own. From the moment he began his political career in 1843, Pettus had styled himself as an uncompromising radical, the rough-hewn representative from the Kemper County piney woods who made a show of lacking the refinement of the Mississippi River elite, to the delight of his constituents. His politics formed a heady mix: a reformist agenda balanced by an unbending support of southern independence. Pettus argued often and publicly that secession was the only remedy to protect Mississippi from conniving abolitionists and a grasping federal government. His passion for this issue, not to mention the length of time Pettus spent squarely in the secessionist camp, often came at great expense. When, in 1850, talk of southern sectionalism had matured into a public convention convened to seek southern independence, Pettus traveled to Nashville to take part in the debate and absorbed a body blow to his political fortunes when the convention fell apart. As a result, Pettus found himself as something of an outlier, even within his own Democratic Party. He did not seek reelection in 1857, but as sectional talk matured into concerted action, it was not long before Pettus acquired that most precious of political titles: principled soothsayer. As circumstances converged to make secession more of a reality, latecomers to southern independence found that men like Pettus already occupied the high ground. As a result, when Democrats gathered in Jackson to nominate a candidate for governor in 1859, the secessionist Pettus was the front-runner. Though his nomination was contested—by those who voiced strong opposition to his unstinting secessionist platform and by many in the state's slaveholding establishment who thought Pettus too much of a populist for such an august office—he stood for election as the preeminent candidate for southern independence. To his supporters, Pettus was a paragon of manly action and determined resolve. According to one Democratic newspaper, Pettus was nothing less than a bright beacon for state's rights. "Forcible in debate, fearless in maintaining his principles, wise and discreet in council," Pettus was the only man for the job. In the election, Pettus won with more than two-thirds of the vote. Wasting no time, in his inaugural address Pettus called for another southern convention, one he now believed would not fail. In the months leading up to the 1860 presidential election, Pettus confidentially wrote to southern compatriots with the élan of a seasoned revolutionary who had found his moment. "I have reasons for hoping that nearly all the slave holding States will meet us in Convention," wrote Pettus to South Carolina governor William Gist in April 1860, "should a Black Republican be elected in November."[2]

Even though his hard-won efforts all pointed to success, letters that crossed Pettus's desk that spoke of revolution—not by his compatriots but by abolitionists and slaves—would have given any zealot pause for thought. It was the soft spot of the secessionist argument that even though men like Pettus believed that the broad swathe of the white South supported the idea of independence, they could never shake the doubt that their own house was not yet in order. All turned on the same questions that had brought the nation to a precipice. If, as secession's supporters argued, citizens owed their most basic loyalty to their states rather than to the American nation, could this venerable tie between states and individuals hold firm once Mississippi became part of a broader Confederacy? Moreover, in a world where slaveholders worried constantly about the loyalty of not only their white neighbors but their own bondspeople, it was hard to believe that if secessionists attempted to go it alone, the rest of the region would follow. Bluster obscured most of the worry, but only just. What was needed was coordinated action, savvy electioneering, the resolve to do all that was necessary to see secession carried out, and the willingness to silence those who stood in the way. If loyalty could not be cajoled, secessionists reasoned, it could be coerced, a time-honored idea in a region dominated by black bondage and white mastery.[3]

The history of how the American South became the Confederate States of America is a story that has been told many times and very well at that. While early studies of secession hewed closely to the idea that its founding was the inevitable product of a long-simmering southern sectional identity, more recent work has shown just what a stage-managed production secession was and, by turns, just how close secessionists came to a humiliating defeat. Several excellent case studies have also focused on how secession played out in individual states. What gets lost in this work, however, is that secession and the creation of a new Confederacy were different historical creatures: once independent, states needed to be subsumed in a broader Confederate state if the secessionist project was to survive a war. Yet while secessionists may have assumed that a Confederate nation would simply pool the collective loyalties of southern citizenship to states in a cocktail of heady nationalism, this process was not simple or straightforward. Building a nation came into conflict with long-held ideas about where citizens had naturally directed their loyalty.[4] All the same, secessionists put long-held theories of government into practice, the same theories that had undergirded debates over citizenship, decades before secession became a reality. At bottom, secessionists sought a compact with citizens that riveted citizens to their states. It was this idea that would become part of the battle men like John Pettus would wage to ensure that the Republic of Mississippi would last.[5]

It would not take long, however, before war and a much larger process of national state formation overwhelmed John Pettus and his republic. Beginning early in the Civil War and building to a crescendo as the American military invaded the state, the Republic of Mississippi would quickly become a shell, with the flimsiest of claims to sovereignty and with, perhaps most importantly, the most tenuous of holds over the loyalty of the populace. Both the United States and the Confederacy would test entirely new and far-reaching policies that expanded national governments into powerful nation-states. These emboldened states bore down hard on the Mississippi Valley, carving the region into pieces. In the maelstrom that ensued, the relationship between Mississippians and Pettus's republic dissolved, along with his government. John Pettus's best laid plans for a strong state would falter and falter quickly. While the battles waged by American and Confederate armies would do much of the damage, it was the inability of Pettus and his government to sustain the tie with the people—the inability to sustain the loyalty of the populace to the idea of an independent Mississippi—that sapped Pettus's government of much of its power. By the last months of the Civil War, John Pettus became a stateless fugitive. Hounded by the American army, cut loose from the Confederacy, he left Mississippi in almost the exact state foretold by the letter he received just days after he took office. His government would be tossed into a revolutionary crucible, forged by powerful nation-states, that would ultimately set Mississippi and the Cotton South alight.

WHEN DELEGATES TO THE STATE'S SECESSION convention made their way to Jackson to decide Mississippi's future, most traveled through counties, towns, and hamlets that had been wilderness only three decades before. While the oldest settlements along the lower Mississippi River dated back to the early eighteenth century, much of the rest of the state had been Indian Country until the 1830s, when two enormous seizures of Creek and Chickasaw land opened up eastern and central Mississippi for development. The territory—carved into plots, sold on the cheap, and gobbled up by speculators—touched off a rapid expansion of the state. Fully thirty new counties were formed between 1833 and 1836, more than doubling the geographical size of the state while rapidly expanding the state's population, free and slave.

The speed with which Mississippi grew created sharp social and political divisions. One of these was a disparity between economic wealth and political power. By 1860, 43 percent of slaveholders in the state who owned more than forty slaves lived on plantations that lined the Mississippi River. These planters, not surprisingly, still owned the lion's share of the personal wealth in the state, in comparison with the inhabitants of the hill country in the north-central part of the state as well as of the piney woods counties that lay farther south. It was a familiar economic gap, between the haves and the have-nots. Most other cotton states in the South wrestled with a similar division. But to a degree even more pronounced than in other Cotton South states, white Mississippians crafted a democratic political culture that was intended to mask this division. State legislators brushed a thick gloss of egalitarianism over a disparity of wealth between whites that most could see but few recognized publicly. A state constitution, ratified in 1832, laid the groundwork to unite new counties with the old, with mass democracy acting as the salve to heal whatever rifts remained.[6] The standard-issue constitutional provisions of the early republic—the easing of restrictions over voting and office-holding, as well as making most public offices subject to popular election—were intended to make poor and moneyed white males alike equal members in the state's body politic. To be sure, older forms of control ensured that elite planters still ruled. But a tense marriage of economic power and political interest welded Mississippi's political culture together, right up to secession.[7]

What buoyed the enthusiasm of delegates to the state's secession convention, particularly those who believed independence was the only way forward, was the steadfast belief that whatever divisions remained, cotton and slavery were the foundation of the economy of the region, the nation, and indeed, the world. By 1860, the state contained an enormous plantation complex that produced nearly a third of the nation's cotton crop, planted and picked by more than 436,000 slaves. As a result, the wealth generated from cotton and slaves influenced the culture and the politics of Mississippi in profound ways. No matter where they lived, regardless of their training or their profession, whites believed that all in the state wanted a share of the cotton spoils. "A large plantation and negroes are the ULTIMA THULE of every Southern gentleman's ambition," declared the *Vicksburg Sun*. "For this the lawyer pores over his dusty tomes, the merchant measures his tape, the doctor rolls his pills, the editor drives his quill, and the mechanic his plane—all, all who dare aspire at all, look to this as the goal of their ambition."[8]

Unity of ambition does not always translate into a unity of political purpose, however, and despite the confidence of some delegates, most worried that the state lacked the broad support necessary to build a new, independent Mississippi. It was this concern, even among the most ardent secessionists, that weighed on the minds of those who made their way to the state capitol. One of them was Absalom Dantzler, a lawyer, minister, and father of four who lived in Jasper, a county in the piney woods near Jackson. Jasper was fast becoming part of Mississippi's plantation complex, though the county in the 1840s and '50s bore all the hallmarks of a raucous frontier. In that environment, men with the connections could make their mark and amass a fortune with dizzying quickness. For his part, Dantzler had parlayed his training as a lawyer and his communal standing as a preacher into a seat in the state legislature and the ownership of some thirty-eight slaves. Despite his position, Dantzler had misgivings about secession, though these concerns had quickly morphed into resignation that a political tide worked against anyone who stood in the way of Mississippi's independence. Dantzler worried that "a State of fearful derangement" gripped legislators he saw on the

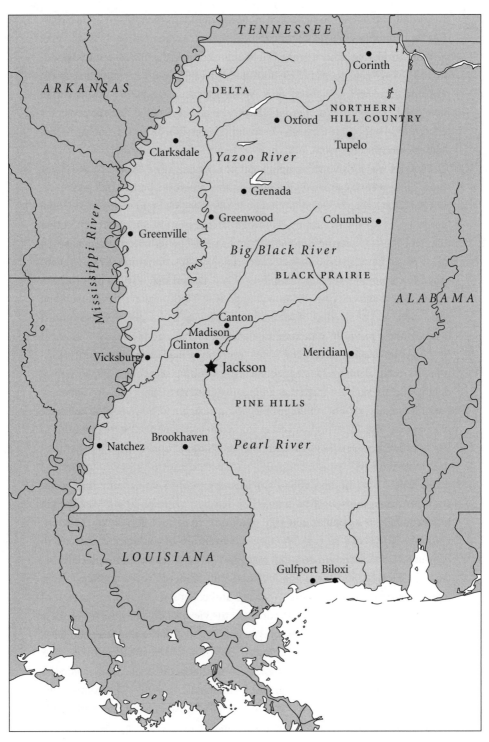

Map of Mississippi

streets and in the boardinghouses around the capitol in the lead-up to the secession convention, men who decried the election of Abraham Lincoln as the final northern insult to southern pride. Dantzler looked past the fire-eater grandstanding to the challenge to come. He admitted with uncommon candor that "most probably times will be harder" once Mississippi seceded, harder perhaps than most people had ever experienced. Though he had concluded that slavery's protection could only come through Mississippi's secession, he hoped that calm, cool deliberation would win out over chest-thumping, frenzied action.[9]

Dantzler was not alone. A significant bloc of delegates elected to the state's secession convention pressed for a slower, more measured path to independence. At a public meeting in Vicksburg in late November 1860, opponents of disunion built support for their cause by claiming that secession was rash, an action that threatened to detonate the American republic before patient negotiation had even taken place. Once in convention, cooperationists (as they came to be known) called for a popular vote on the question and argued that any attempt to push secession through the convention without a vote would set a newly independent Mississippi on the shakiest of foundations. William Barksdale, a cooperationist delegate and a player in state politics, declared that any action that would result in Mississippi leaving the United States "must be ratified by the States [in] which it is proposed." Though he stepped back from calling secession a perversion of democracy, Barksdale argued that an independent Mississippi that did not enjoy the full-throated support of the people would struggle to survive. In the absence of a popular vote, "croaking and disappointed demagogues will seize upon this to stir up groundless opposition to that new constitution," hobbling the independent state in its infancy.[10]

Barksdale was shouted down. For Mississippi's fire-eaters, only immediate and irrevocable secession would do. They defeated a motion to put Mississippi's independence to a popular vote by a margin of 70 to 29. Efforts made by cooperationist delegates—first, to organize a convention of southern states later in February 1861 and, second, to adopt secession only after conventions in Alabama, Georgia, Florida, and Louisiana followed suit—suffered the same fate. Under intense pressure, cooperationists wavered and collapsed. "I have, to the best of my humble ability, endeavored to carry out the views of my constituents in these respects," claimed Walker Brooke of Warren County. "I have acted in good faith, and with no desire to make a factious opposition. I have failed." All the same, Brooke made it clear that no matter his convictions, the convention needed to act quickly. Failure to do so, he claimed, "would make ourselves obnoxious to the scorn and ridicule of the world." With the weight of history sitting uncomfortably on their shoulders, delegates ratified an ordinance of secession by a wide margin, with only fifteen votes against. When the result of the vote was read before the convention, secessionists seized the moment and unfurled a silk flag bearing a single star. Remarking that the flag was the first to be displayed in honor of the newly independent Republic of Mississippi, William Barry, president of the convention, called for the entire delegation to rise in applauding their bold bid for nationhood. None dared remain in their seats.[11]

Even before the vote had been tallied, supporters of secession used the agitprop theater of a flowering independence movement as a scrim behind which they laid the groundwork for a new republic. Destroying their connection to the United States, however, proved far easier than building something new. For some, the ties of allegiance that connected white southerners to the American nation were easily shorn. Robert Flournoy, a delegate from the eastern black prairie county of Pontotoc, argued that the simple passage of the secession ordinance absolved every citizen of Mississippi from allegiance to the United States. As many supporters of secession knew, the finicky work of examining such an important question slowed the speed with which secessionists wanted to take Mississippi out of the United States. The convention did create a committee on citizenship to examine the issue more carefully. But when the report from the committee was presented to the convention, the results were less than clear. J. M. Dyer, a delegate who had supported secession and had sat on the committee, argued that any debate over citizenship, in Mississippi or anywhere else in the would-be Confederacy, should remain broad and ill defined. Despite the rushed way in which secession was put to a vote, Dyer saw no reason for similar speed on the question of citizenship until a confederacy was formed. He remarked that even when the time came for such a debate, delegates should not adopt any measure that might limit anyone from becoming a citizen. Estimating that nearly a half-million southerners remained in the United States, Dyer argued that no impediment should be placed in front of them to stop their return. "There were also Northern people who were as true to the South and its institutions as if born here," claimed Dyer, and any policy that required these individuals, loyal or not, to take an oath and publicly avow their allegiance to Mississippi would be an empty gesture. If traitors lived within the new republic, "an oath will not restrain them. If they are base enough to come here and act the part of spies, they will not hesitate, to commit perjury. If such come here, we will deal with them promptly and decidedly. . . . They will find no protection in an oath of allegiance."[12]

In both the convention that decided on independence and the meeting of the state legislature that followed a few weeks later, representatives worked long hours to cement secession in law. Absalom Dantzler cautioned his wife that she should not expect him home for many weeks, as legislators worked to "make many changes in the Constitution so as to adapt it to the new position which Mississippi has assumed as an independent republic." In the end, Dantzler's warning proved too hasty. In all, the state legislature met for only seven days, even though the number of revised statutes and amendments made for a furious session. To this, an additional session in July added forty-seven separate acts, making it one of the most productive periods of lawmaking in the state's history. At no point, however, was the subject of citizenship discussed. Whatever misgivings some might have had about the way Mississippi took its leave from the United States were buried in the verbiage necessary to harmonize state law with the Confederacy, or to change the time that the Wayne County probate court was held each year.[13]

If the lack of time spent on the relationship between the people and an independent republic spoke volumes about the mindset of lawmakers, it would also prove prophetic. In the absence of a clearly defined relation, voters outside the legislature stepped into the vacuum to define what citizenship in a newly independent Mississippi meant to them. While some secession delegates counseled caution, circumstances outside the convention made loyalty to the cause a point of conflict, backed by the threat of violence and the application of state power. Even as the secession ordinance was being printed in newspapers all over Mississippi, ordinary supporters of the cause resorted to language that made it clear that opposition to independence required radical measures to suppress dissent. For some, the medical metaphor was apt. "I live in a healthy neighborhood, if my County is sickly," wrote one man to Pettus, "but I am happy to say a great change is now going on here. . . . Thank God we now our [sic] loose from Yankey sin & I breathe . . . deeper now." Calls to cut the disloyal from Mississippi like a cancer gathered pace, particularly once the government began to organize the state militia in earnest. Armed units merged with vigilance committees to create a powerful armed wing of the secessionist movement that made no pretense of dealing evenhandedly with those who counseled deliberation or calm. "There is, in our neighborhood, a man whom we regard as being dangerous, or at least he is opposed to our southern movements," wrote the citizens of Hair River to Pettus in May 1861. The letter detailed a militia company that had been organized in the community, with a vigilance committee attached that had instructions to "ferret out all disloyal persons in our boundaries." The letter named three persons in the community who had been public in their support of Lincoln and who hoped that the United States would abolish slavery. Deeming these persons enemies of the state who ought to be clapped in prison for their views, the Hair River vigilance committee sought advice from Pettus as to what they should do, particularly with one unidentified man who made no secret of his allegiance: "He is going at large and we want to get rid of him."[14]

Secessionist concerns about the loyalty of whites were also connected to a concern about whether slaves would be loyal to masters and their cause. It could hardly have been otherwise. For many white southerners, ideas about loyalty were made meaningful through slavery, and for supporters of southern independence, the region's most important asset was also their most vulnerable. While many spoke openly about the undying support of slaves for their masters, rumors of plots by slaves forced as many slaveholders to confront the irony of seeing African Americans as at once the most loyal and the most revolutionary persons living in their midst. Some whites laid their hopes for a southern future on the participation of slaves in a war for independence. One slaveholder in Jefferson County wrote John Pettus in early January 1861 demanding the repeal of a state law that made it illegal for slaves to carry firearms. The planter reasoned that it was better to allow planters to "drill and practice their own slaves" as military units to defend plantations and the state, than to pass up the chance to make effective use of a servile population and allow them to fall under the influence of abolitionists. In contrast, Pettus received a letter from the same county four months later that called for greater vigilance from the state government to police slaves on and off the plantation. The letter disclosed plans of an insurrection, to be carried out on July 4th, "with an eye to burning plantations and threatening white women." Slaveholders searched desperately for clues as to black intentions. Even in professions of undying loyalty from slaves, many masters could never fully trust the sentiment. One newspaper account, published in October 1861, recounted the story of a slave who had escaped his master and fled to American lines in Paducah, Kentucky. Presenting himself to U.S. officers, who informed him that "he was free and as good as any of old Abe's white men," the freedman was paid a wage to be a servant. Much to the satisfaction of readers, the unidentified man "tried the experiment of freedom one month, received no pay for services rendered, made his escape and returned to his master, bringing much valuable information." Whether true or apocryphal, newspaper reports that made light of African American intentions betrayed a nervousness that could not be ignored.[15]

In the echo chamber that secession created, worries about the loyalty of slaves merged quickly with broader concerns about the loyalty of the white populace. John Pettus said as much in his message to the special session of the state legislature six days after the secession ordinance passed. In remarks meant to keep the leadership of the new Republic of Mississippi at the ready, Pettus called on the legislature to make the disloyal, white and black, coequal in the eyes of the law. "We have embarked on a stormy sea," admitted Pettus, "and much of the peril which attends our voyage is to be apprehended from the thoughtlessness and passions of our own crew." Pettus called for order and attention paid to the rule of law, but he also sought and secured stringent laws from the legislature to punish both the planning and the carrying out of insurrection, so that white and black alike did not take circumstances into their own hands. In making this demand, Pettus made no distinction between which group posed the greater threat. The loyalty of slaves and the loyalty of whites, in and out of Mississippi, became part of the same dark threat in the secessionist imagination. In mid-February 1861, Fulton Anderson, Mississippi's appointed commissioner to the state of Virginia, turned that worry into high melodrama. As part of his address to the Virginia legislature, Anderson asked delegates to recall John Brown's raid on Harpers Ferry. He reminded Virginians that treasonous abolitionists had encouraged insurrection, "to give your dwellings to the torch of the incendiary and your wives and children to the knives of assassins." While the attempt, in Anderson's mind, proved a failure, it only showed the resolve of the men who now controlled the White House. Still, in a speech that dripped with menace, Anderson stopped short of impugning the loyalty of slaves. To do so would have tripped a wire that held southern society together. "True that your slaves proved loyal," remarked Anderson, "and by a prompt execution of your laws you vindicated your dignity and exacted from the wretched criminals the just forfeiture of their lives." Whether the statement was an artful dodge or an enormous blind spot, secessionists could not reckon honestly with the loyalty of blacks any more than they could with that of whites. It exposed all at once how secessionists had achieved southern independence.[16]

Even among the loyal, mobilizing support for secession proved a challenge. Not only did secessionist leaders find it hard to keep abreast of the faithful who took matters into their own hands, but building a new republic demanded that leaders confront two key fault lines in the state's political system. One of these was the uneasy division between the settled and the frontier portions of the state. For elite planters, politics in Mississippi had long been a tense mismatch between democratic rhetoric and slaveholder power. Even though the geographical expansion of the state had encouraged the spread of slavery, mutual interest had never completely unified whites in common cause. River planters had never completely squared their status with the political marriage between them and their perceived inferiors in state government. Even the most ardent supporters of secession could not help but notice that establishment newspapers, such as the *Natchez Courier*, saw the secession convention as proof that mass democracy was little more than a tyranny. The state, claimed the paper, was then "governed by an oligarchy of Ninety-Nine. . . . If the people have invested them with dictatorial and sovereign power, so be it. The people will wake up one of these days, from that sad delusion." Though the state's Whig Party organ had long since taken its finger off the popular political pulse, its opinion reflected a long-standing view among the elite in Mississippi society, around which secessionists would have to tread lightly.[17]

The other fissure in Mississippi's political system lay in the distribution of power between the state and the county government. In this respect, planters and hill country farmers alike agreed, though their agreement did not bode well for any secessionist who looked to build a stronger, more lasting base of power. More than in most states, power in Mississippi's government was firmly rooted in county seats. The state constitution effectively created a small state government, with key powers ceded to Boards of Police that acted as the local organ of power in communities. The chosen name of these bodies reveals a good deal. Though the state legislature retained the right to organize a militia, local governments possessed their own armed forces, and at moments throughout the antebellum period, Boards of Police were not shy about using them, particularly on the enslaved. On the institution that mattered in Mississippi, the balance of power between the state and the local wings of government was heavily weighted in favor of counties. Constitutionally, legislators in the state legislature had no means to emancipate, much less intercede in the treatment of slaves, and except in cases where slaves were tried in courts for murder, local control held sway. Boards of Police controlled who served on slave patrols and when they were called into action, and though by 1850 the state legislature had stripped county government of this particular power, it handed this authority not to the state but to local justices of the peace, thus maintaining, even with a slight alteration, the ultimate balance of power in favor of localities. What resulted was a system of government in which the state deferred at the best of times to counties. This relationship was designed in such a way as to not disturb the local networks of power and influence that elite men possessed in their communities.[18]

Set against this backdrop, the challenges facing secessionists were manifold. Even though popular support for Mississippi's independence was evident in many parts of the state, translating that support into a project of state-building proved difficult. Two problems presented themselves to John Pettus. The first had to do with the state's military preparedness. In December 1859, only one month after taking office, Pettus had spearheaded an effort to secure an appropriation for the state's defense that amounted to $150,000. This money had been earmarked for the purchase of a cache of weapons to be used at the state's discretion. For supporters of secession, however, a January 1861 report from the state's adjutant general, W. L. Sykes, on the status of this purchase did not make for easy reading. The report stated that the government had signed a contract with Connecticut's Eli Whitney for a stand of some 1,500 rifles. The agreement fell through, however, largely because Whitney had held most of the shipment back, fearing federal inspection. Only 60 of Whitney's rifles reached state armories, and when they did, a close inspection of them found that they were merely "old guns fixed up." Once secession had been declared, the convention issued an ordinance that gave Pettus broad new powers to tax citizens and issue treasury notes to further fill its military coffers. But in part because of the precedent set by the debacle over guns, the governor found himself disempowered by the creation of a militia board that would hold ultimate authority over the raising of troops. The rebuke proved stinging. The members of the board, who counted themselves as some of Pettus's keenest political rivals, were given a power equal to that of the governor's office.[19]

Pettus was also pressured to assert state control over the growing number of military units that were offering their services for a coming conflict. In the weeks following secession, the state government was inundated with formal and informal offers to raise companies of armed men, in excess of the eighty the secession convention allowed. Even before the convention met, some sixty-five companies had already been organized in the wake of Lincoln's election, as popular enthusiasm for Mississippi's independence swept men into the service by the score. Yet, once the companies were mobilized, the older divisions between state and local power became apparent. For one, in keeping with custom drawn from militia service, companies insisted upon their prerogative to vote for the officers who would lead them into service. Though they had often been little more than honorary titles, prior to the war officer positions in the state militia conferred cultural capital that counted as hard currency in most communities. Officer elections offered communities the opportunity to engage in a thoroughly stage-managed reaffirmation of the status quo: the wealthy and the powerful curried favor, while those lower down the social ladder paid their due to local elites. What these officer elections were not, however, was a clear affirmation of state control over the men who were signing up to serve. The enlistment effort shone a bright light on an antiquated and thoroughly disorganized system. One letter writer claimed that "men who could not even rank and size a company or go through the Manual exercise with a musket" were seeking high military office, "where the lives of thousands might be sacrificed to their ignorance." John C. Higgins, an officer in the state militia, complained to Pettus in mid-January 1861 that "the people seem to be careless & believing the Malitia will now be called out are too apt to permit the different responsible offices to be filled by men in some instances entirely irresponsible and in many instances wholy unfitted either intellectually or morally." To remedy the problem, Higgins called upon Pettus to reorganize the militia and create a thoroughly capable fighting force in its place.[20]

Had military necessity been the only consideration, the governor would have acted. However, to do as Higgins and others demanded—to rebuild the militia while centralizing the government's control—was more than Pettus could manage. To boldly assert authority over the state militia, Pettus would have had to cross an unspoken line between state and local power. In the absence of a clear connection between the state and citizens, necessity dictated that Pettus accept reality. He could hardly tamp down white enthusiasm for war, even if he had wanted to. For this reason, local control over the militia became a poisoned pill state officials were bound to swallow. Companies looking to serve required the executive stamp of approval to be mustered into the state army, but the circumstances that surrounded how these fighting forces were organized and how they were led was left up to communities. To maintain the enthusiasm of the populace and to retain the favor of those in whose hands real power lay—particularly in 1861, with a gubernatorial campaign only months away—John Pettus's state military was his to lead in name alone.[21]

Maintaining the loyalty of the populace and paying due respect to local power brokers meant accepting the services of whoever signed on, in whatever form they offered it. Though the state lacked the means to pay for services, Pettus could refuse a request from a regiment to join the service only at the expense of his own political fortunes. In the absence of state power, however, local battles between clannish groups took center stage whenever regiments were formed and elections were held. "Our Captain has forced us into Camp and says he has the Power and authority to confine us to it," claimed James Gates to Pettus in June 1861. Having been mustered into service by their commanding officer before the state had even called their regiment to serve, Gates and his company were forced from their families, with threats of retribution if they did not comply. "Now I want to know if I am forced and compelled to comply with such Rules as the above where we are not getting any Pay for it all and be harassed and abused by our Officer when they as I conceive have no Power over us at all." Gates prevailed upon Pettus for help, claiming that were Pettus to come to his aid, Gates would bestow the greatest of favors "that any Governor ever did to one of his Subjects."[22]

The language writers used in these letters reveals something both unusual and important about the way people imagined their relationship to the state government. While it would be easy to dismiss the pleas of supplication and the rhetorical poses of the benighted as part of an attempt to stoke the ego of men like Pettus, there is more in these letters. What they reveal is a vernacular of subjecthood, patronage, and political friendship that was woven into the political culture of the state. It was a language connected to the webs of fictive kin that effectively connected communities, a political transubstantiation of informal favors and debts, historical allegiances, social obligations, and cultural rites that bound individuals to act, whether they be powerful or not.[23] For instance, John Pettus received many letters in the first year of the war that prevailed upon him to act so that he might help those who counted themselves as friends. The man from Marshall County who wrote to request weapons from the state arsenal to help organize a home guard asked that Pettus grant his request so that the governor "may do the state some service, and oblige many, many of your friends." This language of friendship contained many meanings. The very term indicated an imagined connection between the governor and the writers. At the same time, the political language of friendship suggested a group identity. By claiming to speak for a group rather than themselves, letters carried more weight. The "Friends of Soldiers" in Jefferson County who wrote Pettus in mid-August 1861 asked that all necessary provisions be made to allow enlisted men to winter with some small comforts while away. In the hands of some writers, however, friendship masked but could not hide political repercussions if a request was not answered with action. A doctor who sought an appointment asked Pettus to help him secure a post as a surgeon in the Confederate Army. Should there not be a vacancy, J. G. Love hoped that Pettus would keep his name in mind, and he made it clear that more than his own aspirations hung in the balance: "I and my Friends will regard it as a great favor if you will confer the honor the first vacancy that does occur." Pettus did not need a good reason to refuse these requests. As it happened, 1861 was an election year. A false step at such a tense moment might spell disaster for his chances to retain the governorship. As one letter writer made clear, with a mixture of obsequiousness and determination, "In times like the present that tries both soul and body, our noble and protective Governor must overlook his gallant people's demands and treat them as kindly as possible."[24]

The clever imagining of Pettus as a potentate to a white southerner's knights-errant was a calculated move. But the need to abide by the terms of an antiquated militia system while at the same time stoking the passion for war and maintaining loyalty to the state made for political misery. Writing from Lauderdale County, perilously close to Pettus's home, one man informed the governor that "almost every man in this part of the State" opposed the governor's concentration of troops, particularly as soldiers were not being properly provisioned or paid. "I have heard a great many men denouncing you for ord[er]ing them out and further for telling them [to] remain in the Service of the State." Democratic newspapers attempted to shore up support, but the tone of the endorsements read more like commiseration. Though the editor of the *American Citizen* claimed that the governor had many detractors, "we do not know what Gove. Pettus has done that he could have avoided; and what left undone that he could possibly have done, to engender this feeling of opposition to him." Allowing that it was impossible for any incumbent to hold office without brooking the ire of some, "especially if he goes straight forward according to the dictates of his own judgment and conscience," the editorial counseled understanding for and fidelity to Pettus. In a desperate bid, the governor put pressure on the state legislature to shift responsibility for troops from the state to the Confederate government in August 1861, but not until days before the election did Pettus convince Jefferson Davis to mobilize state troops into national service. The effect was immediate. In the October election, Pettus carried every county but four, by more than 26,000 votes. He took key slaveholding counties like Adams without trouble— a county that had been cool to his election two years before—and only in the counties around the capital did opposition forces gain any traction. Much of the reason for Pettus's success lay in the unwillingness of the electorate to upset a fragile state only months after it was created, but Pettus's reelection owed a good deal to the state government's inability, or unwillingness, to organize absentee voting for soldiers in camp. Had they been given the chance, many soldiers would have undoubtedly vented their spleen at the polls. With their absence from the voting rolls, Pettus was spared.[25]

Even though Pettus's political career was given a new lease on life, the struggle to command an army in the field and the ceding of that command to the Confederate nation-state had consequences for the Republic of Mississippi. Having equated support for secession with support for the state government, Pettus and other secessionists assumed that the loyalty of the populace bound white southerners to the state of Mississippi. Faced with the prospect of having to cede authority over the military to the Confederacy, the chaotic expressions of loyalty that had propped up Mississippi's secession would now be pulled in one direction: the project of national survival.

The decision to bring Mississippi troops into national service saved Pettus from electoral defeat, and he used his success at the polls as the pretext to justify dramatic action. Pettus was not often given to long-winded oratory, but his message to the state legislature in November 1861 was sweeping and lengthy. In it, the governor lashed out at the ties that had held his power in check. Pettus reminded the legislature that by the end of the year, the state had raised and handed over more than 23,000 troops to the Confederacy, and Pettus was determined that they should be provisioned and supplemented with an additional fighting force. Making it clear that these troops and soldiers still being mustered represented "a larger proportion of the adult male population than any State or nation has sent forth to war in modern times," Pettus took aim at the architecture of government that had hemmed him in. He called for a bold reworking of virtually every aspect of military policy. He asked the legislature to alter the current system of county-level taxation that funded the provisioning of troops, a practice that had proven a disaster when the state government had been forced to accept so many into the service at one time. Pettus also argued for the harmonization of soldiers' pay with that of troops serving the national government and the dissolution of the Military Board, which had so powerfully curtailed his authority. "The magnitude and duration of the war in which we are engaged, I fear, have not been fully appreciated," Pettus claimed at the close of his address. Describing the conflict as do or die, he called on the legislature to do all that was necessary to fully and completely mobilize the state for total war: "Let the legislative action of the State speak this to our friends and foes as the action of our troops on the field has spoken it, and the conflict may be shortened and victory will be insured." If the power of states is determined at least in part by their control over the use of legitimate force, Pettus aimed to balance the scales.[26]

Pettus's decision to dramatically alter the structure of the military cleared ground in ways that would have been unthinkable only a few months before. What he sought was to enlarge the state's power over that of counties, in wartime circumstances that would make it nearly impossible for localities to refuse the effort. But this attempt to restructure the power of the state government paled in comparison with the additional mobilization of the population that Pettus envisioned. As has long been the case in the history of state formation, threats to sovereignty attend massive expansions of state power. For Pettus, just such an opportunity was made possible by American incursions in Tennessee in February 1862 and the massing of troops along Mississippi's northern border. In reaction, Pettus ordered all able-bodied men into the service to defend both the southern coast and the northern hill country in and around Corinth and Meridian. He also empowered local Boards of Police to round up all men who could serve. In a late February address reprinted in newspapers all over the state, Pettus tipped his hand at even more radical action. "Our fate is in our hands. It is with ourselves to decide the alternative. That decision should be, as I believe it will, Liberty or Death. . . . I am unwilling to visit upon the escutcheon of the State the stigma which would be implied in resorting to the draft until every other means had been exhausted." The mere mention of conscription was a barely veiled political threat. Coming as it did a month before the Confederacy would institute the first conscription act in that state's young history, it showed just how much Pettus was ahead of the curve. It was a powerful card that Pettus waved in front of his opposition to show how far he was willing to go to protect his government from disaster.[27]

This moment—of Pettus at his most confident and bellicose—would be the high-water mark of his political career, though in a crushing twist of fate, this same moment would mark the beginning of his swift fall from grace. Relinquishing control of much of the state military to the Confederacy sapped the state government of armed power, a consolidation of authority that would, in time, bring Mississippi's state government firmly under the aegis of the Confederate state. What had been a reciprocal, if tense, relationship between a state and a nation would become something altogether different. To achieve this end required a change in the way citizens made sense of their connection to the national government. Since this change came at a time of threat, circumstances demanded that Mississippians think in new ways about the utility of state power and their level of acceptance of it as a fact in their day-to-day lives. In this way, the need to consolidate authority over people and resources went together with a process of Confederate state formation that effectively sapped the state of Mississippi of its power and, in time, its sovereignty.[28]

Battles over loyalty became more forceful as the state and national governments consolidated their power, and as American troops threatened the Mississippi Valley. The combination of forces attenuated the spectrum of loyalty, as whites inferred from the political debate taking place in Jackson and Richmond the broader intentions of both states. John Pettus received letters from elderly men who offered their services, not as soldiers but as informants who would find those "in our midst who despise our cause" and bring them to justice. Others asked the governor for some direction as to whether there were state laws that would punish people "for Expressing unfriendly feelings towards our Government." The terms of loyalty also took on an added dimension once conscription became a growing reality. A man from Itawamba County, in the northeastern part of the state, offered the services of both him and his friends as volunteers, to avoid being drafted into the service and suffer the ignominy of being tarred as conscripts. As invasion gave the war a more visceral aspect, newspapers offered stark reminders of the challenge ahead. Whereas Mississippians viewed the war a year before "as a kind of frolic," most were now disabused of their simple belief in inevitable victory. "With the experience of the past twelve-months—its successes and its reverses—with a clear knowledge of the nature of the war and its terrible cost in life, health and money," claimed an editorial in the *Daily Mississippian*, "we are all the more thoroughly confirmed in our unalterable determination to brave all and suffer all as long as God gives us life, before we will give up the invaluable boon our fathers bequeathed to us."[29]

A determination to succeed in the face of long odds was a sentiment shared by most Confederates by the middle of 1862, though as a national identity matured, not to mention national power, older loyalties began to quickly melt away. For some, a shared spirit of sacrifice brought the necessity of national, rather than regional, identity to the forefront. For others, time spent in newly occupied territory brought home the problem of remaining loyal to one's state in a war between nations. By July, the Delta county of Bolivar had become a no-man's-land between the Confederacy and a growing American force massed a few miles away in Memphis. U.S. forces had taken New Orleans earlier that April, and the Mississippi River became the nexus point for a welter of divided loyalties and onrushing armies. In this environment, the politicization of loyalty, started during secession, intensified, and with it, counties along the river became centers of disaffection and torn allegiance. One man caught in the middle was W. R. Stewart. In his letter to John Pettus, Stewart stated his belief that it was the duty of all "loyal good citizens" to provide information about the actions of others who might mean the nation harm. Stewart proceeded to disclose details of persons in the county who enjoyed too close a relation to the United States. He reported the unsubstantiated rumor that one neighbor sold 400 bales of cotton to merchants behind American lines, as well as "supplies for their men of vegetables, fresh meat." For the past three months, this individual's sympathies were well known in the community as not having been "with our cause, and he does all he can to embarrass the raising of Partizan companies here and report says has furnished the yankees with full information of the whereabouts of all the cotton in the county, and the names of all prominant Secessionists." Stewart asked Pettus whether the government had cause to arrest the man. Loyal Confederates in Bolivar had grown "very uneasy about his conduct." In closing, Stewart made it clear that so long as Confederate authorities routed out dissenters, the nation would prevail. "We want no domestic enemies amg us," Stewart concluded. "We can handle the yankies if you will keep off our own who give their aid."[30]

Stewart's concern for the nation rather than the state signaled a seismic shift. From the moment that the Mississippi government ceded authority to its armed forces, claims of sovereignty in the face of a growing Confederacy and advancing enemy armies began to lack resolve. By the end of 1862, talk of preserving the Confederacy superseded that of maintaining the state government, leaving officials like John Pettus struggling to assert their authority. "The cause," as so many called it, became less an effort to prepare states like Mississippi for war and more a battle in which loyalties to the Confederacy and a maturing Confederate citizenship assumed pride of place. American incursions into northern Mississippi and along the river worked in tandem with the increased power of the Confederacy to sap the state government of power. National conscription and confiscation acts worked to sustain the nation at the expense of individual states, leaving them without the means to assert control over territory or the people who lived in it. It could not have escaped notice that when, in July 1862, martial law was declared in northern Mississippi—to assert military authority and prevent illegal trading—a Confederate adjutant general issued the diktat, not John Pettus or a representative from his government. The terms of the order also elaborated a new rule of law that clarified just how justice was to be conducted in the state. In the name of national self-preservation, "private interests must be subservient to the public good." With citizens of the state meant to offer their dutiful obedience to military authority, the order threatened those who would upend the Confederate project from within: "Disloyalty must and will not be countenanced. The credit of the Government must be sustained." Those who read the order were left in no doubt just which government's interest would be paramount. The result of this application of brute federal authority left Pettus powerless. A writer to Pettus who hailed from Jackson County on the south coast complained that an impending American invasion was wreaking havoc with slaveholder authority in the region. Pressing Pettus to act, Charles Howell called the governor out. Speaking of slaves and supporters of the American cause in the same breath, Howell charged, "I want them to know that we have a governor that has some power."[31]

By the fall of 1862, letters calling on Mississippi's chief executive to show some intestinal fortitude went without answer. At the head of a government reduced to a cipher by the end of the year, Pettus and the state legislature did what they could in an environment of growing hysteria. Desperate for help, in need of food, and left bereft by national conscription laws that protected the wealthy from military service, correspondents flooded the governor's office with letters from all over the state, seeking assistance, redress, and an outlet for their rage. Letter writers called on Pettus to uphold the law, enlist "stray gentlemen soldiers," and provide for destitute families caught in or near occupied territory. The sheriff of Panola County wrote Pettus with American forces on the approach, asking for advice as to what he should do with his jail, filled as it was with runaway slaves who would undoubtedly join the enemy if freed. By the time the state legislature met in special session in December, a once-bold Pettus offered only beleaguered predictions of a dim future. To the surprise of no one, Pettus told the legislature not only that Mississippi had become a theater of the war, but that the "struggle is now for her existence as a State." Acting quickly but with scant funds, the legislature passed a variety of measures to prepare for the worst, while at the same time acceding to the pleas of constituents to provide relief where possible.[32]

If the autumn of 1862 represented the point at which the state of Mississippi began to crumble, by the spring of 1863, American occupation and the rapid growth of the Confederate state knocked the remaining pillars out from under the Republic of Mississippi, rendering it a failed state. Supportive newspapers that had once called for Pettus to act more forcefully to prepare the state for war now accepted the reality that nation trumped state in importance. "The Confederate authorities should at once call all stragglers to the field," wrote the editor of the *American Citizen* in March 1863, "and Governor Pettus should disband the militia without further delay." The paper called on Pettus to return militia to their homes, so that they might grow crops and feed the nation. The editorial did not need to mention that by doing so, the state would lose its last claim to autonomy in the process. Officers in the state's own militia now actively doubted the state government's hold on sovereignty. Major General S. J. Gholson, writing to the state's adjutant general, James Hamilton, asked for written authorization to secure supplies from Confederate storehouses. Gholson reasoned that "as the State Troops are really in the Confederate service," no argument could be made against the attempt. Though he made no mention of it in his missive, by the time Gholson put pen to paper, Mississippi's state government had already suffered the ignominious loss of the state capital. The American capture of Jackson in May 1863, along with the Confederate surrender of Vicksburg two months later, left John Pettus's government in tatters and on the run.[33]

At a hastily convened meeting in the eastern town of Columbus in early November 1863, legislators presided over a government that was rushing headlong into oblivion. Resolutions passed that session disclosed that fully twenty-four counties lay in enemy hands, including some of the wealthiest parts of what had counted as Mississippi when the war began. With the tax base shrunken, tax collectors in short supply, and the bulk of the state budget earmarked to provide for the families of soldiers, the government had little to appropriate. Perhaps the only indication of a legislative pulse came in the form of a second wartime gubernatorial election, held where possible the previous October. In a landslide victory, lawyer, planter, and militia commander Charles Clark, an establishment darling and longtime enemy of John Pettus, assumed the governorship, securing nearly 12,000 votes, even though his home county of Bolivar lay behind American lines. Even this successful handoff of elected government did little to convince legislators of the state's prospects. Resolutions passed to investigate the legality of Confederate impressment agents, who were seizing property and provisions, were matched by attempts made by legislators to inquire into whether they could, as elected members of government, draw Confederate salaries "which are lucrative."[34] With few options, the legislature also passed a resolution reaffirming the state's connection to the Confederate state, with reassurances "of the faith of the people of Mississippi in the justice of their cause and their determination unabated to sustain to the uttermost the principles that led to their separation from the United States and the establishment of the Confederate Government." While the resolution pointedly claimed that the expansion of the national government had come at the expense of individual states, in a manner unintended by the compact that had formed the nation in the first place, the text lacked muscle. It argued that truly free governments "founded in jealousy and not in confidence" possessed constitutions that carefully circumscribed state power. The re-articulation of secessionist principles, made bankrupt by the war, left the impression that Mississippi's state legislators were now biting the hand that fed them. Government in Mississippi was now sustained by Confederate power, as one of a growing number of failed states in an embattled southern nation.[35]

Once in office, Charles Clark took up the role of Confederate functionary in all but name. He received copies of letters not directed to him, informing him of military policies already decided and Confederate directives adopted for his state without his consultation. Clark also received correspondence from people asking for help to save them from a national government that cast a very long shadow. Writing on behalf of a Lafayette County woman caught carrying goods purchased from family across enemy lines, local official William Delay relayed that Confederate officials had refused to relinquish the goods, citing a military order. As Delay put it to Clark, cases such as these left state power hanging by a thread. In his reply, Clark attempted to shore up his authority and that of his government, but his fatherly chiding of Delay for not throwing his weight around did little to solve the problem: "Do not let your civil officers say they cannot do their duty. They *must* do it or *resign*." Clark received reports of state troops being forcibly conscripted into national service, despite the governor's public order to the contrary, and letters hastily written by slaveholders complaining that Confederate officials were impressing African Americans into military labor, creating ample opportunities for escape.[36]

Clark presided over a breakdown of social order within Mississippi's shrunken borders. A Perry County sheriff complained to Clark that threats to his life prevented him from collecting taxes, while Confederate deserters acted as an ad-hoc rival state in the southern piney woods. Though D. W. Bradley allowed that soldiers had been sent to the county to arrest them, deserters controlled significant territory. Unless something was done, Bradley argued, they "will ride & burn out many loyal citizens in this county." Letters such as these attested to not only a breakdown of order but the extent to which the vacuum that had been created by the collapse of the state government had been filled by more than just rival nation-states. While historians have often interpreted these deserter communities as an index of the slow collapse of the Confederate state, it is worth noting that the timing of their development more closely tracks that of Mississippi's collapse as an independent power. While the angst of deserters found fertile soil in Confederate disaffection, it was the failed Republic of Mississippi that created room for the dissent to grow in the first place.[37]

Perhaps more important than this, however, was the state government's inability to protect those who remained steadfast in their loyalty to Mississippi itself. From the beginning of the war, this issue had lain behind many of the problems that faced Mississippi's state government. The opaque political connection between the state and individual citizens, assumed when the state seceded, in fact proved to be a stumbling block in the state government's battle with counties, an obstacle only overcome by stoking the enthusiasm for war. Like all political relationships between persons and states, the expectation that citizens would serve as soldiers brought with it the obligation on the part of governments to ensure the protection of communities and vigilance in the protection of citizens' rights. When that broke down—when the state ceded control to the national government and collapsed under the weight of American occupation and the Confederate accumulation of resources—the bond that had wound around loyal citizens and the state after secession dissolved and, with it, the legitimacy of the state government itself. If loyalty is the obligation that states demand of citizens, then the expectation of protection is its corollary. Caught between two giant armies, both with the stated prerogative to impress slaves and property to serve their own ends, by the end of 1863 the state of Mississippi could not sustain the loyalty of its populace because it could not protect them. As a result, the state government under Charles Clark's command melted into the background.[38]

A government was not the only thing that cracked under the pressure of occupation. Local communities also became ever more divided, as personal circumstance and sheer survival forced many individuals to discard their citizenship to Mississippi and the Confederacy and swear oaths to the United States. The issue was important enough that Charles Clark addressed the problem in his inaugural address to the legislature in November 1863. It was telling, though, that while Clark allowed that some "taking counsel of their fears" had sworn oaths to the United States, he believed that "the great heart of the people of Mississippi" remained loyal to the cause. This politically expedient division—of material circumstances that compelled some to swear loyalty out of necessity versus the true hearts of the people, which remained pure—made no distinction, by 1863, between Mississippi and nation. One had clearly subsumed the other. Yet for those behind enemy lines, occupation had all but severed the last bonds, cutting some whites loose from the Confederacy, leaving them stateless. Writing from American-occupied Natchez, the new editors of the *Courier* wondered whether, "with the Northern lines of the army still advancing, does it not behoove the candid Southerner to examine his position?" The farther that Confederate armies receded, "and every day widening the breach between you and their former claims," the more white Mississippians faced being a suspect class in occupied territory.[39]

With the ties of loyalty severed and citizenship to the state government emptied of its meaning, perhaps the only institution that connected white Mississippians to their state government was a shared belief in the continued perpetuation of slavery. In all southern states, the conviction that slavery would ensure the prosperity of the region lay behind the argument secessionists made in favor of independence. But here too, war, emancipation, and the needs of the Confederate government shook the slave system to its foundations. Confederate confiscation legislation, passed in March 1862, signaled a shift in policy with far-reaching consequences. Mississippi's legislature followed suit, with a law that allowed the impressment of slaves only with the express consent of owners. It was hotly debated throughout the 1862 session but did finally pass, with strict limits. Even though later iterations of Confederate law expressly instructed military officials to impress slaves into the service within the confines of individual state law, in practice, competition between the Confederacy and the Mississippi government allowed two separate claims on slaves to mature, to the detriment of slaveholder authority. Opening this door also created opportunities for the massive expansion of state control over the slave population, and military orders published the following year made it clear which state would have ultimate control. In an order published in late October 1863 written by Adjut. Gen. Samuel Cooper, the Confederate Army authorized the impressment of male field hands between the ages of seventeen and fifty, so long as slaves made to serve did not amount to more than 5 percent of a given county's slave population. This military directive moved well past Confederate legislation, but in Mississippi at least, it became the law of the land.[40]

By the later stages of the war, Charles Clark spent a good deal of time fending off the advances of Confederate officials who had designs on slaves in the counties still under his authority. In all his correspondence, the message was the same. To remove slaves in what was left of Mississippi would have disastrous consequences, Clark argued, not only for the morale of those who remained loyal to the cause but for the slave system itself. Begging one official not to lay a hand on slaves west of the Pearl River, Clark claimed that impressing more slaves would be damaging, given that "slaves there are easily claimed and have facilities for escape to the enemy, and that portion of the State has heretofore furnished a large amount of labor for the R.R. and the fortifications at Vicksburg and Port Hudson and elsewhere on the Miss. River." The Confederate impressment of slaves, combined with the impressment of horses, wagons, foodstuffs, and soldiers, became part of the same insatiable desire for resources, and Mississippians took note that from the outside looking in, both American and Confederate states seemed part of the same scourge. Reacting perhaps to the political reality that he faced with every slave or soldier forced into national service further weakening the state's hold over its citizens, Clark argued that the demands of the state placed his government in an untenable position. "Conscription and impressment are necessary," he wrote, "but unless a wiser policy is pursued, they will become odious."[41]

Not until the final wartime session of the state legislature did Charles Clark bow to necessity and take up the challenge of winning support for the full-scale conscription of slaves in the state militia, as laborers or "in any capacity in which they might be found effective." He prefaced his comments by underscoring his distaste for the measure, but in his address, Clark provided his own last-ditch solution to what had become an endemic problem that weakened the slave system in every part of the state. For Clark, the possibility of drafting African Americans into the service solved several problems at once. The state would secure slaves more forcefully, under the watchful eye of armed officers, while at the same time keeping slaves from running to enemy lines to further bolster enemy numbers. Clark argued that once in the military, black men would be biddable. "Steady, firm, but kind discipline, such as good masters enforce, is all that is required." Perhaps more importantly, securing slaves in the state rather than the national service had the added advantage of sustaining what was left of the state government's authority, though at no point was it clear that any legislation would, by this point, supersede the power of the Confederate prerogative.[42]

In the end, the legislature took up the measure in committee, but a resolution allowing for black enlistment died on the house floor by a single vote. As close as the vote was, the idea of enlisting African Americans in the military was explosive enough that even a state on its knees thought defeat better than putting the future of a slaveholder's republic in black hands. Though the Confederate cause was barely drawing breath, the committee tasked with drawing up legislative language on black enlistment had their report scrubbed from the record, rather than leaving their words and, presumably, their support for the idea open to public attack.[43]

THE CONFEDERATE SURRENDER THAT WOULD FOLLOW in the weeks after the legislature adjourned could not hide the fact that the Republic of Mississippi had died several months before. As in many failed states, the inability to enforce the rule of law left much of the region in bedlam, as small vigilante groups and ad-hoc paramilitary organizations filled the void and imposed their own rough justice. The chaotic way in which order collapsed in Mississippi served as a bookend to the equally chaotic way in which the state had declared its independence.

Armed with a determination to turn secessionist dreams into reality, the architects of the Republic of Mississippi had overlooked a great deal. The creation of an independent republic depended upon a presumption of supremacy over localities that in no way reflected reality before, during, or after Mississippi declared its independence. Preparing the state for war also overlooked the government's tenuous hold over the military. And though few secessionists could have anticipated it, the national project of Confederate state formation would, in short order, engulf Mississippi and render its state government superfluous. More fundamentally, though, secessionists never honestly reckoned with the inchoate understandings of citizenship that had suffused American politics in the decades before the Civil War and would emerge fully flowered in the arguments of fire-eaters who pushed Mississippi out of the United States. Secessionists had assumed that support for their cause equaled a common spirit of civic kinship. Because more was not done to hold citizens fast and to make being a citizen of Mississippi meaningful—the loyalty of those who took up the state's defense was not ensured and citizens were not protected—the authority of the state government and the presumed loyalty of white southerners to it proved too weak to withstand war and the creation of a wartime Confederate nation.

By turns, if the Republic of Mississippi collapsed under the pressure of armed conflict and the rapid development of the Confederacy, it was within that larger nation-state that new ideas about citizenship and loyalty would flourish. There, white southerners who served the nation would encounter a new definition of what it meant to be a citizen, forged in the same war but with very different materials.

CHAPTER THREE

Schools of Citizenship

Consider the imagined world laid out for Confederate recruits as they perused a soldier's manual: Hundreds of canvas tents, arrayed in straight lines, separated by thoroughfares in a well-appointed camp. Regiments grouped together, in the order that soldiers should expect to follow one another into battle. Hierarchy and order to be observed at all times. Adjutants and surgeons camped to the left of a regiment, quartermasters and assistant surgeons to the right. Every soldier mindful of his number, called out when the rolls were taken at reveille, retreat, and tattoo. No less than 22 paces separating regiments. Regimental camps no more than 400 paces across. Four washerwomen assigned to each company. One ration per day. Latrines dug daily, at a safe distance from camp. Regular drills to ensure that soldiers honed the economy of their movements in the firing of a weapon. "Useful occupations and manly exercises" to be encouraged, providing the sort of diversion that might "repress dissipation and immorality," with the strict observance of religious services every Sunday. Discipline respected above all. Police guards to ensure order. Camp guards to keep the wayward from straying. Capture, confinement, and courts-martial if soldiers fled camp in the calm between battles. Death by firing squad all but certain if soldiers absconded during an engagement. Soldiers made symbols of national ambition. Armies turned into the manifestation of all that a new state self-consciously proclaimed to the world.[1] Buried among the pages of these soldiers' manuals was not only an ideal army but an ideal Confederate States of America.

It would be foolish to take soldiers' manuals as mirrored reflections of what it was like to have been a Confederate soldier. The military ideal portrayed in these manuals rarely matched reality, though that is not the only reason why we should read them. By the middle of the Civil War, scant resources and punishing military campaigns forced Confederate soldiers to sustain themselves with whatever they had to hand, as armed representatives of a republic that fought a modern war on the cheap. Yet even though all the manuals and military regulations now read like something of a pipe dream, they still hold value, less for what they tell us about the day-to-day experiences of soldiers and more for what they tell us about a process of state-sponsored social, cultural, and political acculturation. In barely four and a half years, the Confederate States of America built an army and a nation at the same time, and the development of both taught a lot of white male southerners how to be soldiers and citizens of the new republic, all at once.[2]

Much like the development of the army and the nation, Confederate citizenship evolved on the fly. From the moment the republic was founded, discussions about and debates over what connected white southerners to the nation were overwhelmed by an outpouring of popular enthusiasm for southern independence and war. Drawing upon the ready images of nationalist iconography and the white-hot nationalistic rhetoric that swept much of the Western world by the middle decades of the nineteenth century, the architects of southern independence adopted a broad understanding of citizenship and civic belonging, all to keep the passions of the populace at a rolling boil. Founded as it was after decades of confusion about understandings of national citizenship in the United States, the hazy legal relationship that connected individuals to the new nation was folded whole into the Confederate project without ever being scrutinized. Yet as war outdistanced the inchoate language of nationalism, the needs of the Confederate state quickly changed the terms of citizenship, along with the shape of the state itself. As the nation grew, white southerners in and out of the military confronted the coercive power of a modern state and the obligations that bound people to them. The impressment of property, the conscription of men, the burning of cotton stocks, and the seizure of slaves all combined to warp—sometimes violently—what it meant to be a Confederate citizen. War also warped the bundle of obligations that Confederates owed the state. The centralization and bureaucratization of government power pressed those who counted themselves as loyal to the Confederate cause and bore down even harder on those who were not. Even compared to the more well-resourced United States, the Confederacy became a powerful, centralized state. That it emerged as a full-blown leviathan is all the more incredible, given that the stated goal of the secessionist project was to break away from the kind of overweening power of centralized control that the southern nation embraced by the middle stages of the war.[3]

The Confederacy was an epic gamble. This much is clear from the most recent work on the subject. Yet because we know that it would collapse—that the Confederacy would join the long list of failed states whose demise peppers the history of the nineteenth century—scholars often underplay the work undertaken by Confederate leaders and functionaries, who built a foundation for their state that would ironically outlast the state itself. In particular, the efforts made to develop a close, lasting bond between the Confederacy and its citizens reveal the ingenuity of the endeavor. Coming as it did at a moment when liberal nation-states all over the world were in a tender stage of development, the Confederacy proved to be the product of creative state-builders. While their work was certainly not without blemish, some things lasted. Perhaps most important of all, to win the conflict, Confederate officials, officers, bureaucrats, and preachers redrew the lines of loyalty that connected citizens to their communities. As a nation founded on the principle of small government became a behemoth of centralized national power, loyal Confederates created a kind of idealized citizenship that, by the end of the war, sat at the center of southern civic life. Even though the state itself was riddled with contradictions, citizenship as a title and loyalty as the glue that held it together would bind southern society, while at the same time driving a sharp wedge between the loyal and the disloyal, well after the Civil War ended. As American officials would learn all too well as their army seized southern territory—and particularly as the war came to its indefinite, chaotic end—loyalty to a failed Confederate state continued to maintain a grip on the white southern populace, making it all the harder for Americans to render their nation whole.[4]

Returning to the Confederate army camp for clues, this chapter examines how a state built a military, how that military taught white southerners how to be soldiers and citizens, and what this history reveals about state formation at a pivotal moment in world history. Though development of the state was often haphazard, by the war's middle stages the Confederate Army became a school of citizenship, an institution within which soldiers were taught powerful lessons about not only the sacrifice necessary to securing the independence of their nation but also the coercive power of a modernizing state. The collective experience of being a soldier in the Confederate Army filled an important gap, between the hazy definitions of what citizenship meant in the new republic and the reality of what circumstances demanded from southerners to bring that new republic into being. By the end of the conflict, incoherent definitions of what being a Confederate meant had hardened into a stark and often brutal set of obligations. Along the way, white southerners learned all too well what it meant to be citizens in a modern state, with wartime powers ceded to a national government that extracted resources from a squeezed populace. This power was evident in the way soldiers were trained, the way they prayed, and how they were treated when they fled the ranks and deserted. By drawing sharp lines between the loyal and the disloyal—by turning the loyal into ideal citizens and the disloyal into stateless cowards—and by injecting these demands with a hot dose of evangelical fire, the Confederate state created a powerful kind of citizenship that would outlast the Civil War and leave a lasting mark.[5]

WHEN DELEGATES FROM SIX SECEDING STATES met in the capitol building in Montgomery, Alabama, in February 1861 to convene the first Congress of the Confederate States of America, all who gathered on the floor of the assembly were aware of the enormity of the task before them. For many, the meeting represented the culmination of a long-held fantasy: an opportunity for arch secessionists to don the garb of the American founding fathers they venerated and to knit the frayed ties of a southern union into a new state of their own design. The solemnity of the occasion was matched by the determination to move with the same speed that brought the six states out of the United States, and it was hoped that others would follow. Once delegates agreed on an agenda and presented their credentials in a public show of pomp and popular consent, Congress completed the nation-making tableaux for the packed gallery and then moved quickly into secret session. Behind closed doors, delegates took all of seventy-two hours to decide on a set of principles and present a provisional constitution for the new nation-state.[6]

Just like the American Constitution, the Confederate version concerned itself most with the distribution of powers and the careful enumeration of federal authority, with the question of what connected citizens to the new state set to one side. Unlike the American founding document, the Confederate version gave the federal government no clear powers to naturalize citizens. With the exception of clauses stipulating the origins of individuals seeking high office and a privileges and immunities clause lifted from the document they had turned their backs on, the Confederate Congress deferred in every case to individual states.[7] What's more, at no point did Congress deliberate in a journaled session over the question of whether the Confederacy should have a clear clause defining citizenship in the new nation-state. To have done so would have upset the idea of the Confederacy as a loose federation of independent republics, a proposition that lay at the center of the secessionist argument. All the same, citizenship still popped up at key moments throughout the first Congress. The way that the question of citizenship was dealt with spoke volumes about how Confederates understood the relationship between the state and its people.

Deliberations over the qualifications for high office, for instance, caused a good deal of consternation. The provisional constitution's requirement for the presidency called for holders of the office to be either persons native to the Confederacy or naturalized citizens of a Confederate state once the new national constitution was adopted, with a residency requirement of fourteen years. In deliberations over the final text, however, members of Congress found room to argue that citizenship requirements for the holding of public office did not do enough to reflect the unusual circumstances of the Confederacy's founding. With Upper South states still wavering on secession, any attempt to tie the presidency to citizenship determined from when a candidate's home state left the Union might imperil future presidential candidates from holding office if they hailed from less than fulsome parts of the country. To this, South Carolina delegate Thomas J. Withers put forward an amendment that restricted the presidency to only those persons who were natural-born citizens "of one of the States of the United States." Withers's amendment, with a definition contingent on membership in another sovereign nation, posed problems too. In this, it was a nonstarter and was quickly struck down. But at every stage of the Congress's early deliberations, those who sought a broad definition of citizenship and those who sought a sharper constitutional edge to the title remained at odds in the Confederate government.[8]

The final text of the constitution made it clear that citizenship in the new Confederacy was fungible. Even if President Jefferson Davis remarked in July 1861 that the early battles of the Civil War had "repudiated the foolish conceit that the inhabitants of this Confederacy are still citizens of the United States," few in Congress could have looked to the government's founding document and found evidence of what might replace it. Though a requirement to hold national office offered some guidance as to citizenship, states could define the title in whatever way they chose. On the question of the executive branch, the final draft of the constitution also devolved into abstraction. It stipulated that the Confederate president was to be a natural-born citizen or a citizen at the time the Confederate constitution was adopted or a citizen born in the United States prior to 20 December 1860, the date of South Carolina's secession convention. One of the only parts of the text that did not suffer ambiguity on the issue of citizenship was in the enumeration of powers extended to the nation's judiciary. There, the document insulated Confederate citizens and states from the reach of American law by making it impossible to be sued by a foreign state. This stipulation, as well as the privileges and immunities clause, would be the only clear protection imparted to persons who claimed citizenship in individual states.[9]

The failure to articulate a clear definition of citizenship was not a failure of Confederate statecraft. For one nation born among many in an era of liberal revolution, capacious understandings of citizenship abounded, not to mention in the republic that so many white southerners were in such a hurry to leave. What Confederate leaders assumed, with some justification, was that the broad, ill-defined way that they understood the connection between white southerners and the nation-state would be countered by the cold racial logic of white supremacy and a fiery brand of nationalism. The Confederacy was to be a slaveholder's republic, with protections for white privilege placed at the center of the body politic. As Vice President Alexander Stephens made abundantly clear, the Confederate nation rested on the indisputable truism that African Americans were in no way the white man's equal, and in what passed for a debate on the question, the nation's leadership expressed themselves most clearly and forcefully on the racial composition of the ideal citizen.[10] Moreover, if racial determinism defined the citizen, gender circumscribed the community of citizens even further. Even if worries about the loyalties of slaves worked like an undercurrent to influence how Confederates thought about their most prized possessions, and women were held up as flat symbols of the nation's virtue, being white and male were the only stamps of political membership that mattered. Finally, if one of the goals of nineteenth-century nationalism was to drape a civic religion over the modern state, then Confederates certainly worked hard and with a good deal of success to dress their nation in finery. As historians of the subject have amply demonstrated, a liquid Confederate nationalism plastered over many of the cracks in the new nation's edifice, as well as many of the divisions in southern society. While the nation's leadership held no firmer a grip on the articulation of national identity than other leaders engaged in a similar pursuit—Confederate nationalism retained a conservative, restorationist core from the outset—a white southern nonslaveholding majority could at least see something of themselves in a nation constructed by the racial, gendered dreams of slaveholders. Shorn of the radicalism that emanated from the European revolutions of 1848, home, patriarchy, faith, slavery, and a martial spirit all combined to form the foundation of the Confederate nation.[11]

Founding a state on the fly does not allow for patient deliberation, but it did not take long for the ambiguities of Confederate citizenship to find the perfect vessel in the form of the nation's armed forces. The structure of the army reflected the political realities in a country founded on the principle of limited national power. While the republic's constitutional blueprint certainly allowed for the possibility that the Confederate state could pull rank and assert itself, the stated assumptions about how the army was to be raised and how that army was to be governed respected individual states and their authority. What became clear early on, as Congress met in session in the spring and summer of 1861, was that the raising of an army offered the opportunity to sharpen what being a citizen in the Confederacy meant. Early in the April session, a bill on citizenship and naturalization relating to the Confederate Army offered a path to citizenship for foreign-born noncitizens who volunteered to fight, by automatically turning them into citizens. The act was in keeping with an older republican ideal that dated back to the American Revolution, mixed with the long-standing hope of Confederate legislators that many Americans would flock to their banner once the fighting started in earnest, either out of southern ancestry or ideological kinship. The underlying justification for the bill retained the broad understandings of citizenship that had long been a part of secessionist thinking, but the implications of the legislation welded national belonging to the national army.

The passage of the bill into law was by no means smooth. Though read in April, deliberations on the bill were postponed until May, and it was not made law until August, as arguably more pressing matters of state kept it from consideration. Once it became law, however, it was followed by other legislation designed to confirm the Confederate Army as the preeminent institution for both the making of war and the creation of citizens.[12] By the end of the first legislative session, laws regulating citizenship, even without a definition of what the title entailed, made military service not only the primary means through which the new state bestowed citizenship but also a crucible in which persons of suspect loyalty could prove themselves. A law "respecting alien enemies" made all males over fourteen years of age who hailed from the United States but lived within Confederate borders to be liable to apprehension, detention, and potential expulsion, except in cases where these persons made a declaration of their intention to join the Confederate armed forces. Should these persons be deemed loyal, Confederate service would effectively wipe clean their past and make them citizens in good standing.[13]

By making military service a path to citizenship, the Confederate state joined a long list of republics that made military service the key to civic membership in the body politic. But in so doing, both citizenship and military service were predicated upon the basic loyalty of the individual, and in this, Confederate officials faced a challenge. At least as far back as the American Revolution, the republican ideal of citizenship held that service to the state in times of war presented the clearest indication of the loyalty of the individual, a sacrifice of one's life and limb that the nation could trust. Citizens who offered all to their country, preferably of their own volition, became paragons of civic virtue, and for this reason, the relationship between the military and citizenship conferred a cultural and political power to soldiers in a republic that almost nothing else could.

However, what made military service problematic for the Confederacy was that in a conflict many white southerners took to be an ideological struggle—for regional self-determination, state's rights, and most importantly, the perpetuation of slavery—conferring citizenship on soldiers proved both shaky and ephemeral. In a military that rested, at least at first, on the nation deferring to localities to raise troops, questions persisted about where the true loyalties of soldiers lay. To build a national army in the truest sense of the phrase demanded an effort by Confederate authorities on all fronts, to make being a national soldier meaningful and, by extension, to make national citizenship meaningful as well.[14]

From the moment it was founded, the Confederate Army was a patchwork of a fighting force, with a primary connection to states and counties and, at least at first, the loosest of relations to the national government. As the Confederacy needed to raise an army with all due haste, the national government accepted troops into the service in whatever form individual states offered them. This posed several challenges. For one, a division between Confederate troops and "volunteers" offered up by individual states led some in the national service to pull rank on state troops. For another, in accordance with traditions stemming from the militia tradition throughout the South, soldiers were permitted by custom to elect the officers who would lead them into the service. Though the practice made for an unclear chain of command, as well as an officer corps with several unfit members, Confederate officials could hardly refuse.[15]

The result was a difficult balancing act. While Confederate general Braxton Bragg counseled his staff to allow all regiments to elect their own officers to lead them into service, so as to not upset customary privileges that had been accorded troops in state militias, it was not long before Bragg was complaining that the custom was making it difficult to maintain any semblance of order. It was also not long before Confederate officials came to appreciate the irony of being required to accept soldiers into the service in whatever form they were offered by states, while at the same time footing the bill. Secretary of War Judah P. Benjamin made it abundantly clear by December 1861 that his department would not "give a musket to a man enlisted for less than the war," and states that had made alternate arrangements had better pay to provision them if they were to be counted as reputable fighting regiments. This tug-of-war between necessity and sovereignty would prove one of the defining tensions in the Confederate state from the earliest stage. While national officials initially treaded carefully around the prerogatives of localities, circumstances emboldened Confederate officials to wrest more power from states, in the interest of continuing the war. Still, the battle for control of the military exposed a deeper issue. In a wave of letters that crested as the terms of service for some Confederate regiments came to a close at the end of 1861 and the beginning of 1862, the challenge before officials of a nation-state with a tenuous hold over its own military was set in bold relief. A regiment of Virginia militiamen who had been raised by their state but who now found themselves in the Confederate Army pulled no punches about the limits of national authority or where their loyalties lay: "We were mustered into the Service of the *State of Virginia*, not into that of the *Confederate States*."[16]

It was with these concerns in mind—the need to raise a truly national army while at the same time raising the prerogative of the nation over that of individual states—that the Confederate government began to consider a system of military conscription.[17] In his February 1862 message to Congress, President Jefferson Davis suggested that in its rush to meet American armies on the battlefield, the Confederate state "had attempted more than it had power successfully to achieve."[18] It was in this spirit that conscription was debated, and the result was to be an expansive piece of legislation. To provide the necessary political cover to legislators to draft the bill, a procedural rule in the Senate was changed that made all deliberations affecting foreign relations and public defense best done behind closed doors. While the rule change did not pass without opposition, working in secret session allowed legislators to act quickly, and by early April, a draft conscript bill had been drawn up for consideration.

The conscript bill allowed the Confederate state two key powers. The first furnished the nation with a proper modern army to carry out a thoroughly modern war. It curtailed the customary practice of officer elections by stipulating that conscripted regiments would be led by officers appointed directly by the Confederate government. If existing regiments agreed to reenlist for two years, they could retain their right to elect their officers as necessary; thus a large carrot was dangled in front of soldiers who weighed the virtue of enlisting for the duration of the conflict. Should the war take a turn for the better, soldiers already in the army would also be among the first to be relieved from duty. What these concessions and stipulations were all in aid of, however, was a national government's will to power. By giving the Confederate government control over the nation's officer corps, the conscript bill placed the prerogative of the nation-state at the center of the armed forces.[19]

The second key power in the conscript bill was much bolder. It made white men between the ages of eighteen and thirty-five subject to compulsory military service and under the direct authority of the Confederate state. The new law allowed the national government to sweep away many of the competing structures of communal loyalty and the prerogatives of smaller states that had checked federal power. The act put the officers of local and state government in the employ of the Confederacy as conscription enrollment officers appointed directly by the secretary of war. If those called to serve refused to answer, the legislation extended the remit of military law to arrest and try citizens as deserters subject to military rather than civilian courts. Finally, conscripts would join existing regiments and would be assigned at the discretion of the War Department, though the legislation stipulated that they would be placed in fighting units organized from their home states. While historians rightly point to the long list of exemptions and the reaction of Confederates to them as evidence of the kind of broad disaffection that would weaken the nation from within, other aspects of the legislation are equally important and revealing. They show a Confederate state acting to dramatically enlarge its authority over the populace within its borders. This act, along with the suspension of habeas corpus and the expansion of the state's power over property, marked the moment when the Confederate state came of age.[20]

The rapid growth of the Confederacy's power had a ripple effect. Even before conscription had become law, soldiers who had caught wind of it counseled family and friends to act before it was too late. George Furniaful, a Mississippi soldier writing from Savannah, Georgia, in early 1862, directed his sister to "tell the Boys to look out for the draft or they will be caught." Furniaful disclosed that talk of the bill among soldiers was rife. He also detected a change in the relationship between officers and enlisted men as a result of the enlargement of Confederate control over the military, with officers acting "very much above us these days," a good deal more than Furniaful thought appropriate. For many, the reaction to conscription was a mixture of anger and resignation. It is reasonable to suggest that many soldiers bowed to the inevitable and offered their loyalty to the nation-state more out of expedience. Whether a Confederate soldier was in earnest, however, could not hide the realities of what the Confederate state was attempting. What Furniaful glimpsed was a deeper shift in the relationship between the military and citizens.[21]

The time-honored ideal of the male citizen volunteering to fight was replaced with something altogether different: compulsory service to the national government. As one writer argued in a letter to Confederate secretary of war G. W. Randolph, "Volunteering in legal and in [a] real sense means tendering your services to the State," and there could be no such thing with a system of conscription in place: "the act itself, irrespective of the will of the Subject, puts him in service." Once military service was changed from a volitional obligation of citizenship into a coercive expectation of the state, it was not long before a flood of letters overwhelmed the Richmond offices of the War Department, testifying to the deeper implications of the law. Some charged that conscription would undermine morale, forcing men into the service in companies made up of individuals not from their community. The worry about what would happen to an army where conscripts fought alongside men "who are strangers to them" was a common complaint, though the concern largely missed the point. It was one of the objects of conscription that both power and the traditional lines of loyalty in the Confederate military were to be rerouted, or rewired, connecting soldiers not to their states or counties but to the nation-state directly. Though citizens all over the Confederacy petitioned the national government to secure the prized exemptions that could keep slaveholders, blacksmiths, doctors, and plantation overseers out of the military, conscription sought to sever older ties and create new ones, placing the national government at the top of Confederate loyalties.[22]

Conscription also trained the power of the state on the foreign-born living within Confederate borders. Responding to the question of whether unnaturalized foreigners were subject to military duty, Confederate attorney general Thomas A. Watts claimed that a capacious definition of citizenship allowed for an equally broad remit for the national government to claim the services of would-be soldiers. Watts interpreted the key clause in the conscription act that referred to "residents" of the Confederacy as bringing foreign citizens within the ambit of military service. So long as an individual owned a fixed domicile within the nation's borders—thus allowing that person to enjoy the protections of the state—that individual ought rightly to be obligated to serve in the state's defense. "By remaining here," Watts argued, "receiving the protection due to him as a resident, he is presumed to have elected to consider the Confederate State as . . . his domicile, and is bound to share the burdens as well as the benefits which attach to his condition." Watts's extension of federal power had a clear political advantage. It did not apply to a significant number of people to invite backlash. But the shift in the political winds was unmistakable. "The rapidity with which the Confederate Ship of State is drifting toward the rock of consolidation," wrote an editorialist in the *Richmond Examiner*, "that same rock on which the Union split and went to wreck, is alarming."[23]

The disaffection and sweeping alarm that met Confederate conscription brought white southerners into contact and conflict with a state of rapidly expanding power. Only three months after the conscription act was passed, President Jefferson Davis's aide-de-camp William P. Johnston issued a stinging report on the effect that forced military service was having within the Confederate Army. Conscription and the prolonging of enlistment terms for soldiers who had signed on to serve for only twelve months had, according to Johnston, been an unmitigated disaster. Soldiers "drafted for the war into companies, which experience has proved distasteful to them, engendered a spirit of bitter discontent, which in many instances was fanned by designing men." Moreover, by continuing the practice of allowing some to appoint their own officers, regiments were replacing able men with candidates "grossly incompetent and unable to pass an examination of their duties before the most indulgent boards." "Their legal successors were equally unfit," Johnston went on, "and some regiments seemed tending towards disorganization and anarchy."[24] With division driving a wedge between soldiers and exemptions from military service laying bare the true interests at the heart of the Confederate project, conscription threatened not only social revolution but the mangling of national citizenship as well. "The Conscript Act will do away with all the patriotism we have," wrote South Carolinian J. W. Reid as the legislation made its way through the Confederate Congress. "My private opinion is that our Confederacy is gone up, or will go soon. . . . A more oppressive law was never enacted in the most uncivilized country or by the worst of despots."[25]

Conscription tore a hole in the fabric of southern civic life. Yet out of the creative destruction that went along with the dramatic expansion of state power and the older bonds of citizenship that lay in ruin, something new emerged. Hesitant at first—and hemmed in on all sides by the disaffection that would grow as the war wore on—the Confederate state created a hot-house environment within which loyalty and devotion to the nation-state could intensify. By teaching white southerners how to be modern soldiers and citizens at the same time, the Confederacy constructed perhaps its most lasting monument in the form of the thousands of loyal soldiers who would, even after the war had ended, decry the "lost cause" as a cause not yet lost.

The experience of being a soldier taught Confederate men all they needed to know about what being a citizen of a revolutionary republic meant. This was the fond hope of the nation's architects, and were they to have read the letters of Mississippi's John Baird, the founding fathers of the Confederate nation would have been pleased. Baird was a young man from a moneyed Mississippi family who hailed from Noxubee County, on the state's eastern black prairie. Baird's family had taken full advantage of life in a prosperous plantation economy and had amassed a fortune. By 1860, they owned property in both Noxubee and on the Mississippi Delta, a fortune sufficient to send the young Baird to Virginia's Bethany College, where he was studying when Abraham Lincoln's election encouraged renewed calls for southern independence. Like many white southerners, Baird approved wholeheartedly of Mississippi's swift secession convention, and he poured his enthusiasm for independence into a letter he wrote to a friend. Should his home state leave the Union, Baird argued, it would be nothing less than "the noblest act of her existence," and for his part, the young Mississippian hoped to come to its defense. It was, Baird claimed, a simple question of honor. Better to declare independence than "crouch ourselves beneath the step of abolitionism." Once Mississippi seceded, Baird joined the fight. He signed up to a regiment in a Tennessee brigade under the command of Gen. Benjamin Cheatham. In time, Baird secured leave to join a regiment from his home state, the 9th Battalion of the Mississippi Sharpshooters. No matter which unit Baird fought in, however, his enthusiasm for the national cause endured. He joined the fight so quickly that he failed to win the support of his father before signing up to serve. Writing to his "dear lost boy" in June 1861, Baird's father informed him that at the risk of family acrimony, he ought to do his duty and defend his nation and his family's honor. Nothing less would do.[26]

In spite of John Baird's yearning to take active part in the cause, it was not long before his enthusiasm was tempered by some harsh lessons. By the spring of 1863, he had experienced a good deal of combat, seen friends killed in action, and watched as towns burned in the wake of enormous armies. He wrote to his father that while it pained him to say it, "if this conflict lasts much longer I will feel paid to give my little fortune" for a substitute to serve in his place. Yet for all of the drudgery of a soldier's life and the horror of battle, his service in the Confederacy had taught him something important about what it took to make a nation and what it meant to be a citizen. "The Major portion of the Army seem more determined than ever on liberty or independence," wrote Baird to his father in the late summer of 1863, though he allowed that a good many men were deserting the army. For the young soldier, deserters made a mockery of the cause, no matter the excuse, and the harshest of military punishments would be too lenient to deal with them: "I do wish they would took [sic] them up & shoot them down like dogs for they deserve nothing better." By then, Baird had come to see desertion as something more than a mark of dishonor. It was an affront to the sacrifice loyal men were making in every engagement. Without the full support of all, "we are a ruined nation without doubt. This is a time that can not cope with a part of our strength, but every shoulder must be put to the wheel & immediately at that."[27]

For many who served in the Confederate Army, service in the military was not simply a test of one's virtue. The army was itself an institution—and the military camp a vital space—in which white southerners like John Baird became Confederate citizens. It was a learned thing, tested by conflict and rooted not only in the shared experience of being a soldier but in the myriad ways the Confederate state consolidated its hold over the those who served. It was a formative revolutionary experience. Military service taught soldiers lessons about the meaning of sacrifice and the tools at the disposal of a modern state to rule over its populace. And in the day-to-day experiences of being a loyal soldier—not to mention the examples made of the disloyal—the Confederacy turned its armies into schools of citizenship.

Thumb the manuals printed for soldiers during the Civil War and the outlines of this school are clear enough. Like the primers that nineteenth-century Americans like John Baird would have been familiar with when they had been young, manuals instructed soldiers on not only the letter of military law but the habits and manners of sociability, the lessons of citizenship, and the grammar of state power. Manuals published quickly in 1861 presented a vision of military life dominated by respect for property and hierarchy, Christian morality, and southern manliness. Soldiers were directed to "execute with alacrity and good faith, the lawful orders of the superiors appointed over them," to respect not only their commanding officers but the nation-state for which they fought. This was a loaded direction for Confederate soldiers, who by the end of that year were fighting with the national government to retain the right to elect officers. All the same, the stated character of Confederate military authority was to be firm but judicious. Officers of every grade were "forbidden to injure those under them by tyrannical or capricious conduct, or by abusive language." Perhaps most importantly, most soldiers' manuals contained the official oath of allegiance all were required to swear to be mustered into the Confederate Army. Soldiers pledged to serve the nation-state "honestly and faithfully against all their enemies or opposers whatsoever" and to obey the orders of officers, the president of the Confederacy, and the Articles of War.[28]

Even though the rhetoric of secession encouraged soldiers to see themselves as volunteer revolutionaries swept up in a broad, nationalist movement, manuals made it clear that armies were no less than the embodiments of state power. Though soldiers had not read the work of Carl von Clausewitz, many Confederate manuals repeated his dictum that war was politics by other means. It would be easy to think that this was an empty phrase for soldiers who had not been schooled in the finer points of military strategy. The lesson to be learned from this bit of military wisdom, however, left no room for doubt that soldiers were to see themselves as the tools of government. Soldiers, like armies, one manual argued, were in no way independent of the will of the state. War was a "tool of politics, without any mathematical foundation, a hazard of possibilities, probabilities, luck and ill-luck," and soldiers were the physical manifestations of the Confederate state from the moment they donned a uniform. From a modern perspective, this might not seem a particularly surprising view. From the perspective of the mid-nineteenth century, however, this was an innovation of statecraft. The idea of soldiers as state possessions worked against not only the volitional rhetoric of manly service that encouraged so many to enlist but the kind of revolutionary struggle so many white southerners believed they were engaged in. Not for the first time in its short life, the Confederate state draped an older history over a very new and innovative enlargement of state power. Though leaders trumpeted the new nation as a throwback to the time of Washington, the Confederate state had a lot more in common with iron-fisted Bismarckian consolidation.[29]

Military manuals brushed a thin veneer over a world of soldiering and chaotic war. Life in a Confederate Army camp was a constant swirl of people, smells, and noises, long stretches of boredom broken by moments of abject terror. In this way, the rhythm of a soldier's life was at once tumultuous and dull, cramped but often lonely. "Well today is Sunday," wrote South Carolinian Isaac Alexander to his mother and sister from a camp near Corinth in the spring of 1862. "Sunday is like any other day here, there is the same amount of work done," Alexander confided; "it is either picket duty, guard at the trenches or Fatigue duty." For the young soldier, the steady stream of obligatory duties gave his life a sense of order and some semblance of calm. No matter the sadness of being so far from home and family, there was "always something to keep a man going." For others, the sheer variety of pastimes open to soldiers—some sanctioned and most not—provided ready diversion. "Camp life you doubtless imagine to be very dull, and you wouldn't be far wrong," wrote one soldier in a letter published in a Mississippi newspaper, "but there are many ways of puttering in variations; cards, backgammon, draft, and chess often serve the purpose of giving different parts to the opera."[30] Idle time led also to discussions of politics, particularly in the run-up to officer elections, or when the passing round of worn newspapers or old rumors from home encouraged Confederate soldiers to wonder aloud about the future direction of the country. As in most armies, the opportunity for political debate was unavoidable. For officers, however, the discussion of politics represented a constant threat to the morale and cohesion of a military unit.[31]

What served as the counterpoint to the idle chatter of soldiers was a culture of religiosity that saturated the rank and file. While it is certainly true that not all soldiers took an active part, it cannot be denied that religion played a role in shaping the lives of most Confederate soldiers.[32] It was a familiar institution. It connected soldiers to their families and communities back home, and it was often a yearning for the familiar that brought soldiers into the fold. Stationed with his two brothers in a Virginia encampment in the early summer of 1861, Harry Lewis made his religious devotion a balm to soothe the nerves of his mother back home in Woodville, Mississippi. "I went to church Sunday, or rather to the churches, for I went to two different ones and heard a part of two sermons and an exhortation," wrote Lewis. "Camp is a bad place for religion it is true but Dear Mother it is not so bad as I expected." The fiery sermon from the regimental pastor, the determination of the proselytizing faithful, the pamphlets, second-hand Bibles, religious camp meetings, and obligatory Sunday services all gave Confederate Army camps a familiar set of rituals around which day-to-day life revolved.[33]

Religion also added weight to the Confederate state-building project. By the end of the Civil War, faith in God and faith in the nation had hardened into something particularly potent: a righteous belief that the Almighty looked with favor on the Confederacy, providing the nation-state with the rationale to rule. At first, religion bore no such imprimatur, but it is hardly an accident that an upsurge in organized religious revivalism, well under way by the autumn of 1862, came about as the Confederate state tightened its hold over the national military. The *Confederate Baptist*, a newspaper printed in Columbia, South Carolina, eagerly published reports of soldiers' gathering interest in a faithful life. The autumn of 1862 witnessed "a season of refreshing from the presence of the Lord," and many soldiers throughout the army devoted themselves to colportage, or proselytizing through the distribution of pamphlets and religious tracts. If religious newspapers like the *Baptist* are to be believed, soldiers who made their way through camp with godly literature found receptive audiences everywhere. "The camp is a place of trial," wrote one editorialist in mid-December 1862, "but it is no less a school of virtue; and the soldier may entitle himself to the admiration of his country, not only by the toils and perils of the campaign, but by the high qualities which those toils and perils have developed and nurtured." While the effectiveness of these efforts is impossible to measure, the effortless mixing of religious imagery and metaphor in the way that Confederates talked about their struggle and the future of the republic is hard to ignore. At a camp near Fredericksburg, Virginia, in late 1862, T. D. Gwin addressed troops before battle with a rousing call to arms. "The happiness, freedom and independence" of all white southerners, "as well as the military glory and honor, the foreign recognition and permanent establishment of our new and heaven-born Republic," all hung in the balance. Placing their trust in the Almighty, "for the emancipation of our spirits to the bright world above, let us fall with our feet to the enemy, our backs to the field of battle, and our faces to the smiling heavens." For Gwin, those who fell were more than friends and comrades. They were martyrs who had offered up their lives in the service of "our new and heaven-born Republic."[34]

The mixture of religious language and national rhetoric added a richness and texture to Confederate political culture. In the face of growing want and in reaction to government calls to dampen opposition and face a common foe united, organized churches called for an end to doctrinal difference, so that devotees of all faiths could "unite our efforts for the salvation of souls" and the survival of the nation. Pastors of all denominations played a vital role in the articulation of a broad, ringing statement of Confederate purpose. Reaching for a familiar canvas to set the southern republic against, Rev. James Henley Thornwell argued that white southerners were fighting to uphold all that was righteous and godly about the original American republic. "We are not revolutionists," corrected Thornwell, "we are resisting revolution. We are upholding the true doctrines of the Federal

Constitution. We are conservative. Our success is the triumph of all that has been considered established in the past." Combining Confederate dogma with religious meaning, Thornwell tore a page from the Bible and called on all white southerners to act in accordance with the teachings of Christ: "We can never become aggressive; we may absorb, but we can never invade for conquest, any neighboring State." If Confederates were successful in the establishment of their independent republic, Thornwell argued, "the peace of the world is secured if our arms prevail. We shall have a Government that acknowledges God, that reverences right, and that makes law supreme." The only group who ought to feel the contempt of a faithful nation were those fellow Confederates who stood in the way of God's plan for the Confederacy and shirked their responsibilities to the nation. For them, "public contempt should whip them from their lurking holes, and compel them to share the common danger. The community that will cherish such men without rebuke, brings down wrath upon it. They must be forced to be useful, to avert the judgments of God from the patrons of cowardice and meanness." When national unity lagged, faith buoyed the Confederate cause.[35]

Sermons that called for religious sacrifice for the greater good of the nation-state became a foundation of national Confederate citizenship. The quintessential Confederate soldier was not only an individual riven to his post out of a sense of manly duty. He was a godly one as well: a paragon of martial prowess and Christian virtue. Even if few measured up to the ideal, by the later stages of the Civil War, the elevation of the Christian soldier to a national symbol provided the state with an ideal citizen. Devotion to the cause, particularly when faced with long odds, melded easily with the symbol of the Christian soldier to provide the Confederacy with a potent talisman of the country's civic religion.[36]

It was a religion at its most powerful when citizen-soldiers sat in judgment of their own. Speaking before a brigade of North Carolinians in February 1864 at a ceremony to execute twenty-two members of the brigade who had deserted to American armies and had been captured, Rev. John Paris called on those still loyal to appreciate the distinction between their righteous sacrifice for the nation-state and the righteousness of executing men who made a mockery of their suffering. According to the Confederate Articles of War, soldiers who left their post to desert to the enemy were to be punished with death, and for Paris, there was a lesson embedded in the sight of the condemned men who awaited the firing squad. As he made clear, "The true christian is always a true patriot," and any soldier knows that "patriotism and Christianity walk hand in hand." Paris argued that the deserters who stood before his congregation did more than just turn their backs on their nation. They also turned their backs to the solemn oath that all Confederate soldiers took to faithfully serve the state and ensure its future no matter the cost. By fleeing their army and their nation, the condemned men had broken that natural allegiance "that every man owes to the government of the State which throws around him the aegis of its protection." Deserters at the firing line, argued Paris, ought to have no courtesy extended to them. Their actions had placed them beyond the pale. All good men, "all true men, and all loyal men who love their country," should mark their deaths with nothing less than a hearty "Amen!"[37]

The aggrieved words of an army preacher hint at a deep well of national sentiment about loyalty—to the cause, the nation, and the Confederate state. At the heart of this conviction was a dichotomy between the devoted soldier and the disloyal deserter. Since ties between soldiers and their states had been severed with the consolidation of the army, and the terms of citizenship had been rewritten with compulsory service in the military through conscription, it fell to Confederate civilian and military leaders to keep their army together, no matter the cost. However, beginning in earnest in 1862, Confederate soldiers fled the army in significant numbers. Accurate estimates are difficult to verify, but the best work on this subject suggests that by the end of the war, more than 100,000 soldiers had deserted. Whether they sought to return home to families threatened by the war, had lost heart in the cause, had grown tired of fighting in a conflict that many had come to see as a rich man's war, or were fed up with army life, deserters sapped the Confederate Army of soldiers when they were needed the most.[38]

Desertion exposed some deep cracks in the Confederacy, and historians have certainly focused on them. They have examined what motivated soldiers to leave, made much of the total numbers who fled their posts, and used Confederate desertions as a human index of national resolve. Of equal importance, however, are the lengths to which the Confederate state went to stop the flow of deserters from the army and what the state did to keep the many more who remained. This effort—haphazard though it may have been—shone a bright light on the limits of the Confederate state, but it also illuminated a broad shift in what it meant to be a Confederate citizen. By the end of the war, loyalty to the state formed the nucleus of a new ideal of citizenship, and the figure of the disloyal deserter loomed particularly large as the citizen's opposite. The lessons that the state attempted to impart to those who remained, about what it meant to be a Confederate citizen, were particularly sharp and often gruesome. In camps all over the American South, there was no purer lesson of civic devotion than for soldiers to behold the punishments meted out to deserters. By the end of the conflict, captured deserters became symbols of shame, disloyalty, and treason, as well as physical manifestations of state power.[39]

From the moment that desertions became more commonplace in the Confederate Army, officials, pastors, and political leaders wrapped the issue in evangelical language and suffused it with the menace of state retribution. The Reverend Basil Manly Jr., a South Carolinian who taught at the Southern Baptist Theological Seminary, published a short piece on the subject that blurred the line between sin and national disloyalty. In his account, Manly recounted the story of a Confederate soldier named Charles whose family lived in American-controlled Virginia. Whether driven by a longing for home, a "dislike of camp restraints, or the fickleness of a boy," Charles cast his oath of enlistment aside and deserted his post. In chancing an escape, the young soldier and traitors like him had done more than imperil the cause of the southern nation. According to Manly, "They left the Lord, they left his people, they left his ordinances, they left his ways, they cast his book aside, they put his laws behind their back, they cut themselves off from Him and His." By equating disloyalty to the nation with disloyalty to the Almighty, Manly argued that just as those who countenanced sin still had the opportunity to be saved, so too could wavering Confederates seek redemption, if they wanted it. Ultimately, a soldier's thoughts were his own; it was his actions that mattered. For those who had taken the next step and "cast the fear of God behind you," Manly argued that deserters needed to be made aware of the cost. They had forsaken not only their country but their faith: "You have gone forth from God's people, because you were not of them. And what now? The vows of God are upon you. You have broken them; but the shattered links still cling around your soul, and cannot be shaken off."[40] In the evolving civic religion that had become the beating heart of the Confederate state, desertion cut the individual loose not only from the nation and its protections but from all of the bonds of church and faith that wound around southern communities. Having broken their covenant with God and the nation, deserters were to be treated as stateless, faithless persons and nothing more.

There was always the faint hope that deserters could repent for their sins. For Manly, even those who fled their post ought to be welcomed back into the fold once they had been punished: "There is salvation even for such as you, with Him who 'is able to save unto the uttermost.'" For soldiers who deserted early in the war, Manly's religiously inspired lenience echoed faintly in War Department policies. Sensitivity, for instance, in punishing Confederate soldiers with the lash reflected a common concern about the morale of an army in which many, if not most, equated whippings with the kind of punishment doled out to slaves. Other officers and soldiers also hoped for evenhanded justice. Harry Lewis, who was stationed near Fredericksburg in the winter of 1862, was called as a witness to the court-martial of a member of his company. Though Lewis confided to his mother that the man was by no means a friend, the accused had fled the army because of an illness, and as a result, Lewis was "confident he will be lightly delt with by the

Court, as he has ben a fine soldier, effective on the battle field as well as at camp save in this affair alone."[41]

It would not take long, however, before the Confederate military dealt with deserters in a manner that left little room for mercy. Around the same time that Confederate conscription became law, the increased power of the national government over its army began to influence how the military dealt with desertion. "I have juste saw one of the Worst sight that I Ever saw in my life," wrote one soldier to another in the late summer of 1862. He had just witnessed a man shot for desertion, and the sight of a condemned soldier killed by his former comrades sickened him. As Capt. W. M. Butt put it, "it was a nuff to see our Men shot bye the yankees but it is Worse to see them shote by our one men. It is more than I Ever Expected to see in My life bee fore."[42] Not only the severity of the punishments doled out by courts-martial but also the increasingly creative ways in which deserters were punished were disturbing. Some of the punishments were standard military fare: marking time on a barrel, the docking of pay, solitary confinement, hard labor with a ball and chain around the ankle, and unremitting fatigue duty. But it was not long before even more of an example was made of deserters. By the spring of 1863, the Confederate adjutant and inspector general's office was inundated with documents relating to courts-martial convened all over the army, and the punishments these tribunals meted out to the guilty spoke to something more than just rough military justice. As punishment for desertion, Lieut. P. C. Harper of the 25th Louisiana Volunteers had his crime, name, place of abode, and the sentence of his court-martial printed in every soldier's newspaper and in every newspaper published in his home state. Even though insufficient evidence was brought against them to secure a conviction, three soldiers from a Mississippi regiment stationed in Mobile were placed under surveillance without their knowledge. Capt. Jonathan Becker of the 38th Alabama was sentenced to forfeit his pay and allowance for the duration of the sentence, was placed on a barrel morning and night and made to wear a sandwich board on which were written the words "deserter" and "swindler," was tattooed with the letters "D" for deserter and "T" for traitor on each hip, had his head shaved, and, after punishment, was drummed out of the service.[43] As the number of desertions increased, there appeared to have been no punishment in which the spectacle of the sentence was not taken into account. One newspaper correspondent noted that by the spring of 1863, punishments for desertion and almost every transgression of military law had become both more public and more laden with meaning. The writer described the scene of one man who was sentenced to wear a barrel shirt in front of his regiment: "The barrel is placed over the head of the defender, his arms being put through holes on each side. The barrel is marked in large letters,

'Absent without leave,' 'I deserted my colors,' and other sentences to describe the nature of the offense. The culprit, feeling like a drowned rat, is then led up and down the line or stationed in front of his regiment during dress parade." Shamed by the military and condemned by the state, captured deserters played a symbolic role in the Confederate Army equal in power to that of the loyal Christian soldier. They became living symbols of what could happen if soldiers did not reckon with their duty to the nation and offered stark reminders of what the Confederate state could do to men who offered nothing less than their complete devotion.[44]

By late 1864, as American invasion shrunk the Confederacy and successive losses on the battlefield made defeat a growing reality, a variety of increasingly shrill pronouncements rapidly clarified the ideal of citizenship forged in the nation's army. When the public spectacle of punished deserters failed to staunch the flow of men from the military, the War Department issued circulars calling for the redoubled efforts of local sheriffs and conscript agents. A conscript officer who failed to do the hard work of arresting and rounding up AWOL Confederate soldiers was "a traitor of the deepest dye." Even if locals in his county might support his inaction, "the curse of God and his country will fall upon him." By the early spring of 1865, entreaties in soldiers' newspapers continued to trumpet the cause as divinely inspired, even if defeat seemed certain. "We require a united people," claimed an editorial in the *Army and Navy Herald*, "people that will listen to not terms of conciliation short of complete independence; people who will decry all prattlings about peace until our enemies shall tender it upon such terms as will be alike just and honorable."[45]

This kind of faith fed a collective delusion about a future in which Confederates would become loyal citizens of a failed state. This was particularly true of soldiers who found that the experience of serving the Confederacy had left a lasting mark. "Some of our Southern people are much disheartened," wrote a soldier to his cousin Eliza Caldwell, "but the army is in good spirits and confident of our ultimate success." All the same, the soldier allowed that after four years of service, life as a Confederate had ruined him for a life after war: "I feel that I am fit for nothing else but a soldier." Perhaps most tellingly, even in southern territory occupied by American forces, a veneration and idealization of Confederate citizenship seems to have matured into something altogether different. Reporting on the situation in northern Mississippi for the Freedmen's Bureau, S. H. Melcher declared that young men and injured veterans continued to wear their Confederate uniforms and took part in school exhibitions and amateur dramatics that venerated victorious Confederates laying waste to American armies. Melcher was candid. He reported that whites in the region "hate any man who is not in favor of the rebel cause and in favor of vagrant and apprentice laws, which will reduce the freedmen" to a condition akin to slavery, even before the Confederate surrender.[46]

REFLECTING ON THE CONFEDERACY AT THE moment it collapsed, writer William McDonald joined southern leaders and writers in a fit of soul-searching over what had gone wrong. With their government on the run and their army in tatters, Confederates looked back to the recent past for clues about what had led to their nation's defeat and what the future might hold. For McDonald, "there is always much mystery about great revolutions," but as he and so many other Confederates raked the embers of their nation in the search for answers, it was not the Revolution of 1861 but one that occurred two years earlier that seemed the real source of southern destruction.[47]

In a slim volume—part history, part wounded polemic—McDonald laid before readers a blow-by-blow account of John Brown's raid on Harpers Ferry. With chapters devoted not only to Brown's early life but to a history of the abolitionist movement, to which Brown was so devoted until his death, McDonald was keen to lay all blame for the war at the feet of ruthless abolitionists who had backed white southerners into a corner and all but dared them to bolt the Union. As McDonald had it, abolitionists and not secessionist supporters were the real rebels in the conflict. It was they who connived to unlawfully and violently upend southern society, and it was their party, firmly installed in the White House by 1861, that sought to finish the work that John Brown had begun. Though the ironic twisting of a familiar history was not new, what made McDonald's account unusual was the tone deployed and the words chosen. The writer was at pains to make it clear that what opponents of slavery did to the South and to the Union was treasonous. "It was then seen that they had banded to destroy the delegated majesty of the established constitution, and to exalt in its stead, not a new constitution modified," but a majoritarian dictatorship bent on pursuing power for "party interest and sectional hate." Republicans, "with treason in their hearts," took an oath to uphold a Constitution they had no interest in upholding, all the while placing white southerners in the position of having to remain loyal to the United States by leaving it. Now, in defeat, southerners might endure the infamy that comes from being the citizens of a failed state and surrender "every principle for the maintenance of the right of which she first drew her loyal sword." But there was little to be done but accept a life as "a homeless, penniless wanderer, with no resort but to forever abandon her native soil, or drag out a dreary life of bondage to the hated northerner."[48]

In the way McDonald cast southern defeat, one can detect all the stock metaphors and familiar language of the Lost Cause. Yet because the collapse of the Confederacy fed a collective outpouring of self-pity, one can see both a profound set of pressing questions about the place of former Confederate citizens in a postwar American republic and a deeply divisive politics of loyalty in full bloom.

Though the Confederacy would dissolve, the bonds of loyalty forged between that nation and many of its citizens would prove more lasting and, ultimately, stronger than any tie that may have connected white southerners as citizens to the United States before the conflict started.[49] Particularly as the doctrines of free labor and a debate over the nature of federal power in the defeated South took hold, loyalty and the veneration of one's citizenship to a failed state grew in importance. Looking more closely at the roots of this loyalty, one can see a process of state-sponsored education that centered on the Confederate military. It was certainly an imperfect process. While many loyal Confederate citizens refused to bend even in defeat, many white southerners abandoned the southern nation or fled the army, and some even actively sought the nation's downfall. Yet for those who remained—for those who were loyal, committed themselves to the nation, learned the hard lessons of what could befall the disloyal, and survived the conflict—the hothouse experience at the center of the Confederacy's experiment in citizenship made an indelible impression. When the Civil War began, citizenship in the new Confederacy was an inchoate thing. By the time the war ended, it had become a hardened set of obligations and alliances. It was a bond of devotion between a modern state and a people, and it would complicate any attempt made by the United States to bring white southerners back into the national fold.

CHAPTER FOUR

Defining Loyalty in an Age of Emancipation

In the pages of *Harper's New Monthly Magazine*, readers in the winter of 1861 were treated to an article on the life of America's most notorious traitor, Benedict Arnold. Written with a patient eye for detail and adorned with lavish pen-and-ink drawings, the piece made it clear that in Arnold's life, readers could glimpse what citizens should expect if they abandoned their principles and turned their backs on their country. The article examined every facet of the infamous man's story, from his Connecticut boyhood and his exploits as a revolutionary soldier to his galling inability to rise through the ranks of the Continental Army and his decision in 1779 to switch allegiance and serve the British Empire. Throughout, the piece depicted Arnold as vain and ambitious, brimming with confidence, quick to anger, and sensitive to every slight. While the sketch of Arnold's life did not overlook his accomplishments as an American soldier, the sting in the tale came at the close. The history recounted that after the Revolution, no matter where Arnold went, the taint of his cowardice and disloyalty trailed him, souring all of his relations. Even after he became a successful merchant in royalist New Brunswick, living life "in a style of ostentatious profusion," his past and his "haughty deportment made him very unpopular." Burned in effigy by loyalists, labeled a traitor by those whose cause had been his only a few years before, Arnold was marked by his past as a man without honor. He was driven by the desire for wealth rather than patriotic loyalty, and fate dealt him a hand in life that he had richly deserved. Readers should expect nothing less if they considered a similar fall from civic grace.[1]

Published only seven months into the Civil War, the message in the story of Arnold's life could hardly have been clearer. By the time Americans read the article, Arnold's posh extravagance, arrogant presumption, and act of unforgivable treason could have easily stood in for the depictions of wealthy slaveholders that by then saturated American popular print. Certainly once the Civil War began in earnest, magazines and newspaper dailies churned out copy that cast white southerners as traitors to be scorned, individuals whose loose allegiances and skin-deep convictions had led them to toss their citizenship aside in the vain hope of national aggrandizement. Writing in Horace Greeley's *New York Tribune*, one contributor hoped that the idea of the nation's flag having been "polluted by traitorous bands" of secessionists would send flocks of northerners to volunteer in a "patriotic rush." By the end of 1861, the *Tribune* had become an index of national loyalty and republican paranoia. From its pages came a torrent of commentary on treason that offered no quarter to all but the most steadfast. "The principle of free speech," wrote one *Tribune* editorialist in the summer of 1862, "affords no justification for the traitorous license which is increasing among us."[2]

Motivated by their anger, a bellicose nationalism, and the desire for revenge, Americans drew new meaning from old stories in a debate that convulsed the country. It was a struggle in and out of government over who could be counted as loyal, what rights the disloyal ought to possess, and what citizenship meant in what was left of the nation. Sectionalism and secession had sparked it, but the battle over loyalty had grown into a titanic struggle by the close of the war's first year, particularly as the Confederate state tightened its grip over its population, in and out of the military. Americans faced the prospect that even if the United States prevailed, reuniting the country with those who had disavowed their citizenship as Americans, there was still the gnawing doubt whether the republic would ever, should never, be as it once was. If white southerners pledged their loyalty in word and action to another nation, any reconstituted American nation would have to deal with this perfidy in a way that would satisfy those who had been true to the republic. Particularly as the body count from a growing list of battles piled high in the collective American unconscious, the desire to punish those blamed for the carnage would, in time, turn into a lust for vengeance that would not be easily assuaged. Loyalty—the kind of loyalty that men like Benedict Arnold threw aside so lightly—was under the national microscope, and it forced Americans to confront the hard reality that even if successful, the United States could not endure without a fundamental change in the relationship between individual citizens and the republic.[3]

Ideas about and professions of loyalty also took on added importance because of how the debate changed the way that Americans reckoned with not only new ideas about citizenship but new obligations to the nation-state. That the national government grew so quickly and assumed so many powers with such dramatic speed compelled Americans to stand up and take notice. When they did, the obligations at the heart of citizenship, and not simply the rights that citizens enjoyed, assumed a new primacy. To serve—to offer one's life to the state, to sacrifice for that state, to be loyal at all times, and to suffer the consequences if one's loyalty was found wanting—became part of a new reality that Americans ignored at their peril. Treason was a crime perpetrated not against an individual but against the state, and at a time of war, declarations of loyalty and accusations of disloyalty were anything but empty words. They had to be proven to the satisfaction of government, and only months into the Civil War, no one could mistake the fact that that same government would stand in judgment as loyalty's ultimate arbiter.[4]

Yet while administrators and political leaders drew sharp contrasts between the loyal and the disloyal, sorting the patriots from the Benedict Arnolds proved so much easier in theory than in practice. Though treason stood out as the only crime made plain in the American constitution, the loyalties that lay at the heart of the transgression were ephemeral. They were emotional acts, committed at tense moments and interpreted by others at a point of fevered national drama. To prove loyalty required assurances not only from the accused but also from their friends and neighbors, who were, in turn, required to demonstrate their own loyalties. What's more, to judge the value of loyalty, some yardstick was needed against which to measure it, and coming to agreement over how loyalty was to be measured proved as hard as the acts in question. Particularly as the war intensified and as U.S. forces began to occupy more Confederate territory, the problem of loyalty became that much harder to solve. American officers, provost marshals, and government officials learned hard lessons on an almost daily basis about the problem of demanding the loyalty of individuals in occupied communities, where the line between the United States and the Confederacy was constantly shifting and porous. And even if the pleas of the loyal were in earnest, trusting them proved difficult. This lack of trust created a gap between law and national feeling, between stated war aims and the reality of life in the occupied South. Even if the purpose of the government was to speed the return of southern states into the nation—to "resume their allegiance to the United States," as Abraham Lincoln stated in his Reconstruction plan at the end of 1863—tidy national plans for a unified future had to square with the mood of the loyal in the rest of the country. By the war's middle stages, many Americans demanded their pound of flesh, not to mention a more stringent, more unsparing set of rules regarding citizenship that would, by the war's end, leave white southerners in no doubt that their failure in national independence would make them outsiders in a postwar republic.[5]

In a world of shifting loyalties, the only thing steadfast, particularly in the South, was the national affinity of persons whose fortunes and freedom would become the focus of the war. African Americans had long looked to the impending conflict between North and South as the culmination of a biblical deliverance. But they began the war as bit characters in a larger national drama. White southerners may have worried about their intentions, and many Republicans might have hoped that they would lend a hand in destroying the system that kept them in chains; but both American and Confederate governments did not count slaves as more than a people to whom history happens. They were persons of interest, not combatants of value.

Yet as the war dragged on, slaves made their intentions crystal clear. They fled plantations by the thousands and surged towards U.S. lines whenever and wherever the opportunity arose. What's more, the potential they possessed as weapons of war offered African Americans opportunities to prove their value and their loyalty, all at once. Stepping boldly into the conflict, particularly once it grew into a war for emancipation, slaves joined a long list of Africans in the Americas who used their wartime service as leverage to win them concessions when the conflict ended. Casting their lot with the United States and Lincoln, many African Americans endured the hardship of war by proclaiming themselves as loyalty personified, devoted not only to the perpetuation of the republic but to the state that had become, by 1863, devoted to destroying slavery. In so doing, many slaves throughout the South anticipated the emerging vision of the South as a colonial possession by presenting themselves as loyal subjects, if not yet citizens, in a southern world where the allegiance of whites was never certain. They learned important lessons about how the American state worked, what it wanted from them, how it could be used, and what loyalty to the state could win them. In the broader world history of emancipation, African Americans asserted themselves in ways that were canny, bold, and unprecedented. They would, in time, convince the American state of their value, creating a relationship between themselves and a government that would reverberate in national politics for decades. They would prove themselves as loyal to claim rights as citizens when the conflict ended.[6]

This chapter draws the history of American emancipation together with the story of how the federal government became a leviathan to show the ways in which loyalty became fused with citizenship during the Civil War. Following the development of debates over loyalty in Congress and the many ways in which freedpeople used loyalty as a wedge to pry open the body politic, the chapter examines how the war etched a new definition of citizenship into the cornerstone of an emergent, new republic. Staring through the prism of loyalty, Americans would discern in the refracted light some cold conclusions about their nation-state and the place of African Americans in it. By the end of the war, loyalty would crystallize into both a set of hard obligations and a high bar against which all were measured and many were found wanting.

IN A SPECIAL SESSION CALLED TO order in the spring of 1861, the U.S. Congress presided over a government besieged. With seven states out of the Union and more to follow, discussion in both the House and Senate turned predictably to the nation's response, particularly once war with the Confederacy became a reality. But as the ensuing debate made clear, the threat of armed conflict was matched by worries about threats from within. Senators, for one, faced the question of what to do with fellow members who hailed from states that wavered on the edges of a shrunken American republic. The problem this handful of representatives presented to the federal government turned a matter of procedure—of whether to allow members to sit as part of a legislative quorum—into a soul-searching debate that revealed just how quickly ideas about citizenship and Americans' obligation to the state were changing. Over the next year, congressional discussions about loyalty would sweep the government and the nation into a frenzy. Worries about the allegiances of officials and the sympathies of citizens would send the American national government into a period of purge that would only grow in intensity as the war wore on.

Loyalty and the redefinition of American citizenship emerged early in the Civil War and swept unlikely characters into the spotlight. Take the brief career of U.S. senator for Texas Louis T. Wigfall. A die-hard secessionist who had agitated for southern independence as long as anyone in the emergent Confederacy, Wigfall had earned a reputation as a political brawler, first in his native South Carolina and later in Texas, where he emigrated in the late 1840s following the Mexican War. But his election to the U.S. Senate in 1860, before Texas had seceded, presented him with an opportunity. In the wake of his election, Wigfall stated publicly that he deemed himself a foreigner in the United States, without any tie of allegiance to the national government, though in his campaign he did not make it clear whether he would swear an oath if he were elected.[7] In response, when Wigfall won his seat, senators presented a resolution in March 1861 calling for his expulsion even before news of Texas's secession had reached Washington. Given his views, expulsion was hardly a worry for Wigfall, who would in time take his seat in the Confederate Congress. He could have renounced his election, yet the chance to puncture a hole in what remained of the Union was too good to pass up. By seeking his removal before the secession of his state was confirmed, the debate presented to Wigfall the chance to force the hand of Republicans in Congress to accept the Confederacy as an independent nation. It also allowed secessionists to refute the Republican argument that the war was being fought simply for national preservation.

The Constitution set requirements to hold office based on an individual's age, the length of time a representative had been a citizen of the republic, and whether the representative had taken an oath. A man like Wigfall satisfied most of these requirements, save the last one, which had been little more than an empty ritual. For Congress to argue otherwise—to suggest that loyalty was the most important requirement for the holding of federal office—upset the Lincoln administration's delicate definition of the war as an insurrection of citizens rather than a battle between the United States and a nascent Confederate nation. Yet it was the presumed secession of the state Wigfall represented and, most importantly, his public declaration of disloyalty that assumed the greatest importance in the debate that followed. According to Connecticut Republican Lafayette S. Foster, the Senate owed it to the Constitution and the integrity of the national government not to allow Wigfall his place. If war was to ensue between the United States and the Confederacy, resulting in the "tearing down and trampling in the dust the national flag," the republic would be vulnerable to attack not only from Confederate forces but from disloyal elements within the country who would seek to harm the national government. Federal power was, for Foster, indivisible, supreme, and in danger. In this context, though, it was not simply the act of a southern state seceding from the republic that cut representatives like Foster to the quick. What mattered as much was an individual making a mockery of the United States by disavowing his loyalty to the country while seeking to take his place in the nation's legislature. While Wigfall's temerity struck northern members of Congress as begging for strong action, southern representatives still serving in the Senate hit on the issue of allegiance as laying bare the tenuous nature of national citizenship and the righteousness of secession. Virginia Democrat James M. Mason allowed that should Texas secede, Wigfall's demand to be counted as a member of the Senate would be null and void. The presumption, however, that his lack of allegiance to the nation was enough to cast Wigfall out of the Senate was a draconian overreach by Republicans and ought to be called out as little more than partisan grandstanding. If anything, Mason argued, Wigfall was acting in concert with both the law and his conscience. All Americans owed their ultimate allegiance to their states, not the nation, and when pressed on this point, all right-thinking people would hold fast to their connection as citizens to the state of their birth. The federal state, claimed Mason, was a "mere temporary agency," a man-made and therefore inherently flawed thing that lacked a fixed, natural, historic hold over its people. An individual state, in contrast, possessed a deep, abiding license to the allegiance of those born within its borders. The news of Texas's secession made Mason's point and Wigfall's case moot. Once open to debate, however, talk of loyalty quickly spread.[8]

At the heart of the question of loyalty was a simple but profound issue in American politics. If citizens owed their allegiance to their states rather than to the nation, what right did the national government have to protect itself from internal or external threat? Though the Constitution gave the national government the means to act when threatened by treason, the flimsy tie between it and citizens in popular politics left the federal state open to attack. Almost immediately, the threat posed by wavering loyalties prompted calls not only to expose dissenters within the republic but also to offer full-throated support for a new kind of national state, one empowered to protect itself, prosecute a full-scale war, and command the obligation of all.

The writer who leaped at this new idea with complete abandon was Anna Ella Carroll. The daughter of a wealthy Maryland planter, Carroll was a politician of consummate skill. By the time the Civil War erupted, she had been a player in politics for more than a decade. She had sided with the Whigs, but when that party fell apart, Carroll took up the banner of the Know-Nothing campaign and wrote a ferocious set of pamphlets about Catholic influence in her native state that propelled her to the upper echelon of anti-immigrant politics. Ever the operator, Carroll felt just how much the political wind had shifted by the mid-1850s. When the Know-Nothings dissolved, she changed tack and moved to the Republican Party, early enough to be counted as a stalwart. By the time Abraham Lincoln was elected president, she had made her name as a backroom pamphleteer and a knowledgeable political advisor who had the ear of many in Lincoln's cabinet, including, in time, the president himself.[9]

Anna Carroll's greatest assets were her agile legal mind and her incredibly sharp pen. In unadorned, powerful language, Carroll honed the case against the South to a knife's point. To her, what supporters of secession had set in motion was nothing less than a coordinated act of treason. For Carroll, what made secession all the more diabolical was that it was a coup d'état orchestrated by a small "conspiracy of official persons" who left loyal white southerners "wholly without the means of effectual opposition." With national pride trampled by secessionists, the national government had done little to protect itself or to prosecute the traitors in its midst. Little wonder to Carroll, then, that loyal Americans felt powerless. Yet, as she laid out in great detail, it was clearly within the power of the national government to act boldly.[10]

What Carroll envisioned was a state freed from the box of small government that antebellum politics had put it in and a volitional definition of citizenship that turned older ideas about the title upside down. She trotted out the timeworn arguments over the Constitution's ratification as proof of how long-simmering the argument over the appropriate size and scope of the national state had been in the republic's history. But in the war powers vested in the executive branch of government, Carroll saw the outline of a state very different from the one imagined by most Americans, a state fixed with raw, coercive authority. As she argued, the right to declare war against enemies foreign and domestic was collapsed in the text. The Constitution, she claimed, placed "the two cases of war, the one being internal, and the other external, in the same predicament as to power." Within this ambiguity, the executive possessed not only the right to make war but the right to suspend the writ of habeas corpus, giving the nation-state power at once over an army and the civilian population. All this power was automatically enacted, according to Carroll, whenever the nation was in a state of war. Yet what made civil war different from other conflicts lay in the acts of loyalty individuals chose to proclaim, for or against their former government. "No man," argued Carroll, "becomes a part of the insurrectionary force unless he actually joins it. . . . No one is an enemy to the government unless he *voluntarily* casts off its authority." By defining secession and southern independence in this way—not as a collective act of automatic repudiation but as an individual, deeply personal renunciation of allegiance—Carroll reworked an older debate over citizenship that had defined politics in the United States for decades and created something new in the process.[11]

In Carroll's mind, the ties between individual states and citizens mattered little at a time of national peril. If anything, war laid bare the deepest of connections between citizens and the national state. Moreover, the secession of a state was not coequal with white southerners casting off their citizenship to the national government. A state might secede, but it was within the power of white citizens to choose whether they would follow. Hard bonds connected Americans to the state, and if they chose to remain loyal to it, their rights as citizens would be respected. "The duties of allegiance and protection are reciprocal," concluded Carroll, echoing a time-honored theory of governance. "Hence, if the supreme power of the nation should not, within a reasonable time, afford that protection which is their Federal right to its own citizens of the South, they will forever be released from their allegiance." But should white southerners choose to become Confederate citizens, they would become enemy noncombatants. If they renounced their loyalty, they would be offered no recourse to rights as citizens or to rights over their property if the national government deemed it expedient. Personal acts alone would, for Carroll, determine the shape and ferocity of war. It was a conflict that, for her, existed between the nation-state and whomever renounced it. To deny the state allegiance, "voluntarily assumes the character of a public enemy. By the same conduct he also reveals the profound hostility of his heart towards the Federal authority, and the obstinate determination of his will to resist it."[12]

Carroll's definition of loyalty and her imagining of a powerful state that commanded obligation would become part of the national debate and would quickly find its way into public policy. By the beginning of 1862, congressional investigations into the loyalty of representatives began to circle around not simply persons from states who wavered at the edges of the republic but individuals who lived within the United States whose convictions were deemed suspect as well. When Benjamin Stark, a Democrat and a proslavery advocate, was appointed to fill a vacant seat in the U.S. Senate by John Whiteacre, the governor of Oregon, Republicans in Congress sought to block him. Citing his support of slavery as proof of his disloyalty, the debate over his membership echoed Anna Carroll's arguments. According to Charles Sumner, the qualification to serve in government that was paramount was loyalty; all other prerequisites paled by comparison. "If an applicant here is disloyal, or if there is reasonable ground to believe him to be disloyal, it seems to me that, under the Constitution of the United States, he should not be admitted to this body until the question of his loyalty" has been resolved beyond reasonable doubt.[13] Even though a lack of evidence cleared Stark of any wrongdoing, by the time the debate was over, loyalty had ascended to something that approached the spiritual, as senators spoke of not allowing the purity of the government to be diluted by disloyal persons in their midst. Lyman Trumbull, who claimed to be in favor of "investigating disloyalty anywhere and everywhere," thought so little of Stark, even after his name had been cleared, that Trumbull threw him in with Confederates as part of the same sickness that threatened the nation. Traitors, Trumbull railed, "may achieve a greater triumph over this Government, do more to destroy its institutions, and to subvert the Constitution, by sending their traitors here to-day armed with thirty years of life, nine years citizenship, and an inhabitancy of the States in rebellion, with credentials from their traitor Governors, than by continuing this war."[14]

The debate in Congress over loyalty reached a tipping point in the spring of 1862 and dovetailed with the publication of a House report that same session. The report showed how quickly concerns about loyalty had become a witch hunt. A select committee on the loyalty of clerks headed by Wisconsin congressman John Fox "Bowie Knife" Potter had been convened the previous year when Congress directed all federal employees to take a new oath of allegiance. In practice, the Lincoln administration allowed each member in the cabinet to tailor the oath to his own department, with any person who refused to take it subject to dismissal. Potter's committee, however, was formed to give the new oath added bite. The committee was set up with the power to examine and expose all who refused to submit to this new declaration of allegiance. Potter sought and received lists of persons who had refused the oath from all federal departments. Given the tenor of the moment, it was not long before the lists grew to include any individual suspected of disloyalty. Any and all information was fair game, and in time hundreds of separate investigations were taken up, resulting in a dense report ninety-two pages long.[15]

Once furnished with lists of suspected persons, numbering 550 in all, the committee set to work in late August 1861. It met on an almost daily basis, making inquiries and interviewing the associates of those suspected of doing harm to the republic from within. The committee tipped its hand in the report and assumed the broadest mandate to investigate and prosecute individuals deemed unworthy of government office. At a time of civil war, the committee claimed, "disloyal men will be constantly seeking the confidence of the government, in order to betray its secrets, and to enjoy its patronage, and it would be strange if they were not often successful." Painting a stark picture of a state marbled with enemies, the committee aimed to extract anyone who might do the government harm. To undertake this kind of surgery, the committee focused on examining charges against individuals leveled by "respectable and responsible citizens" and collecting testimonial evidence under oath. The committee allowed that there was always the chance that "partisan or personal feeling," not to mention professional avarice or grudge, might compromise the testimony that was often drawn from other clerks in a suspected individual's own department. All the same, while some loyal citizens may have unjustly become the focus of investigation, the committee argued that an unfairly tarnished reputation was worth the price if it inoculated the national government. It was "a light exaction to make of men of doubtful loyalty, that they be reduced to the level of the great mass of their fellow-citizens by removal from places of trust and power."[16]

Even for those who charged that the committee acted as little more than a partisan body, the report still made for uncomfortable reading. Four witnesses testified against James Wright, a clerk in the Judge Advocate's Office who hailed from Maryland and had denounced the government at a public meeting. J. T. C. Clark, employed in the Quartermaster's Department, was charged by the committee for stating publicly that he hoped the Confederate Army would capture Washington "and murder every damned black republican." Lieut. Col. William Maynadier, a confidant of Jefferson Davis when the Confederate president had been the secretary of war, assumed a post as assistant to the head of the Ordinance Department. He was accused of selling 20,000 stand of arms to the Confederacy, with an informal agreement to furnish much more. While these cases justified the committee's existence, others straddled a very fine line between acceptable evidence and hearsay. Edmund Brooke, a chief clerk in the Paymaster-General's

Office, was marked as suspect for merely agreeing with a minister from a George-town parish who elected to omit a prayer for the president of the United States from his Sunday service. Robert Dodge, a paymaster in a private firm contracted by the War Department, was found guilty of suggesting that southerners would assassinate Lincoln before he was inaugurated. This utterance, as well as the Dodge family's well-known secessionist sympathies, was enough to convince the committee of the threat Dodge posed to the republic. Viewed through the looking glass of loyalty, even personal hesitation on the part of suspected persons regarding their allegiance brought swift condemnation. John Mattingly, a clerk in the Post Office, was accused of agonizing over whether to take the new oath of loyalty, as well as having been seen raising a glass to Jefferson Davis and the success of the Confederacy at a Washington watering hole. Mattingly's fate was sealed when the circumstantial evidence against him congealed with the help of Postmaster General John Miller, who was satisfied with his secessionist credentials. Though the committee allowed that they were unsure of the evidence in support of Miller's claim, a high-ranking official in the Lincoln administration leveling a charge of disloyalty was enough to turn opaque testimony into something flawlessly clear. Political position, as it happened, created its own hierarchy of loyalty, making everyone lower down the pecking order potentially suspect.[17]

Congressional committees and the expanded powers of federal agents turned the state inside out while at the same time giving it the justification to grow. Ad-hoc authority invested in the hands of Secretary of State William Seward—who famously boasted that with the touch of a telegraph hammer, he could order hasty arrests and indefinite imprisonments of any person in any part of the country—made all suspected persons subject to summary detention. Even for those who stood with the United States in its war against the Confederacy, the fusion of loyalty with citizenship was a worry. The very word "loyalty" had, according to one writer in the *North American Review*, undergone a thorough renovation. It no longer denoted a person's fidelity to the law but had, more worryingly, come to equal "fidelity to the sovereign or executive head of the nation." Political and national devotion—to the national government, to the Republican Party, and to Lincoln himself—had become commingled, and it was in this sense, as much as in any other, that Americans confronted the power of the state and their relationship to it. Between the end of 1861 and the middle of 1862, Congress turned an incredible array of legislation into law, expanding federal power while at the same time creating programs designed to etch the principles of the ruling Republican Party into the foundations of the country. Income and comprehensive sales taxes, used to raise money for the war effort; the Homestead Act, to provide loyal Americans with land on the continental frontier; the Morrill Land-Grant

Act, to build educational institutes for the promotion of a modern economy; and the Militia Law, to furnish the armed forces with conscripts all encouraged the growth of the national government. By the end of the conflict, the federal government's revenue had doubled while at the same time consolidating the nation-state's authority. What's more, where it could, the national government made personal loyalty the minimum qualification for any connection between citizens and the state. In 1862 alone, and largely on the strength of the select committee that had investigated federal employees, Congress moved in several directions at once to shut the door of the national government to anyone who possessed anything less than the spotless credentials of a devoted republican. Suspect citizens in the District of Columbia were, by May 1862, subject to investigation and the swearing of oaths in order to vote, foreshadowing what federal officials would require of suspect Confederates in the occupied South. Tightened regulations made anyone who gave aid to the enemy—by taking up arms, offering food, or allowing farm animals to be drafted into the Confederate cause—ineligible to sit as petit or grand jurors, with a complex oath to be taken even by those who satisfied the loyalty requirement. In July, Congress made all persons connected to public service, civilian or otherwise, subject to an oath of loyalty to hold any office or to fulfill any contract with the national government. Whether individuals were lining up to vote in the nation's capital or vying for a growing number of lucrative federal military contracts, the implications of the debate over loyalty, in and out of government, were unequivocal. What had started with worries had hardened into a steadfast conviction. Personal allegiance had, a year into the war, become the prerequisite for citizenship in the American republic.[18]

An indication of how much loyalty had permeated American politics can be found in the discussion over what to do with the South if the United States prevailed. From the moment loyalty erupted as an issue in national politics, the debate over it had always focused attention and ire on former citizens who had cast their lot with an enemy nation. By 1862, however, the harsher light that had been cast on the question had, along with the progress of the war itself, encouraged loyal Americans to see disloyal Confederates with harder eyes. Particular scorn for slaveholders remained, but as the conflict entered its second year, the debate over loyalty encouraged many to paint all white southerners with the same brush. As the suspect class of traitors expanded, so too did the horizon of possibility for what an emboldened national government could do with the occupied South. In an article that asked, "What Shall We Do With Them?" one writer in the *Atlantic Monthly* in the spring of 1862 encouraged readers to set southern disloyalty against a larger, historical canvas. Reaching back to recent history for clues as to how older, venerable nations and empires had brought order to chaos, the writer asked readers to imagine the United States as Great Britain, and the Confederacy as India under Crown rule. The writer playfully allowed that the conquered Indians were "in complexion, much nearer akin to that portion of our Southern citizens which has *not* rebelled," but in the application and character of British power on the Indian subcontinent, the writer argued that Americans might find a useful corollary. Setting the creation of the Confederacy alongside the 1857 Indian Rebellion, one principle of politics and power became plain: "The restoration of the lawful authority over rebels does not restore them to their old *status*. They are at the pleasure of the conquering power. Rights of citizenship, having been abjured, do not return with the same coercion which demands duties of citizenship. . . . Every wrong-doer is *ipso facto* a rebel. He forfeits, according to due course of law, a measure of his privileges, while constrained to the same responsibility of obedience."[19] This leap of historical logic contained several new ideas. Framing the war not as an armed conflict between two parts of the same nation but as a war that could, with American victory, turn defeated Confederates into colonial subjects set the conflict on entirely new ground. The very idea was explosive. Having made the point, the writer admitted as much by backing off, blaming slaveholders for the war and arguing that the American occupation of the conquered South should revolve around the punishment of former masters for their civic and moral sins by abolishing slavery. Yet the depth of the anger directed at secessionists and the Confederate South more generally hints at the more radical possibilities that sustained an undercurrent in American thinking about the war's hoped-for end. Coming as it did at a high-water mark in the debate over loyalty, the imagining of the South as a colonial possession—and white southerners stripped of their status as citizens—foreshadowed federal wartime policy.[20]

The dark future predicted for individuals who carried on the war and did not return to their old allegiances hardened quite quickly. For Confederates who held fast to their allegiances as independent citizens of an enemy state, many writers in the popular press called for the American republic to be unsparing. "We will give everybody time to pack up. We will make up a little purse for any especially hard case which the removal may show. But stay and be plague-stricken," and the nation would no longer suffer the instability. "This rebellion has placed the North [in the position] where it must conquer, for its own best interests, and dignity, and the salvation of free institutions," claimed an editorial in the *Continental Monthly*. "It must conquer, to command future friendship and that respect without which Union itself is a mockery." Disloyalty ought to be met with appropriate, sustained punishment. Traitors stripped of their citizenship, with the occupied South secured as a colonial possession, was the only insurance to prevent the American republic from ceaseless division.[21]

The idea of the disloyal Confederate South as a future American colony—whether as tentative metaphor or nascent policy—accelerated as Congress sharpened policy toward rebel property. In many respects, property confiscation and emancipation went hand in hand with the colonial future that many imagined for secessionists and their supporters. To soften the ground for emancipation, Attorney General Edward Bates issued a public opinion on the place of African Americans in the republic. While Bates allowed that national citizenship had long been amorphous and ill defined, he offered a ringing argument in favor of emancipation and African American rights to protection by arguing for the natural and irreducible claim to the title of citizen for all persons born in the United States, regardless of race or status. In so doing, Bates argued that while the Constitution fell silent on a specific definition of citizenship, a broad understanding of the title left ample room for freedpeople. All the same, Bates made it equally clear that while all persons born in the country should be counted as citizens, personal actions, like treason, ought to preclude individuals from the title. Civil war had changed the very precepts of the relationship between Americans and the nation-state. "Citizenship of the United States is an integral thing," wrote Bates, "incapable of legal existence in fractional parts." While historians focus on the broader implications of citizenship in Bates's argument for freedpeople, the foundation of the attorney general's argument rested on the distinction between citizens and noncitizens following lines of loyalty, not the color of one's skin. While all African Americans ought to be deemed citizens by virtue of having been born in the country, those who had worked to upend the republic could not reclaim the title so easily. Because they had joined an enemy state, their status was forfeit.[22]

Having laid down a marker on citizenship, Congress also moved in other directions to support the government's claim to other property of the disloyal. As part of the debate over what became the Second Confiscation Act, representatives supporting the legislation set the need to punish disloyal Confederates alongside the demands of the national government in war. Though the debate over the seizure of Confederate property prompted the act, some in Congress detected an imperial tone to the legislation that made them squeamish. "The national Government, from a weak and feeble enginery, has grown to become a formidable sovereign, swaying a great continent, and shaking the earth with the tread of its armies," claimed Missouri Democrat John W. Noell in May 1862. "Who now seeks the humbler service of a State, save as a training ground and a portal to the imperial and dazzling service of the sovereign?" While Noell allowed that the power of the nation was manifest over that of individual states, it was a perversion of national principle to carve up the South into imperial provinces, "placed under the dominion of the great proconsuls whom the President shall send forth in armed pomp and sway over them." Noell was clear that loyalty ought to govern all action in the occupied Confederacy. The rebel leadership should hang, and all who served in a position of prominence in government ought to be banished, their property seized and disposed of at the pleasure of the United States. But Noell held firm to the idea that the majority of the white southern population had been coerced into secession and would revert to their old allegiances with patient, sympathetic clemency. Others found the colonial metaphor more appropriate. Kansas Republican Senator Samuel Pomeroy suggested in a debate over African American colonization that the national government should consider a similar program for disloyal slaveholders. Better, Pomeroy argued, to banish disloyal slaveholders from the country rather than engage in the kind of bloodlust that might remind Americans of the French mob during the Terror.[23]

Even if Pomeroy's idea was never seriously considered, the imperial patina on top of the powers of the federal state and the colonial future that awaited the South should the Confederacy fall could not be ignored. In the final text of the Second Confiscation Act, not only were all disloyal persons found guilty of treason subject to the death penalty—closing the legal circle that had remained open since the Constitution was ratified—but the litmus test of loyalty was enshrined at the very heart of the wartime state. All persons connected to Confederate civilian and military leadership were subject to the forfeiture of all their property, as was anyone who gave aid to the enemy. As historians have recently made quite clear, the sections of the act pertaining to slavery clearly signaled a deep shift in American thinking about the institution, with slaves subject to seizure from rebel masters. The act also retroactively freed African Americans who had already escaped. The second-to-last section of the act offered disloyal persons an opportunity to seek redress through a presidential pardon, though the wording of the section gave Lincoln an immense amount of latitude to decide these cases at his pleasure. In the act's vision of federal power, as well as in its implications, what the Second Confiscation Act heralded was a powerful nation-state that would wield extraordinary power in the occupied South, with loyalty and emancipation forged as a weapon that could be used to beat the enemy into submission.[24]

In many respects, the Second Confiscation Act represented the culmination of a debate about loyalty that had started before the Civil War. The debate reached a tipping point once American and Confederate armies began killing each other with gruesome regularity. Passage of the act allowed for the massive expansion of the federal state while at the same time reinforcing the wedge between loyalty and disloyalty in countless communities. White southerners, no matter their true allegiances, slowly fell into a political and jurisdictional gap. Their citizenship in the Confederacy erased their status as Americans while making them enemies in the eyes of the government. Perhaps most revolutionary of all, the Second Confiscation Act also opened the door to the possibility that with their loyalty, African Americans could claim a relationship with a powerful nation-state more intimate and meaningful than the one their owners enjoyed when the war began. Historians have long pointed to the Confiscation Acts as a turning point in the history of African American emancipation. This is definitely true. Never before in the history of the Atlantic World had emancipation been set in motion on such a scale. But there was something more. Buried in this legislation were not simply the ingredients of black freedom but the possibility that former slaves could forge a bond with a powerful state. Laden with risk and uncertainty, African Americans joined the debate over loyalty by holding themselves up as the most loyal persons in a Confederate South that many were already beginning to view as a colonial possession. With their freedom, freedpeople would step into the gap created by emancipation—a gap between slavery and citizenship—while placing themselves at the center of the most profoundly jarring moment of state formation in the American republic's history.[25]

Barney Alford was too young to understand all of what he saw. He remembered slavery and the world around him as a child would. His account was a retrospective flood of emotions: random images, hazy allusions, fearful moments of physical terror, and warm memories of simple pleasures. The personalities who dominated Alford's memory were stock archetypes: his mother who worked in the big house, his father who drove other slaves in the field, the emotional mistress and the stolid master, the overbearing overseer who squeezed every ounce of cotton from the slaves in his charge, and the slave patrollers who menacingly policed the woods that ringed the plantation. Yet, as in most slave narratives, the Civil War marked a sharp break in the story of Barney Alford's life, and once the conflict was under way, Alford remembered another force to be reckoned with. Not long after the war began, and certainly once the northern army occupied portions of Mississippi around Alford's Pike County home, the United States cast a very long shadow in his memory. Alford remembered U.S. troops making their way up the main plantation road in search of food. When Alford's mistress refused them, the soldiers "just went ter de smoke house en busted open de door en tuk allus our meat en sugar en flour en tuk it wid dem." Having taken all that they could carry, American soldiers set fire to the cotton crop and the gin, and they did little to stop some of the slaves from following them off the plantation. For Alford, the memory was formative. It was a display of power so discordant with what the young boy knew, a show of force that upended any authority to which his master might have laid claim. Having glimpsed the power of the state, Barney Alford saw in it a power to be respected and the possibility of his own salvation.[26]

To see the American state through the eyes of slaves is to confront a series of half-formed impressions. At best, we see the faint outlines of an ill-defined relationship at a moment of social upheaval. Once U.S. forces occupied Confederate territory, however, a picture emerges in the historical record of a people who confronted the possibility of emancipation and the arrival of a new kind of power in their lives. To manage this historic change, slaves needed information about what changes lay ahead and how slave communities might negotiate them. As with most subaltern peoples, knowledge of events and the collective understandings of how circumstances might affect them traveled along well-worn circuits of news and rumor that had sustained African Americans throughout slavery. Snatches of overheard conversation, rumors that swirled around the slave quarter, the interpretation of a slaveholder's furtive glance, and talk on the steamboat dock or in the slave market all became news for the "grapevine telegraph," as so many slaves called it. Though imperfect, this method of carrying information proved both elastic and durable, while at the same time possessing incredible reach by the middle of the nineteenth century. Its lines stretched from urban centers and market towns to plantations, rural hamlets, and remote settlements.[27] Slaves who were able to move across plantation lines or who learned a trade and were hired out by their masters proved natural conduits for the passage of news. Louis Davis, a Mississippi slave from Coahoma County, remembered that any visit to a plantation brought the expectation that news was to be shared. Saturday nights proved particularly good times for the exchange of information, as plantation discipline and patrols were more lax. Davis claimed that few slaves were caught passing news, as white authorities "couldn' tell where they was at, and by morning they was in their beds asleep." Once the Civil War was under way, the grapevine proved to be one of the most important sources for information about battles and troop movements, American successes or Confederate failures. But it also became one of the primary ways through which African Americans learned about the American state, its demands, its expectations, and how it operated.[28]

For some slaves, the expectation that a war over the future of the Union would result in black freedom encouraged a collective rush into the breach. George Washington Albright was only fifteen when the war broke out, but from his home in Holly Springs, Mississippi, he set to work passing news and spreading information about an impending invasion to slaves all over his county. Part courier, part community organizer, Albright gathered slaves together in secret—with knocks, signs, and passwords—to inform them of what he had heard, so that slaves would in turn "find their way to still other plantations, and so the story spread." For other slaves not as bold as Albright, impressions could be gleaned from the nervous movements of masters. Adeline Hodge knew just how close American forces were to her Bolivar County home when her master spirited her and her fellow slaves from the quarter and into the nearby woods. For still more slaves, not until the U.S. Army was on the doorstep did they believe the rumors they had heard. Berry Smith remembered not believing the talk around Scott County that the U.S. military was out to destroy slavery, "until we hard about de fightin' at Vicksburg." In all of these accounts was an understandably human reaction. No matter the consequences, war wreaked havoc, and not all slaves were as certain that the prudent thing to do was to rush into harm's way. By 1863, however, few could doubt that the Civil War held out the promise of irrevocable change. What remained in question was what role slaves might play and what kind of connection slaves might fashion to the state that sought slavery's demise.[29]

Few parts of the Confederate South experienced an occupation as feverish or chaotic as that in the Mississippi Valley. The capture of New Orleans by the U.S. Navy in April 1862, along with the seizure of Memphis later that June, cut the valley's Confederate residents off from their most important waterway. The simultaneous advance of American forces into the interior of Tennessee also turned the divided region into a war zone. With the Mississippi River and northern parts of the valley in U.S. hands by the middle of 1862, the majority of Mississippi's 436,000 African Americans found themselves living on or near a tenuous border between two warring states. Learning all that they could, African Americans played a meager hand of cards to maximum effect. They bore down hard on a weakened system that had kept them in chains, while at the same time seeking every opportunity to push American officials to see their value as combatants. They provided information to the U.S. Army about the whereabouts of Confederate forces, winning the respect and protection of those who saw escaped slaves as vital sources of intelligence. And even though it was certainly true that the sight of entire communities of escaped slaves streaming across American lines brought frustration to decision-makers and dissension in the military ranks, it was not long before the devotion of African Americans bore fruit. Their loyalty would, in time, highlight the contrast between supporters of the American state and the unrepentant treason of Confederates.[30]

At least at first, black loyalty did not figure as the counterpoint to white treason. Just as the slow transformation of slaves in the eyes of U.S. bureaucrats—from property to contraband to persons—limited opportunities for African Americans in the occupied South, it would take time for American officers, let alone the state, to see the political meaning in slaves' words and deeds. However, the problem of securing territory and the growing frustration with the loyalties of whites who lived in the occupied South opened many eyes. As early as January 1862, officers tasked with patrolling the tense border between Confederate Mississippi and

U.S.-controlled territory wrote reports to their superiors that expressed a deep frustration with the steady stream of wagons loaded with cotton that was making its way across American lines. Wagons driven by "owners acknowledging themselves to be disloyal," made a mockery of the conflict, and men like Brig. Gen. I. F. Quinby could take only so much. Quinby wrote that the sight of such treasonous activity was "so manifestly wrong that I have taken the responsibility of stopping and sending back all cotton in the hands of the original owners who cannot produce satisfactory proofs of loyalty."[31]

The loaded phrase at the end of Quinby's brusque note crystallized the problem. Civilian and military representatives of the United States could never completely believe the loyalty claims of white southerners. No matter how many claims were made or how many documents were produced, white southerners' oaths of loyalty had to be trusted, and trust was in very short supply. For this reason, while it was certainly true that, in the words of one historian, loyalty oaths became "weapons ready to hand with which federal officers could combat unrest in newly-occupied areas," they were still blunt instruments in the hands of white southerners. Claims of loyalty, even if documented, relied upon the good reputation of the individual, and if this could not be verified to the satisfaction of officials, oaths would remain as suspect as the people they endorsed. Just like the paper currency of indeterminate origin that Americans traded so often in the decades leading up to the Civil War, wartime papers identifying former Confederates as loyal Americans were difficult to believe and hard to trust. No matter how many oaths were signed and countersigned, they were pale imitations when compared with concrete displays of devotion. Thus African Americans seized on loyalty not only as a means of doing damage to the reputations of their former owners, but as a way to secure a more durable bond with the American state. Particularly by the beginning of 1863, as the Emancipation Proclamation paved the way for black men to fight in U.S. blue, African Americans discovered an opportunity to prove their devotion without the need for empty paper oaths.[32]

In the effort to enlist African American men as soldiers in the Mississippi Valley, freedpeople found one way to prove their value. For this reason, the experiences of U.S. officials tasked with overseeing black enlistment reveal a good deal. It was with them that the depth of black loyalties was measured, and no one appreciated the potential of African American loyalty to the United States more than the adjutant general of the U.S. Army. By the time he made his first trip to organize black troops in the Mississippi Valley, Lorenzo Thomas was a fifty-nine-year-old soldier who had served the U.S. Army for four decades. In that time he had proven to be a true survivor. A paper soldier, more at home behind a desk than in the field, Thomas bore all the requisite scars of a career spent in the bureaucratic trenches of the War Department. For his pains, he had amassed a very long list of enemies. By the time Thomas was put to work raising regiments of former slaves, Secretary of War Edwin Stanton and several high-ranking officials in the War Department thought him little more than a self-aggrandizing snake who could not be trusted. His status as a Delaware-born former slaveholder also made him a man of suspect loyalty. By September 1864, Thomas was beating back challenges to his character from officers who believed that he was too close to disloyal Confederates in Mississippi. It was a charge that never matured into something formal, but the evidence against him certainly did not burnish the adjutant general's reputation in the eyes of the officer corps. No matter the skeletons in his closet, his skills as an administrator gave him intimate knowledge of the inner workings of the War Department. He also possessed the ability to surmount the obstacles involved in bringing black slave troops into the American ranks.[33]

Like many of his generation, Thomas indulged a patronizing, paternalist view of African Americans. Once the Emancipation Proclamation cleared the path for the use of freedmen as soldiers, Thomas made it clear that black troops should be barred from the officer corps, not simply because it was "detrimental to the service" but because it would turn soldiers "capable of much usefulness, into a source of constant embarrassment and annoyance." By turns, Thomas also publicly positioned himself as not only Abraham Lincoln's right hand but a high-ranking protector of African Americans in and out of the military. In a speech offered to troops in Chicago in late April 1863, Thomas made it clear that all persons from "this unfortunate race" were to be invited behind U.S. lines, fed, clothed, armed, and treated kindly. "I shall take the women and children, and the men who cannot go into our army organization," and put them to work on abandoned plantations in the American-occupied South. "Knowing the country well," Thomas went on, "they will be able to track out these accursed guerrillas, and drive them from the land." Even Thomas's detractors noted that while "Adjutant General Thomas makes bad speeches to troops," white U.S. soldiers had begun to see the value in having African Americans serving in American blue.[34]

Even if Thomas lacked the requisite oratorical fire, it was telling that once he arrived in the Mississippi Valley, audiences of freedpeople wasted no time and turned the adjutant general's public addresses to their political advantage. Before a newly organized black regiment that was drilling in a makeshift camp on the outskirts of Memphis, Thomas delivered a potted speech in the late spring of 1863 that quickly morphed into a raucous, call-and-response Sunday service. Thomas told the assembly that while he understood the horrors of slavery, he knew that blacks would fight for their freedom and the United States. "I came here to tell you what the President expects you to do," he called to the crowd. "He wishes

Portrait of Brig. and Adjut. Gen. Lorenzo Thomas, officer of the Federal Army, ca. 1860–65.
Brady National Photographic Art Gallery. Courtesy of the Library of Congress Prints and
Photographs Division, LC-DIG-cwpb-04799.

every one of you who can, to work. You used to work for masters: now you are free—free as I am, good as I am. . . . I know you would rather work for wages than be slaves; you can do more." Describing black regiments already on the battlefield as a credit to their race and an inspiration for black communities all over the South, Thomas thundered, "I propose to arm you. Will you help us crush this accursed rebellion? I believe slavery is the cause of it. President Lincoln has set you free—will you fight?" In response, the black audience urged Thomas on. "Suppose I would give you guns, and you should see a party of guerrillas in the woods, what would you do?" Thomas asked the crowd. "Fetch 'em all in, Massa Thomas!" Thomas then led the audience in a rendition of "Am I a Soldier of the Cross?" that, for a newspaper correspondent who witnessed the event, brought to mind an impassioned revival meeting.[35]

Peeling back the layers of an event like Thomas's speech in Memphis requires an understanding of both context and intention. The African American reaction to Thomas was certainly part of a broader racial theater that freedpeople took part in for the benefit of white northern audiences. The ecstatic reaction of former slaves to the opportunity to serve as soldiers resonated with northerners who saw in the Emancipation Proclamation an opportunity to set the Civil War on a more ideological foundation. But the elated reception Thomas received served the political purposes of freedpeople as well. By taking up the opportunity to fight as soldiers, African Americans in the Mississippi Valley were joining a long list of enslaved people in the Atlantic World who found a path to emancipation in military service. What freedpeople were attempting, however, was not simply to claim rights as liberal individualists, as an earlier generation had done in the wake of the American Revolution. Their politics was different still from the universal rights that slaves and *gens de couleur* in the French colony of Saint Dominque claimed in the months that followed the fall of the Bastille. Though an intellectual undercurrent of rights talk could be detected, the key to what African Americans sought in the middle of the Civil War lay in a hardheaded pragmatism of what slaves needed to do in the absence of a stable, legal status and in the institution to which they offered up their loyalty. By attaching themselves broadly to an ideological cause but explicitly as persons loyal to a state, freedpeople focused their energies and their devotion on an institution they believed would win them protection from white reprisal and would give them preferential treatment as persons who lived in a region shot through with Confederate treason and disloyalty. All too aware of the loaded meaning of loyalty, African Americans would latch onto the project men like Lorenzo Thomas were setting in motion. They would tread a fine line between asserting their rights and subsuming their desires in a broader, deferential bid for access to all that the American state could provide. In response to the

American government's bid for imperial supremacy in the South, many fashioned themselves as loyal subjects. It was a canny move, filled with risk, but it served the purposes of a people caught between slavery and citizenship.[36]

African American expectations of what the American national government could provide were balanced and often overwhelmed by the obligations that military service placed on black shoulders. Though many African Americans voluntarily signed up to serve, in places like Mississippi, Lorenzo Thomas's military recruitment was really forced conscription. The key to the adjutant general's recruitment drive was to empower white officers to organize foraging parties in American-controlled areas, with a bounty to be paid by Thomas's office for every freedman enlisted.[37] Traveling inland and along the Mississippi River, these parties of armed men collected any freedmen they found and placed them under American control, particularly those "Unemployed persons of color, vagrants and camp loafers" whose idleness closer to military encampments made them suspect.[38] The speed with which foraging parties signed up African Americans to serve also mattered more than making sure would-be soldiers were actually capable of serving. Medical examinations of prospective recruits uncovered a host of ailments and degenerative illnesses that would have precluded men from serving, and while the adjutant general's office docked the pay of U.S. officers who knowingly recruited ailing men into the ranks, the measure was never completely effective. "It is astonishing how small a percentage there is of the males fit for soldiers," wrote Lorenzo Thomas to a subordinate at the end of 1863. Though he made it clear that it was the policy of his department to ensure that black regiments had the proper medical staff necessary to care for the sick and wounded, the ultimate medical record of the black enlistment effort was poor at best and grossly negligent at worst.[39]

Once formed into new regiments, African Americans also had to contend with white officers, some of whom would never have been elevated to similar positions in other regiments. Officer examination boards often rubber-stamped the promotion of enlisted men to serve as the officers of black regiments, and the result was disastrous. Speed, once again, mattered more than due diligence. Writing to Lorenzo Thomas from southern Louisiana in the fall of 1863, one colonel remarked that he had witnessed "so much unsavory . . . oppression of the poor black by officers who with only a single qualification were detailed to gather up the unwilling or willing, sick or well negroes apparently with but one object," namely the bounty paid to officers by the adjutant general's office. John J. Mudd reported that he had several white officers of black regiments arrested for misconduct because their actions disgraced the army and the republic.[40] Many black soldiers wrote their own letters of protest. These letters showed not only the depth of their frustration but also how quickly African Americans were learning about the inner workings of War Department bureaucracy. As one unnamed black soldier, who identified himself as "one of the union Colored friends," wrote in late 1863, "it is retten that a man can not Serve two master But it Seems that the Collored population has got two a rebel master an a union master the both want our Servises one wants us to make Cotton and Sugar And Sell it and keep the money the union masters wants us to fight the battles under white officers and injoy both money and the union black soldiers And white officers will not play togeather much longer."[41] Letters such as these made it clear that no matter the depth of black loyalty, the allegiance of African Americans had limits.

The loyalty of freedpeople was also tested in courts of military justice. Courts-martial of African American soldiers exposed a deep fissure between white and black in the chain of military command. Pvt. Edward Williams of the 1st Mississippi Heavy Artillery was brought up on charges of insubordination in March 1864. His case revolved around an altercation he had with Maj. John Davis, a white officer who demanded a pass from Williams for leaving his company. When Williams refused to present his papers and instead cocked a pistol at Davis, he was arrested. At his trial, testimony for and against Williams did not explain the incident but pointed instead to the fact that within his regiment, Williams had been made an acting sergeant. He had distinguished himself in the field and as a scout, and he undoubtedly believed that he was due some respect from a fellow officer, even if the American army did not accept his rank.[42]

Beyond the friction between white officers and black enlisted men, cases before military courts also exposed bigger problems between African Americans and the government. Courts-martial of black soldiers spoke as much, of course, to military discipline as to loyalty, but the decisions rendered against African Americans influenced a broader set of concerns. Some cases spoke to the issue of an American state that expected freedmen to serve, without paying due attention to the obligations African Americans believed that the republic owed soldiers and their families. Pvt. Mose Germain of the 2nd Mississippi Infantry was brought before a court-martial in January 1864 on a charge of desertion. According to the evidence against him, Germain had been absent from his regiment dating back to August. When Germain was asked for a statement, his response was telling. He claimed that he had left because of concern for his family, but that he had been absent for only three weeks, at which point he had joined another regiment based in Louisiana and closer to his home. Regardless of the familial considerations at play in the case, Germain was found guilty, docked pay, and served as a laborer for six months with a ball and chain around his leg. All the same, cases such as Germain's revealed the difficult choices that freedmen faced when they served.

African American soldiers: District of Columbia, Company E, 4th U.S. Colored Infantry, at Fort Lincoln, ca. 1863–66. Photograph by William Morris Smith. Courtesy of the Library of Congress Prints and Photographs Division, LC-DIG-cwpb-04294.

They often left families behind who struggled to support themselves. It was a measure of the peril African American families found themselves in that soldiers chanced desertion and the punishments that went with it to help in whatever way they could. Augustus Harrison deserted his Louisiana regiment for nearly four months, but when brought before the judge advocate, the soldier testified that he had left the army to help his mother and sisters, who had been "run from home to escape the rebels." They had fled without any of their possessions, and Harrison had appealed to his commanding officers for a leave: "They wouldn't let me go as I asked them to, so I tried to go see about them myself." For his transgression, Harrison was sentenced to a year's docked pay and a year's hard labor.[43]

Other soldiers ran afoul of a U.S. Army bureaucracy that proved confusing. Some soldiers absented themselves from regiments because of the ill treatment of officers or perhaps because they wanted to serve with friends or relations. Freedmen had little say in what regiment they joined once they were mustered into the service, and many deserted not to flee the army but to join other fighting units. The haste with which soldiers were mustered and the seemingly random way they were formed into regiments undoubtedly gave freedmen the impression that they possessed some choice, though courts punished soldiers for their mistake. Henry Jones left his regiment to join another in January 1864. At his trial, he simply offered his apologies: "I am sorry I went away, and I will not do it again." For his affront to military order, Jones was sentenced to three months' hard labor. James Brown, also from the 2nd Mississippi, was charged with two days' desertion, as Brown traveled to a camp outside Vicksburg to see his father. During the trial, it became clear that part of the reason why Brown had left was due to his regiment not having been made aware of their obligations as soldiers, laid out in the Articles of War. Despite evidence to suggest that the entire regiment had not been properly advised of their duties, Brown was found guilty and was docked a month's pay.[44]

If cases of mistaken duty proved embarrassing for American military officials, they paled in comparison with cases in which order in black regiments broke down completely. In early December 1863, the 4th Regiment of Louisiana's Corps d'Afrique mutinied in protest at the treatment by their white commanding officer, Lieut. Col. Augustus Benedict, who beat two teenage drummers with a cart whip without provocation. Though they had been lauded by commanders as "among the best disciplined and the best instructed regiments of this class of troops," the regiment reacted swiftly to the beating. They took possession of their rifles and gathered together, calling Benedict out. When he refused, the rage of the crowd spilled over into indiscriminate anger at the republic Benedict represented. According to court testimony, some soldiers shouted that they "did not come here to be whipped" by white officers. Others spurred the armed crowd to "kill all the damned Yankees." In the end, a court-martial found Benedict guilty of using excessive force, only the latest in a long string of abuses during his time in the service. In a swipe at Lorenzo Thomas and his office, Brig. Gen. William Dwight argued that the affair represented "a warning against trusting foolish and passionate officers in high command over these black troops." Interoffice politicking aside, military justice demanded that an example be made of not only a poor excuse for an officer but also the African Americans who threatened him. Six members of the regiment were sentenced to hard labor—some for as many as ten years—while two members of the regiment who were thought to be the ringleaders were sentenced to death by firing squad.[45]

Black soldiers who came before courts-martial experienced state power at its most naked.[46] Yet the problems that lay at the heart of so many of these cases spoke to a gap between what the state was willing to offer African Americans in protection and respect and what freedpeople believed they were due for their willingness to fight and die for the United States. It would take time for African Americans to learn the inner workings of that state, and more time still for them to learn what it would take to place pressure on that state to secure for freedpeople something more than their freedom in return for their efforts. Even by the end of the Civil War, officers made it clear that the only thing black communities could expect from the national government was their emancipation, though ironically, Lorenzo Thomas would be among the first to glimpse something bigger and more lasting in the countless actions of devotion African Americans offered as loyalists.

As early as April 1863, Thomas had begun to use language that would have been familiar to men and women across the country. He called on the U.S. Army to secure and settle occupied territory in the Mississippi Valley for communities of loyal persons. What was unusual about his thinking, however, was that Thomas elided the race of the group who ought to be deemed loyal. For him, African American loyalty played a role from the outset. In a special order issued from Milliken's Bend, Louisiana, Thomas called on his office to work in concert with the quartermaster general and the Treasury Department to ensure that trade and the flow of cotton would return to a pre-war normal. The necessity of settling "a loyal population who will protect . . . the freedom of commercial intercourse" along the Mississippi River became one of Thomas's key policies. The primary object of this effort, as Thomas wrote in a circular later that fall, was to "line the banks of the Mississippi River with a loyal population and to give aid in securing the uninterrupted navigation of the river." At the heart of his plan was to make loyalty and emancipation the weapons that would destroy the Confederacy. But there was more in this plan that spoke to what a future South might look like: an ad-hoc American colony. The loyalty of individual planters would determine whether the United States would seize plantations. Land belonging to men of undoubted loyalty, "especially those who have been so from the beginning of the rebellion, will be occupied and managed by themselves or leased by them to loyal citizens." But to protect plantations and cotton, Thomas envisioned loyal African Americans as not only the wage laborers who would pick the cotton and bring it to market but also the armed soldiers whom he would put to work protecting cotton awaiting shipment and securing cotton abandoned by disloyal planters who had fled their homes.[47]

Like all sharp bureaucrats, Thomas blunted the more radical edges of his free labor policies while at the same time obscuring the fact that by the end of 1863, the Treasury Department, not Thomas, was in real control. Acting as the arbiter of contracts and labor disputes, the Treasury put in place a system that gave freed-people more opportunities to own their own land or to negotiate a share of the cotton crop in lieu of wages, and more responsibilities as independent workers who were required to pay for their own food and clothing. Much of the reason for this shift in responsibility lay with critics of Thomas who felt his plan was not radical enough and too paternalistic to allow the proper development of free labor in the Mississippi Valley. All the same, what the American policy regarding Rebel property aimed to do was transformative, both in what advocates of free labor wanted to create and in the fusion of wartime loyalty and property that lay at the plan's heart. Even though Thomas had his powers over plantations taken from him, his ability to see the relationship between emancipation and loyalty remained key to U.S. policy.[48]

Even if his office was no longer in complete control, Thomas remained a figurehead. To a mass gathering of freedpeople, soldiers, planters, and officers at Goodrich's Landing, Louisiana, in November 1863, Thomas lauded black soldiers in blue as a credit to their race while at the same time commanding black laborers to earn their freedom with sweat and effort. "You must render your employers willing obedience—make them feel that you are interested in the work as well as themselves, and then you will establish that mutual confidence which is the strongest bond between the employer and employed." Yet if the clear purpose of this new plantation system was merely to put freedpeople to work, it did not escape the notice of northern newspaper correspondents that of the roughly forty-five plantations along the Mississippi River that fell within the Treasury's purview by the end of 1863, fully fifteen were operated by African American lessees. Even though his every word dripped with condescension toward African Americans, Lorenzo Thomas did not need to make clearer that which was plain. In a region of the country where white disloyalty was evident everywhere, freedpeople sat on the front lines of a loyal army of emancipation and a new social order.[49]

Thomas would have another chance to mold that new social order, largely because it was not long before free labor in Mississippi was under threat. By the middle of 1864, in occupied parts of the Mississippi Valley at a distance from large concentrations of U.S. troops, a guerrilla war to upend an embryonic free labor system was quickly becoming a full-blown terrorist campaign, and Treasury agents were helpless to stop it. Planters who had sworn allegiance to the United States but who remained firmly wedded to the Confederate cause were directing the actions of armed bands, and black laborers in these regions ran "the great risk of being carried off into slavery again." The problem in Mississippi proved particularly stark in the area along the Alabama border. There, in early 1864, the eastern movement of troops, under the command of William T. Sherman, left the town of Meridian open to an attack that resulted in thousands of African American workers fleeing plantations. After entreaties from Abraham Lincoln that Thomas get a firmer grip on the situation and be "master of the Contraband & leasing Business," the adjutant general acted quickly. In an order issued in March 1864, Thomas ordered the reconstitution of the plantation lease system. He cut laborers' wages, placed the responsibility to feed and clothe workers back in the hands of employers, required laborers to have a pass to leave plantations, and placed the maintenance of order directly in the hands of provost marshals. By the early spring of 1864, the adjutant general's office reported some thirteen black regiments, stationed throughout southwestern Mississippi and eastern Louisiana, at the ready to protect black laborers on American-controlled plantations.[50]

The tug-of-war over the shape and direction of free labor in the Mississippi Valley looked a lot like chaos on the ground. For one, the size of the project was staggering. By the spring of 1864, the plantation lease program directed the development of more than 162,000 acres in eastern Louisiana and southern Mississippi, leased by 287 lessees and worked by nearly 15,000 laborers, who supported a population of freedpeople that numbered more than 44,000. What's more, given the stipulations in Thomas's revised program, it is not surprising that freedpeople protested early and often that their wages had been slashed unfairly. The welcome that Thomas's plan received from northern lessees in the valley also said a good deal about the larger interests the adjutant general was out to serve. On a plantation near Vicksburg, northern lessee Isaac Shoemaker spent much of 1864 lamenting the inefficiency of a system that impeded the development of free labor, not to mention the free flow of cotton. Shoemaker argued that "every conceivable obstruction" had been put in the way of planters when plantation management had been in Treasury hands, and it was only fitting that control be returned to Thomas.[51]

Yet even if the plan suffered from the condescension of its architect, it was in Thomas's vision for the kind of political relationship that freedpeople would have with the United States that a more lasting impact can be seen. One cannot ignore the colonial relationship Thomas imagined between freedpeople, suspect Confederates, and the American state. By the end of 1864, these ideas had hardened into a relation of power that placed that state firmly in imperial control over the occupied South. All the same, it is equally apparent that his efforts—however imperfect—to provide for African Americans proved a key ingredient in binding freedpeople to the Union. One can glimpse his meaning in his general order that reconstituted the plantation system. Thomas argued that men "who refuse to defend their country with the ballot box or cartridge box, have no just claim to the benefits of liberty regulated by law." All persons who sought the protection of the United States could not rely on a previous position of citizenship in the United States. From here on out, oaths of allegiance laid before the nation-state would constitute the only "test of unconditional fealty to the government and all its measures." "Whoever is indifferent or hostile" to the state or its army "must choose between the liberty which foreign lands afford, the poverty of the rebel States, and the innumerable and inappreciable blessings which our Government confers upon its people." The implications of this order were as expansive as the potential benefit to African Americans was revolutionary. By draping a benevolent state over a system of free labor, Lorenzo Thomas placed a loyal black population at the center of a new body politic. Even though the status of freedpeople as something more than the beneficiaries of state largesse lay undone, African Americans stood as the vanguard in a new, loyal, colonial South.[52]

BY THE TIME CONGRESS CONVENED the Joint Committee on Reconstruction in December 1865, the result of a four-and-a-half-year war had left the South not only defeated but divided. Yet in the hundreds of pages of testimony drawn from 144 witnesses, the committee returned again and again to the puzzle of how to weigh the future of the former Confederacy against the disloyalty of past transgressions. By then, attempts by a new president, Andrew Johnson, to remake the South according to his own belief in the deeper tie of loyalty that bound white southerners to the United States had run afoul of Republicans in Congress, who believed that the president's plans made a mockery of emancipation. All the same, the testimony before the joint committee revealed that loyalty to the American republic was in short supply in the South, and elevating those who had been loyal over those who had not would bring order and, it was hoped, stasis. Albert Warren Kelsey, a northerner who had managed abandoned plantations all over the occupied South, spoke for many witnesses called before the committee. When asked about the state of loyalty to the American government in the Fourth Military District (Mississippi and Arkansas), Kelsey argued that the sentiment was nearly nonexistent. "The people there have no attachment to the Union, none of the feelings which we deem patriotic. . . . It seems to me that they have very little of what we have been taught to consider loyalty to the government."[53]

It was a sign of just how much had changed that Kelsey's idea of loyalty to the nation and to the government were one and the same. By the end of the conflict, the growth of the federal state and the power it wielded over the occupied South had made it impossible to distinguish between the two; one had become wrapped in the other so as to become seamless. That had not been the case only a few years before. The Civil War started not only a state's rights revolution but a sea change in the way Americans understood their citizenship. Military service and the state powers that had grown to accommodate the necessities of war breathed new life into the dormant obligations of citizenship while also fashioning new responsibilities to create a new definition of the title. It would be a citizenship different from the many notions of what it meant to be an American that existed only a few years before. This new relationship—between citizens and the American state—would mingle with sharpened ideas of loyalty to turn white southerners into a suspect class and make black wartime service and subjecthood a foundation for the African American bid for citizenship after the war ended. While congressional investigators would wring their hands with worry about what the future might hold, perhaps the only thing certain in the tense months that followed the end of formal hostilities was that the battle over citizenship and loyalty would be fought in a thousand locations throughout the increasingly colonial South between former Americans and their former slaves.

CHAPTER FIVE

Loyalty Under Fire

By the time members of Congress began to debate a constitutional amendment banning slavery in the United States in the final months of the Civil War, questions about emancipation and citizenship had become well and truly tangled. After four years of war—four years in which the national government had ballooned in size and the abolition of slavery had become a weapon used to punish the disloyal in the Confederate South—few doubted that the cornerstones of emancipation needed to be laid by a national state with the power to carry out such a revolutionary reordering of the South and the republic. The Thirteenth Amendment set a price that the disloyal were bound to pay before the country would deign to welcome Confederates back into the Union, with a powerful state overseeing all. As Ohio House Republican James Mitchell Ashley saw it, the war had demolished the secessionist argument that the Union was a collection of independent states. The national Constitution now superseded all other interests, and the national government enjoyed supremacy, clothed as it was "with the sovereignty of the whole people." Just as power was consolidated at the national level, the national government could demand the consolidated allegiance of loyal citizens. "The first and highest allegiance is due from the citizen to the national Government," argued Ashley, and with its armies in command, few doubted that the national government could enforce that duty. Though Ashley spoke with confidence that the Congress and the country supported his assertion, his idea of the nation-state enjoying pride of place in the allegiance of citizens showed just how much had changed. Now on the cusp of defeat, individuals who had thrown off their allegiance to the triumphant nation could no longer claim meaningful rights in a postwar republic. Deemed by many American leaders as wards of the state at best—and at worst as colonial subjects under the direct control of a national government that reigned supreme—white southerners were to be made to pay for their treason with uncompensated emancipation and a process of state-sanctioned mass contrition.[1]

The Unionist resolve to punish Confederates was deepened with the assassination of the Union's chief executive. Abraham Lincoln's death resulted in a collective venting of rage that only sharpened the focus of the loyal against anyone who stood against the republic. "I have hitherto felt that not only the people but the *leaders* of the *South* could be reclaimed to the Union," wrote a former newspaper editor from Tennessee. "I see nothing now but the unrelenting hand of justice to be meted out to all who will not bow to the authority of the Constitution. . . . The assassination of Mr. Lincoln, like the fall of Sumpter, has welded the nation as an iron thunderbolt to be hurled against treason wherever found." While the writer still counseled leniency for those who did not lead the Confederacy, the anger proved hard to channel. "Mr. Lincoln died a martyr to his policy of extreme leniency," wrote a Pennsylvania woman only two days after the assassination. Now that her president had been slain, however, she was filled with hatred, not only for traitors but for "the descendants of traitors and traitor sympathizers," who deserved only to be "shunned as a race accursed for all time to come." The curious twisting of the racial thinking of the day only added weight to what the war had wrought. Not only did Confederates fall outside the American body politic. They ought to be counted as a suspect race unto themselves.[2]

The new president who received these letters knew only too well what loyalty meant. By the time he laid a hand on a Bible and swore the presidential oath at a hastily convened ceremony in a Washington boardinghouse, Andrew Johnson had made a name for himself as the self-professed paragon of American loyalty in the occupied South. When his state of Tennessee seceded, Johnson was the only southern representative in Congress who continued to hold his seat. As he had done so many times before, Johnson bucked his state and his party and had voiced some of the strongest objections to secession. He labeled the Confederacy as little more than heresy, its architects nothing less than traitors. All who sought the breakup of the Union deserved, Johnson claimed, the harshest punishments for their crimes. Johnson's position placed him at the front of Unionist ranks in wartime Washington. When the Lincoln administration sought a military governor for American-controlled Tennessee in March 1862, Johnson was the clear choice. Presiding over a divided state in a position he had held less than a decade before, Johnson poured his energies into isolating Confederate loyalists and purifying

"A Proper Family Re-Union," 1865. Oscar H. Harpel and Burgoo Zac. Courtesy of the Library of Congress Prints and Photographs Division, LC-USZ62-40505.

the population that remained. "Treason must be made odious, and traitors must be punished and impoverished," Johnson famously threatened in July 1862. Proclaiming that "the traitor has ceased to be a citizen," Johnson, as well as other loyal officials, was to ensure that a Confederate could expect "a severe ordeal before he is restored" to any place in the republic.[3]

With a population separated into such stark camps and with the distance from the Lincoln White House to do whatever was needed to bring the state to heel, Johnson attempted to cut treason out of Tennessee. It was bloody work, and loyalty oaths became his chief instrument. For voting in general elections in the state in January 1864, Johnson pushed past the Lincoln administration's language on the subject and drafted a franchise oath of his own. In it, Johnson demanded more than mere loyalty. A citizen had to actively take part in destroying the Confederacy before he could vote. This action and others like it endeared him to many Unionists all over the country, as well as a northern press that had hardly been kind to Johnson before the war. For a man who had found it hard to be heard in Congress, by the time he accepted Lincoln's offer to be his running mate on the National Unionist ticket, Johnson had become a man whose voice now carried.

To his loyal devotion to the Union, Johnson augmented a belief in the preeminent power of the federal state. "The authority of the Government is supreme, and will admit of no rivalry," Johnson claimed as he accepted the vice presidential nomination. "No institution can rise above it, whether it be slavery or any other organized power." With his uncompromising words about treason and his imagining of a new kind of republic where loyalty to the national government trumped all other allegiances, by the end of the war Johnson had positioned himself at the front lines of an ideological war to remake the country. Even as Americans mourned the death of Lincoln, many breathed a sigh of relief as Johnson assumed the presidency. Here was a man who understood the kind of hard-edged governance needed to bring the country together on terms that Unionist victors deemed acceptable. Supporters believed that Andrew Johnson would rain biblical justice down on those who had torn the republic to pieces.[4]

Given the strength of Johnson's ideas about loyalty and statecraft, how all of this goodwill for him could have evaporated so quickly remains one of the most puzzling parts of a puzzling era in American history. So much has been written about Andrew Johnson's rise and fall from power that in the rush to explain why he failed—in the rush to narrate the tragic arc of the Reconstruction story—it is sometimes difficult to see what he tried to accomplish. His catastrophic miscalculations, his vitriolic racism, his vain use of power, and the enormous chip on his shoulder all get in the way of seeing Johnson with clear eyes. He divided Americans when he lived and even more so after he died. Writers and historians have held him up as either an idol of the Lost Cause or a craven caricature of white supremacy. Perhaps, as W. E. B. Du Bois had it, Johnson was a victim of his small-mindedness. With characteristic eloquence, Du Bois argued that Johnson was, after all, the poor white indentured apprentice who could not see beyond his race, a victim of his own ignorance who was "played upon by mighty fingers and selfish, subtle minds," having become drunk "with the heady wine of sudden and accidental success." The tragedy of Johnson's time in the White House, as so many have argued, was that he was a man whose temperament and talents did not fit his moment in power, in sharp contrast to his predecessor.[5]

Yet, pushing past the vitriol of Johnson's presidency, one can glimpse something important in his plan for the reconstituted Union and something equally profound about the opposition to Johnson and his vision for the republic. His obsession with loyalty tells us something vital about the way so many Americans understood citizenship as the country slowly emerged from the Civil War, and something more about how this fusion of loyalty and citizenship began to slowly disintegrate in the months that followed. Even if the ground shifted beneath Johnson's feet, he believed with a fervency that bordered on the religious that only if former Confederates made a deeply personal act of capitulation and sup-plication could the country be made whole. Moreover, Johnson believed that as a loyal white southerner, he was best placed to evaluate these pledges of loyalty and pleas of earnest allegiance. Though his control over Reconstruction was fleeting, his plan for the country brought to fruition a new kind of relation between people and the federal state, one in which Americans were tied fast to the Union and to the national government that Johnson represented.

IN THE MIDDLE OF JULY 1864, Andrew Johnson sent a telegram to his running mate, Abraham Lincoln, with warm words of support for the president's tactful pocket veto of the Wade-Davis Bill. The legislation—more a manifesto—had outlined the Radical Republican position on both emancipation and loyalty in the occupied South, and it had done so in uncompromising fashion. The bill's plan for Reconstruction would have required that a majority of whites submit to the Ironclad Oath in which they would declare that they had never offered support of any kind to the Confederate States. It was a high bar. At its heart, the legislation was based on the principle that having sworn allegiance to a rival nation-state, a Confederate citizen who lived in a Union-occupied area was devoid of political rights and ought to be treated as such. Moreover, the bill also isolated Confederates who served in any meaningful civil or military office as not having any right to citizenship at all. For Lincoln, the bill was an impediment to reconciliation. In the proclamation justifying his shelving of the Wade-Davis Bill, the president stated not only that it was politically inflexible but that its ban on slavery trumped the Thirteenth Amendment, which Lincoln believed would be a more lasting legal instrument to ensure emancipation. For his part, the military governor of Tennessee approved wholeheartedly of Lincoln's action. The pocket veto, Johnson wrote, "is just as it should have been & the real union men" he knew were satisfied with it.[6]

Though Johnson supported Lincoln's decision, the hard-edged language about loyalty in the bill had a lot in common with how Johnson defined the idea as mili-tary governor of his own divided state. Though he could hardly have been called a political ideologue, Johnson believed in the acceptance of personal responsibility entailed in declaring one's loyalty. When he spoke of it, as he did often, he used a language of faith to justify his actions. In a speech to Unionists near Gallatin, Ten-nessee, in mid-July 1864, Johnson warned his audience that Confederates sought to carry out "their hell-born work of treason" unless they were stopped. For the vice presidential nominee, secession and opposition to the national government were nothing less than "the workings of the devil. It was the spirit exhibited by the devil and his angels who had to be thrust out of Heaven for their rebellion," and for this reason disloyalty must "be put down; conquered—utterly subjugated." Half-measures would not suffice. According to Johnson, there was "a great rebellion raging in our beloved country to be suppressed," and the future of the Union depended upon setting the republic on solid ground.[7]

Johnson's unequivocal, Old Testament language made clear that which had become horribly muddled in Washington. The twin projects of national reunification and emancipation had become fused. While many legislators allowed that hard, unsparing tests of loyal citizenship ought to be put in place, there were as many who allowed that if slavery was what caused the war, some allowance should be made for Confederate citizens who had no stake in the institution. For other legislators, the laws of war made all white southerners suspect, foreign persons beyond the pale of citizenship. In a speech at the end of May 1864, Republican Daniel Morris argued that the only sure way to abolish slavery and protect the Union lay in treating all white southerners as subjects—not citizens—in a reconstituted Union. Then and only then could Unionists be assured of the destruction of slavery, with recalcitrant Confederates pushed safely to the political sidelines. Morris's notion of subjecthood for white southerners was riven to military law. He suggested that Confederate secession was akin to an imagined band of naval officers who mutinied aboard an American vessel. "When the malcontents are subdued, should they be restored to command? May they insist upon the control of the recaptured vessel? By their acts they have forfeited this privilege, and yet they are amenable to the laws. They owe the fealty of a citizen without a citizen's rights." This idea of fealty without citizenship—colonial subjects in fact if not in name—gathered strength in Washington. A white southerner who fell within the ambit of Union power might owe and offer allegiance to the state, Morris argued, but even once his allegiance was offered, he ought to have "no voice at the ballot-box, he may not hold an office of trust, nor can he participate as a witness or juror in any of our courts. He is a felon, he wears the taint and the disabilities of a felon."[8]

The surest punishment lay not simply in forcing Confederates to submit to a kind of colonial status in a reconstituted Union. It was also bound up with the destruction of the institution to which the South owed its prosperity, and in this some members of Congress demurred. New York Democrat Anson Herrick urged members to forestall a decision on emancipation before southerners were brought back into the Union. "In their present condition we have no right to impose upon them this proposed constitutional provision, which we know will be obnoxious, even as a punishment for their rebellion." Any postwar Union that permanently dismantled slavery needed the broadest support, even among those whose livelihoods had been bound up with the institution. With a presidential election on the horizon, this debate had become wrapped up in a process of window-dressing for the electorate. But it also reflected a profound division within American society. What price was the Union to insist upon in return for southern capitulation? On this point, Andrew Johnson had a ready answer.[9]

Unlike moderates, Johnson saw no problem with the national government flexing its muscles. He believed that the federal state, in the interest of self-preservation, possessed ample means to protect itself, as well as the obligation to act in the interest of those who had remained loyal to it. While still in the Senate Johnson delivered a hard speech in 1862 against powerful Indiana Democrat Jesse D. Bright, who had been expelled from Congress for acting as a Confederate gunrunner. Never one to blanch at the prospect of skewering a member of his own party, Johnson attacked Bright as a traitor and all who supported him as squeamish cowards. "How is rebellion to be put down without coercion, without enforcing the laws?" Johnson raged. "How is the nation to be protected from insurrection without coercing the citizens to obedience?" As military governor of Tennessee, Johnson put his ideas about the power of the state and the necessity of coercion to the test. In May 1862, only two months after assuming his office, he issued a proclamation in response to Confederate raids on Unionist communities. In it, Johnson made it clear that for every loyal American mistreated, "five or more rebels from the most prominent in the immediate neighborhood shall be arrested, imprisoned, and otherwise dealt with as the nature of the case may require." In situations where property had been stolen or damaged, retribution would be brought to bear on Confederate sympathizers. Property stolen would be answered by the Union with property seized. By June, even Tennesseans who uttered disloyal sentiments could count on their arrest by American troops, their loyalties earning them a forced trip to Confederate lines, where Johnson's government would treat them as foreign spies if they attempted to return home. With a philosophy of power born from the wartime debates about the appropriate use of governmental authority in a time of war, Andrew Johnson trained the gaze of his government squarely on the disloyal of Tennessee. Hardened by occupation, Johnson's view of loyalty was unsparing. But if the methods he used to prop up Unionism in Tennessee revealed a man devoted to the nation, his vision of a future in which southerners would one day be brought back into the United States was much more complex.[10]

In a speech he gave to Unionists in Tennessee at the beginning of 1864, Johnson made the case for the restoration of government, while at the same time delving into the question of the place of American citizenship in the occupied South. On the surface, the speech was unremarkable. Johnson toed a hard line on disloyalty. He claimed that the white southerner who had "engaged in this rebellion, and has got his consent to give up the government of the United States, and with his person attach his fortunes to the Southern Confederacy, or to any other government," had effectively expatriated himself from the republic. Mangling an argument he had made many times—about the Civil War as a rebellion of states within the Union—Johnson claimed that Confederates ought to be treated as immigrants from a foreign country, subject to the laws of naturalization and bound by an oath of allegiance should they wish to become American citizens again. At the same time, Johnson also allowed that a great many white southerners had joined the Confederacy in a "reign of terror." They had been conscripted, were duped, or had offered their allegiances in a fit of misguided, flag-waving nationalism. For them and even for Unionists who thought emancipation too high a price to pay for the republic's survival, Johnson counseled supplication: "Go over there; there is an altar for you. There is President Lincoln's altar if you want pardon or amnesty—if petitioning to the President for executive clemency. If you want to escape the penalties you have incurred by violations of law and the constitution, go over there and get your pardon." Mixing an evocative religious language with a hard wartime politics, Johnson was clearing ground for a process of reunification and citizenship all at once, a bifurcated citizenship in which disloyal southerners would be citizens of a sort, separate from those who had never relinquished their allegiance to the republic. Grounded in a personal act of confession and contrition, but with sharp lines drawn between those whose actions demanded retribution and those whose actions did not, Andrew Johnson was making wartime loyalty the sine qua non of civic membership in the Union.[11]

The only other sharp line that Johnson drew under his new republic was a racial one. Aside from his belief in loyalty to the Union, his other conviction lay in the idea that the United States was a white man's republic. For Johnson, African Americans could not accomplish in freedom what God's law, nature, and good sense had all made perfectly impossible. As so many historians have so clearly argued for so long, Johnson's racism was deep and abiding, even in the context of the mid-nineteenth century. In his 1864 speech on restoration, Johnson made it clear that he was for the supremacy of free labor, regardless of race, though the impossibility of African Americans possessing the skill or the intelligence to govern themselves, let alone a country, was evident for all to see. Johnson suggested that African Americans could be sent abroad, to Mexico, for instance, "where there is not that difference in class or distinction, in reference to blood or color." He also let down his guard in speaking of the American population as being in need of a racial cleansing. "We have not yet fulfilled our mission," Johnson went on. "We have got the negroes to dispose of. We will do that." While his words went a good deal further than those of most Union officials in the occupied South,

Johnson's ideas about freedpeople and their fitness in his imagined loyal republic would have likely been met with approval by white Unionist audiences in Tennessee. By 1864, slavery still existed in the central and eastern portions of the state, and it was not until around the time that Johnson addressed his audience on the question of home rule that the Union government began to tentatively dismantle the institution in the tenuously occupied portions of the state. What was interesting about his comments was that in many parts of the South—including Johnson's home state—African American communities had been engaged in the work of declaring their fitness to be counted as citizens by proclaiming the very same kind of loyalty to the Union that Johnson held so dear. As they would when the war came to its messy end and with increased volume as postwar realities set in, freedpeople argued for entry into the body politic as loyal Americans. In one of the most astonishing ironies, perhaps the most loyal group in the Confederate South were the very people that Andrew Johnson overlooked as a people unfit for citizenship.[12]

Once he ascended to the presidency, Johnson played a slower, more considered game with regard to loyalty. Though he was pushed to act more aggressively, he seemed to take an accurate measure of the moment by keeping his own counsel. His biographer claims that Johnson's deliberate pace was due at least in part to his political acumen. While he continued to publicly issue harsh words of warning against Confederate traitors, Johnson privately sought to bring all of the disparate voices in his predecessor's cabinet into his confidence.[13] There is also evidence to suggest that the slow pace of Johnson's plan for the nation only partly concealed a speedy military reconstruction of the defeated South that fanned out across the region.[14] In Mississippi alone, nearly 15,000 troops held positions in outposts all over the state by the middle of 1865.[15] All the same, for those outside the War Department who seethed with rage, supporters and critics alike parsed Johnson's every word to divine his future actions. The new president was greeted, for instance, with encouragement from those who believed that he would exact retribution not only from slaveholders for the war but also from moneyed Americans who stood against working people everywhere. One letter writer from Philadelphia expressed his joy at the prospect of Johnson in the White House, if only because he believed that Johnson would make war against not only southern wealth but northern interests "who would favor slavery for the sake of having capital control labor." Johnson also received support from African Americans, who urged the president to act in their favor. In a rhetorical move that would dominate their politics in the months that followed the end of the war, freedpeople made it clear that their love of the Union, which had been tested in war and would remain indomitable, made African Americans anxious "to show our countrymen that we can and will fit ourselves for the creditable discharge of the duties of citizenship." "It seems to us that men who are willing on the field of danger to carry the muskets of republics, in the days of peace ought to be permitted to carry its ballots," wrote North Carolina freedmen in an open letter to Johnson, "and certainly we cannot understand the justice of denying the elective franchise to men who have been fighting for the country, while it is freely given to men who have just returned from four years fighting against it." In many respects, these calls for more determined action were encouraged by Johnson's own wartime record. At the close of the war, many Americans had come to see him as the defender of Unionist loyalty, and these expectations generated even higher hopes for what Johnson would do once in office. What Johnson did when he finally took action would surprise many and enrage many more. His Reconstruction plan captured all of the contradictory imperatives of its architect, while at the same time enshrining a particular kind of reunification at the heart of federal policy.[16]

Presidential Reconstruction was formed from two ideas: a vision of the wartime state and the place of smaller polities within it. Both ideas were born from the experience of war, both were mere extensions of policies put in place by Johnson's predecessor, but both were taken up by Johnson and revised significantly. The first lay in how Johnson interpreted the end of the war: less as a sharp break between war and peace and more as a middle stage between the two. While Johnson's Reconstruction plan merely carried over some of the key ideas in Lincoln's wartime policies, the use of wartime presidential powers after an armistice was an innovation. In a broader context, however, there was cause to believe that the Union needed to remain on something approximating a war footing. The assassination of Lincoln was viewed by many northerners as yet another attempt by Confederates to sustain the war. What's more, given the national obsession with punishing Confederate president Jefferson Davis—an obsession that increased once Davis was finally apprehended in the middle of May 1865—there were grounds to believe that a de facto insurrection would continue for the foreseeable future. While conservative elements within the South argued for the restoration of their place in the Union, even they cautioned Johnson from moving too quickly toward peace and ceding too much authority to states that lacked the stability to govern. "I am anxious to see my native State once more in her proper position," wrote John Claiborne from Mississippi in early May. As a member of one of the oldest ruling families in the state, Claiborne could have been forgiven for thinking that his stand against secession in 1861 might broaden his political horizons now that official hostilities had abated. However, even Claiborne believed that, without a strong federal presence, governance in the state was too frail and would undoubtedly collapse. "My opinion is that, for 12 months to come," states like Mississippi ought to be kept "under the immediate eye of the Executive and controlled by military rule." In answer to men like Claiborne and just as he had done in Tennessee, Johnson would lay out a program for Reconstruction in which executive authority would trump all other federal power.[17]

The other pillar of what would become Presidential Reconstruction signaled more of a departure for Johnson: a curious interpretation of the place of seceded states in the Union that would dog Johnson from the moment he made the idea public. Moving away from some of his wartime comments—and in sharp contrast to observers who were arguing that southern states ought to be treated as colonial possessions of the Union—Johnson argued instead for the former Confederacy to become a collection not of failed, independent states but of rebellious states that remained in the Union in a kind of suspended animation. They remained part of the republic even though they had seceded, but their rebellion against the Union had resulted in southern states forfeiting their rights to participation in the political process. This made Presidential Reconstruction a completely different social, political, and economic project from what many Republicans, not to mention civil and military officials stationed in the South, understood as their challenge in the wake of the war. The purpose, as Johnson imagined it, was merely to reunify the disparate parts of the Union, not to remake the South in any meaningful way. State-sponsored programs that sought a dramatic economic change of the slaveholding South to a system of free labor, as well as political change that might bring African Americans into the body politic as citizens, were, for Johnson, not within his power. In fact, what Johnson saw as the immediate future of the South and the nation was not even Reconstruction at all. As he put it to Gen. John Logan at the end of May, "There is no such thing as reconstruction. These States have not gone out of the Union, therefore reconstruction is not necessary." What Johnson saw as his purpose was to animate southern states from "temporary suspension of their government." The only stipulation that Johnson demanded—the only stipulation that seemed to matter to him—was that southern states, constituted by a loyal electorate, appoint equally loyal men to govern. As he made plain to Logan, "provided always they elect loyal men," former Confederate states ought to be brought back into the Union. The war, according to Johnson, not only had vindicated the Unionist view that the republic was indivisible but also had drawn a bright line around the obligations of national citizenship. So long as whites could prove their loyalty, they could become citizens. Should they be incapable of taking the oath of allegiance, they would be treated as a suspect class in American society.[18]

That Johnson charted a path for the republic's future so out of step with so many in and out of government has long made Presidential Reconstruction an enigma. But his ideas remain inscrutable only if Johnson's abiding devotion to the idea of loyalty is removed from the equation. Place it back into the formula, and things become clearer. Johnson believed in the cleansing, transformative, purging power of personal contrition bound up with loyalty oaths. They were so much more than empty words. Reaffirming one's loyalty to the national government was a solemn thing, a public demonstration of one's allegiance to the republic. From the start of the war, Johnson held fast to the idea that the vast majority of the white southern population had remained loyal to the Union. It seemed ludicrous to him to think that secession was anything more than a slaveholders' coup and that, at the first opportunity, nonslaveholders would reaffirm their allegiance to the republic once more. And it was only in the public demonstration of that loyalty, in the form of oaths, that the country could become whole again. In a widely published set of remarks he offered to the Pennsylvania congressional delegation in early May 1865, Johnson claimed that while he would not spare those who had committed treason, "there are also some who have been engaged in this rebellion, who, while technically speaking, are guilty of treason, yet are morally not. Thousands have been drawn into it, involved by vicious influences." For those who had been misled, Johnson counseled mercy. To those "who have deceived—to the conscious, influential traitor, who attempted to destroy the life of the nation, I would say 'On you be inflicted the severest penalties of your crime.'"[19]

While the proclamation that laid out Johnson's reunification plan claimed to extend wartime policies, the obsessive attention that he paid to the intricacies of loyalty was unique to the new president. The proclamation divided the white southern population by extending amnesty and restored property rights to the bulk of former Confederates, except those who fell within the parameters of fourteen exception clauses. The clauses themselves spoke to some of Johnson's most closely held convictions. For those who had served the Confederacy as high-ranking civilian or military officials, left posts in the Union government to assume positions in the Confederate state, traveled from the Union to give aid to the Confederacy, or been members of the moneyed southern elite before the war started, Johnson demanded that all who wanted a pardon make special application. Within these clauses, Johnson made it clear that both the architects of secession and the southern elite he had always despised could only be made citizens again with his say-so. He also incorporated a hazy fourteenth clause that isolated those who had taken a wartime oath but who had not maintained their loyalty to the Union after their oaths had been taken. This gave Johnson some latitude to ensure that individuals in states that had already reconstituted themselves as loyal could have their actions scrutinized with more care. On paper, the micromanagement implied by the proclamation was truly breathtaking. The political power that Johnson retained for himself by being the lone arbiter of loyalty was equally stunning. Johnson's proclamation did not simply make loyalty a center-piece of Presidential Reconstruction; it created a single, one-size-fits-all definition of loyalty that was drawn, at least in part, from Johnson's own self-identity as a southern Unionist. In sum, loyalty was the engine that drove the entire project of Presidential Reconstruction, and only Johnson could make it work.[20]

Historians who have examined the period have often remarked that the proc-lamation was too lenient and naive. It created an easy path for white southerners to reclaim their citizenship, and when twinned with the rapid political reunifi-cation plan set in place by Lincoln and continued by Johnson, it offered ample opportunity for former Confederates to rule their region once again. Yet a closer look at the proclamation reveals a good deal. Johnson's plan was based on the idea that loyalty oaths were powerful documents that bound individuals and their honor to the republic, not to the states of their birth. His devotion to this idea becomes clearer when one considers that at no point in his proclamation did he lay out some mechanism to revoke a pardon once it had been issued. New York lawyer Henry Fessenden urged Johnson to do as much only days before the proclamation was made public. "Such a clause may not be usual in a proclamation of amnesty," Fessenden allowed, "but the circumstances of our national case are unusual; and there is going to be need of something of the sort with the gentry with whom you have to deal." It is probable that Johnson did not insert such a clause into his proclamation for political reasons. But it is just as likely that he did not make his plan more flexible because he believed that an oath taken was a solemn vow. Moreover, Johnson's plan did not create any bureaucracy to deal with the torrent of oaths that was sure to follow the publication of his plan. Rather, as a southerner and a former military governor, Johnson made himself the last word on loyalty. He and he alone would adjudicate every claim. He would be the one to bestow citizenship on former Confederates or deem their treason unworthy of the privilege. Placing himself in such a position also undoubtedly had a political purpose. Extending citizenship in such a personal way would endear Johnson to many would-be supporters. But this was not his only purpose. In his capacity as president, Johnson genuinely believed that he was best placed to judge loyalty. He had spent years affirming and reaffirming his own loyalty to the Union, and setting the loyalty of amnesty applicants against his own, Johnson believed that he could reunify the country one oath at a time.[21]

Johnson's Reconstruction plan had a good many supporters, at least at first. Johnson had few confidants, but those who counted themselves in his small inner circle offered encouragement at the path he had laid out for the country. James Bingham, a friend from Tennessee, wrote Johnson to let him know that his supporters were enthusiastic about both his plan for amnesty and his position on African American citizenship: "Your amnesty gives satisfaction to all fair-minded men, and you have struck the true keynote on reconstruction. Your position on the question of negro suffrage is impregnable." Bingham also believed that loyalists all over the country would sustain him and that his popularity in Tennessee would be equal to that in other states.[22]

If loyal supporters thought that Johnson had hit the mark, others immediately pounced on what they saw as the enormous blind spot in his plan. "You say you believe in democratic government, or consent of loyal people," wrote Tennessean Joseph Noxon, "yet you dare not avow with practical effect the right of the colord man to vote. Are you honest?" Others criticized Johnson's belief in the power of oaths to cleanse the body politic. "It was the principal fault of our late lamented chief that he was too lenient," wrote Samuel Snyder, a milliner from Indiana. "But from the treatment you have had at the hands of the Rebels & from your declarations since your elevation we had a right to expect a little more nerve about you. . . . Are we to receive back with open arms the murderers of our sons & brothers, and forgive all their crimes & thereby make rebelion honorable?" On the question of loyalty, Snyder had no time for oaths. Better, he said, to hang the ringleaders of the Confederacy than to let their treason forever threaten the stability of the Union. If Johnson was asking loyal Americans to rely upon his personal judgement, it became immediately apparent that this kind of trust was in short supply.[23]

The confidence embedded in Andrew Johnson's plan for Reconstruction—the belief that the chief executive was best placed to make the republic whole—was also magnified by the political risk Johnson was taking in issuing a plan at all. With Congress out of session, any plan of such importance that lacked the input of Republicans in both houses would be subject to intense scrutiny. Thaddeus Stevens cautioned Johnson that Congress deemed Reconstruction "as a question for the Legislative power exclusively," and while he made it clear that Johnson's plan would undoubtedly receive broad support, he feared that there was a difference between how the executive and legislative branches of government wanted to proceed. "Better call an extra Session," Stevens urged, "than to allow many to think that the executive was approaching usurpation." Stevens's threat would foreshadow a battle to come. But in so many respects, this was not the battleground Johnson had in mind. His focus was trained squarely on building an imagined community of southern loyalists, and many of the reports and letters that Johnson received in the summer of 1865 favored his approach. Using a language the president would have found familiar because it was his own, many letter writers urged Johnson to stay the course. Writing from Key West, Florida, in early June 1865,

J. George Harris called on Johnson to persevere despite the growing opposition against him. Quoting from Luke's gospel, Harris claimed that just as Christ counseled Martha to set aside the worries of this world and focus on the hereafter, in the occupied South "loyalty is 'the one thing needful.'" Johnson's proclamation, Harris went on, "comes to us like a new revelation. Repentant rebels hail it with joy—but it is like a blister to the skin of those whose loyalty is merely on the lips, for it burns and brings treason from their hearts to the surface." So long as former Confederates were willing to take a step toward the Union, Johnson had laid out a process by which he would meet them halfway.[24]

As Johnson's plans for the South began to be put into practice and as the pleas of white southerners began to make their way to Washington, Johnson's careful imagining of a loyal republic would be sorely tested. He would come under fire, not only from Republicans who believed that his plan left no room for African Americans, but also from those who believed that his terms of reconciliation were too lenient for former Confederate traitors to become citizens once again. Having made his name as the very symbol of wartime loyalty, Johnson presumed perhaps that a nation tired of war would accept his terms. Looking more closely at the effect of Johnson's Reconstruction in Mississippi, however, one can see not only the difficulties that his program of loyalty let loose but also the ways in which loyalty as a prerequisite for citizenship would slowly become discredited.

James Lusk Alcorn was definitely not the kind of white southerner that Andrew Johnson had in mind when he devised his plan for Reconstruction. A Coahoma County planter and lawyer who had settled in Mississippi in 1844, Alcorn had amassed a fortune in land and some seventy-seven slaves by 1860. It was not long before Alcorn, like most planters of his training and wealth, translated his assets into political currency in the Delta. The lure of a political career quickly captured his ambition, and he would represent his county for more than two decades. A Whig to his core, Alcorn was initially cool to secession. However, his political status forced him into the spotlight, whether he wanted it or not. Supporters offered him up as a candidate for the president of the secession convention, though he lost the vote. Alcorn served on the committee of fifteen who drew up Mississippi's secession ordinance, and despite his best efforts to steer a more moderate, conciliatory course—he voted in favor of stalling Mississippi's secession until other southern states left the Union—he was still among the eighty-five convention delegates who voted in favor of the ordinance. His initial opposition to southern independence, however, distanced him from power. Alcorn made many enemies in the John Pettus administration, including the governor himself, and his position following secession was often a lonely one. When the war broke out, he was appointed brigadier general in the state militia, a largely ceremonial position. While his time in that post was brief, he still used his authority to push back at attempts by the Confederate Army to supersede the military authority of the state militia. When this proved a quixotic errand, Alcorn found himself the object of derision in the state's popular press and in the state legislature. Later in the year, he was captured and imprisoned. With his parole from a Union prisoner of war camp in 1863, Alcorn returned to Mississippi. Yet his opposition to the Confederacy did not preclude him from serving in office. He ran for election in the state legislature in 1864, and he continued to serve the state in that capacity until the very end of the war.[25]

By 1865, the collateral damage of the conflict on his property and the loss of his two sons who died in uniform had soured James Alcorn. He had come to see the Confederacy as a disaster. In a dark, angry letter to his wife that he wrote in March 1865, Alcorn heaped scorn on Democrats, on secessionists, and particularly on Jefferson Davis, "the miserable, stupid, one eyed, dyspeptic, arrogant, tyrant," who had venerated the southern countryside as heaven on earth yet had made southern soil "wet with the tears of widows & orphans and the land which he has bathed in the blood of a people once free, but now enslaved." All Alcorn wanted was to see southern leaders like Davis damned and dead. In July 1865, he took the oath of allegiance and filed his application for amnesty a few weeks later, hoping to reclaim his status as a citizen of the United States.[26]

Yet as a man who believed so deeply that the Confederate project was a blight on the South, even Alcorn found it difficult to declare his allegiance to Andrew Johnson and the Union. Rewriting the history of his recent past, Alcorn confronted his decisions and his record of loyalty to the American nation and attempted to scrub both of any treason. He claimed that he had opposed the ordinance of secession "as a question of policy and a question of Constitutional right." His opposition "was active and firm up to the hour of the passage of the ordinance." When, however, Alcorn believed that his position was untenable and when it became clear that his opposition would brook "worse consequences," he yielded to the majority who wanted out of the Union. To burnish his credentials as a loyal representative of his constituents, Alcorn made a show in his application of emphasizing his opposition to the Confederacy during the war. He also parsed both his words and his past actions by making it clear that while he obeyed Confederate law, he had never served the nation in any official capacity. This was, to be sure, a revision of his past, given his position in the state government of Mississippi. All the same, Alcorn hoped that by separating his public self from his private loyalties, he could make Johnson see that he had never allowed the Confederacy to become the object of his closest political affections. Separating heart from head, Alcorn fell upon the mercy of Andrew Johnson, praying that his application for amnesty would be "found worthy."[27]

With its tortured language, buried facts, and divided loyalties, Alcorn's case file joined the 1,113 amnesty applications from Mississippians that made their way to Washington.[28] As a collection of underutilized historical documents, they reveal a deeply personal history of regret and rage, often wrapped in contorted arguments that attempted to obscure or, in some cases, honestly reckon with actions that most Americans would have counted as treasonous. As testimonials that were both legal documents and almost religious confessions, they reflected precisely the kind of supplication that Andrew Johnson envisioned. Aping the kind of talk the president filled his speeches with in the weeks and months that followed Appomattox, they limned the spiritual and the legal all at once in a conversation between a president and would-be traitors. Not all the applications for amnesty met Johnson's standard of loyalty. Petitioners expressed hidden agendas and hardheaded reasons for bidding Johnson to bestow citizenship on them. All the same, the petitions revealed the promise and the deep problems with loyalty as a key to citizenship in the postwar republic.

One of the leitmotifs that ran through the applications was a determination on the part of some amnesty-seekers to remain apolitical, should they be made citizens once more. Despite the fact that he was counted on by Governor William Sharkey as a loyal "Union Whig," Noxubee County planter Thomas Barton wanted no part in politics or elected office, claiming that his chronic rheumatism kept him housebound. Alexander Clayton argued that while he had served his state as a member of the secession convention, the Confederacy as a member of the Constitutional Congress, and the District of Mississippi as an inspector, he had never aspired to high political office. "Before this War," Clayton wrote, "it was my wish to have spent the better part of my life in quiet and retirement." For his part, Clayton regretted the war and the bloodshed, claiming that if southerners "could have foreseen that such a War would have followed," the secession of southern states would likely not have happened. Clayton also styled himself a kind planter. He stated that his former slaves had always said Clayton had treated them kindly, and that he had already contracted his former slaves to work for a wage: "So ends the chapter of slavery with me."[29]

Other amnesty-seekers struck a more defiant pose. L. Q. C. Lamar—the young lawyer from Oxford who would go on to fame in national politics and infamy for the role he played in Mississippi's White Line movement in the 1870s—pointed to his principles as his reason for supporting secession. Hitting the note that so many would strike in their amnesty letters, Lamar claimed that he had been raised to believe "that the Sovereignty of Government, in this Country, resided in the people of the several States." He soft-pedaled his pivotal role in the secession convention, choosing instead to emphasize his war record for the Confederate cause.

For this reason, his amnesty letter echoed so many others in how it took up the mantle of what would become the Lost Cause. Lamar wrote that he had become convinced that the effort to erect a southern nation had ended in "inevitable failure." His only wish was to do his part to maintain "Republican institutions" in his home state.[30]

Mary Parker, an Adams County widow, made no apologies for aiding state and Confederate troops during the war, even though her dead husband and her extended family counted themselves as believers in the indivisibility of the Union in 1861. Refusing to give up her loyalties to the southern cause, Parker still prevailed upon Johnson to extend her a pardon. Having lost her land and her slaves in both Mississippi and Louisiana, Parker made it clear that her ability to provide for her family depended upon her ability to be deemed loyal, even if she implied that her heart was not in it. Andiana Rogers was similarly forthright in her support of the Confederacy. Unlike many male amnesty-seekers, Rogers was clear that her sympathies were with the Confederacy. She made no secret of having sold supplies to Confederate troops when they could have been spared. For Rogers, the fact that she was born in the South made her sympathies naturally tend toward her section, though with the Confederacy's collapse she wished to be restored to the status of an American citizen. Applications from female amnesty seekers are particularly complex. As many of the privileges of citizenship remained beyond women's grasp, this ironically allowed women an unusual degree of latitude in retaining their Confederate sympathies. To work around this difficulty, some women relied on men to vouch for them. To bolster her application, Parker included an affidavit from three men of her acquaintance to further vouch for the veracity of her claim. But the applications of other women, like Parker's, underscored the expedience of filing to claim rights, without ever giving up their wartime loyalties.[31]

Requests for amnesty and declarations of renewed allegiance often relied on intricate personal histories. With counties in disarray, whites who attempted to claim Unionist loyalty in a desperate effort to stave off ruin could do little but offer tortured letters of regret. These letters provide insight into the political imaginations of their writers. By recounting their histories of loyalty to the Union, these writers manufactured a kind of hierarchy of allegiance. Each letter was designed to stake a claim to true fealty, in contrast to the actions of Confederate sympathizers, who were often the writer's own neighbors. John Watson was a member of Mississippi's Union Convention in 1851, the political organization that was formed to block the secession of the state in the wake of the Compromise of 1850. And though, a decade later, he claimed to have been "politically opposed to Mr. Lincoln," he had stood in opposition to secession, an act of bravery that, Watson hoped, would sway skeptical Union officials. When it became apparent that secession would become a reality, Watson acquiesced in favor of the Confederacy. He accepted positions of government office and later would serve the state as a senator in the Confederate Congress. Despite his active involvement at the highest levels of its government, Watson claimed in his plea for amnesty that he was never truly loyal to the Confederacy. He wrote that he was "conscientiously prepared to take the amnesty oath and to assume the duties and responsibilities of a good, true, and loyal citizen of the United States. . . . No one could have been more opposed to disunion than I was, and no one, to the extent of his abilities, labored more earnestly to avert it." By minimizing his influence over a seeming historical inevitability like secession, Watson could deemphasize his role as a leader in the Confederate government.[32]

This claim of secession's inevitability pervaded the pardons and pleas of white Mississippians. Many writers emptied their letters of intention, particularly on their role in the formation of the Confederate government. "My record will show that I offered opposition until secession was consummated and before us," wrote one man from Adams County. "Out of it came a government. Within its limits, was my home. I would not leave it, but resolved to do all in my power to defend it." For some, the clever manipulation of language and the suggestion that the act of having been citizens of another state changed little; it gave former Confederates and their amnesties added weight, even if the passive voice veiled a profound shift in allegiance. A small piece in a Panola County newspaper divulged perhaps more than the editors intended, when the writer told the story of a prominent Mississippi gentleman who called on Judge Advocate General Joseph Holt in Washington. The man recounted the story to Holt of a neighbor who was in search of a pardon. The neighbor had "always been a Union man" and ought to be given amnesty, though Holt replied that it was "a wonder we had a fighting to do down that way; I have not seen or heard of a man yet from Mississippi or Louisiana, who was not a Union man." Speaking for many Unionists who could not bring themselves to believe that southern pleas of loyalty were in earnest, Holt asked, "Who was it that was fighting us?"[33]

Petitioners also disclosed political squabbles and pitched battles between Union and Confederate sympathizers. Letters detailed efforts by loyal Confederates to organize the takeover of local government, while others charged that secession and war had laid waste to the entire state. Trying to raise a militia of Unionists in Tippah County in the autumn of 1865, H. E. Moore wrote of an attempt by Confederate loyalists to discredit him in the county as little more than an appendage of Unionist occupation. "The northern part of the County is Composed mostly of Union men (I mean loyal men)," wrote Moore, in the new political language of the moment, "and many of them too are men who have served their time out in this War in the U.S. Service." Loyalty to the Union, however, had won Moore and his compatriots only derision. As he made clear, the critics of their company claimed that "'there is not any Union and that all union men and men who served in the U.S. army shall leave this Country, leave their homes, land &c.'" In Tippah County, as elsewhere in Mississippi, publicly declaring one's loyalty cut torn communities to the bone while at the same time throwing loyal Unionists open to attack from all corners. Other letter writers prevailed upon officials to ensure that the military occupation of their communities respected their loyalty, even if it was deemed by many to be only skin-deep. Citizens of Noxubee County wrote an overheated petition to Governor Benjamin Humphries near the end of 1865 complaining that the installation of a black Union regiment in the county was an affront to the oaths so many of the petitioners had taken. "We are loyal citizens to the government of the State of Mississippi and to the government of the United States," and it was from both the state and federal governments that newly minted white citizens demanded protection from former slaves in uniform. While the petitioners were careful to insist that the Union officers who led black regiments in Noxubee were able, just men, they objected to being rendered "powerless for our own protection" when faced with the daily threat of African Americans enforcing the Union's justice in their county.[34]

As amnesty-seekers attempted to claim rights on flimsy pledges of allegiance or to explain away their actions in secession and war too easily for Unionists to bear, the idea of loyalty itself underwent a slow devaluation. In part, this stemmed from the problem inherent in Johnson's plan, of a single litmus test of loyalty too inflexible and open to all kinds of manipulations by amnesty-seekers. The ease with which pardon-seekers explained away their treasonous actions demeaned the idea of loyalty as something that could be proven to the satisfaction of government officials, let alone the nation. But the diminution of loyalty also reflected the expanded horizon of possibility that Presidential Reconstruction provided whites in reconstituted governments. Mississippi's hastily convened constitutional convention, which met in August 1865, was principally composed of former Whigs who had either been marginalized by the dominance of secessionists in the 1850s, or who had stepped back from independence at the state's moment of choosing four years before. As they gathered in one of the few buildings in Jackson left standing from the Union occupation, convention delegates stood apart from the small bands of former Confederate soldiers who still walked the streets of the capital dressed in their military grays and who, according to a *New York Times* correspondent, had not yet divested themselves of their "former prejudices and animosities." Yet, isolated as they may have been from those who still clung to their allegiance to a failed state, even convention delegates found oaths of loyalty difficult to endure. "I cannot regard it as lawful," declared George L. Potter of Hinds County, "that our Senators and Representatives shall be first required to take a special oath contained in the acts of Congress—a sort of test oath of loyalty—the sum and substance of which may be stated in this way: that no man can present himself there, as a Representative of a State, who has even smelled the recent rebellion." Loyalty to the Union also smacked of forced fealty to the Republican Party. The partisan agenda that many saw between the lines of the proclamation began to eat away at the fusion of personal allegiance and citizenship. Other members of the convention reached the conclusion that if party ultimately mattered more than an individual's attachment to the nation, the collective political pasts of members ought to mask the taint of treason. R. S. Hudson of Yazoo County argued that the fact that the convention was "almost entirely composed of gentlemen who hold opinions, politically, the very opposite of those of" Jefferson Davis ought to weigh in the measurement of individual loyalty.[35]

Perhaps the most profound result of Andrew Johnson's Reconstruction plan was that it provided white southerners with the means to cleanse themselves of their sins. Hampton Jarnagin of Noxubee County claimed that by constituting a convention that claimed to represent loyal persons throughout the state, presidential amnesty had wiped the convention clean of any wrongdoing. "To-day, so far as humility is concerned," Jarnagin argued, "we stand as if there had been no rebellion, or if we had been guilty of no treason." The power of presidential amnesty without any oversight threw Johnson's plan open to all sorts of liberties taken by those who had taken the oath, giving them free rein to act. The readers of southern newspapers were also encouraged to see the swearing of loyalty as little more than a means to an end. A report in a Coahoma County paper in the fall of 1865 made a mockery of oaths and loyalty by recounting the apocryphal story of a local woman who had traveled across the Mississippi River to Arkansas in search of supplies. When told by the commanding Union officer that in order to purchase anything, she was required to swear an oath, the woman responded that she was brought up to believe that "it ain't right to swear." When pressed, according to the story, she responded, "Well if I must I must, do *d-d-n you*." Darkly humorous stories like this one joined a long list of tall tales involving white southern women who challenged authority and reveled in their unrepentant Confederate pride. Elevated as these women had so often been to the status of a national symbol, stories involving them staring down Union officers had, by the end of the war, become a ready trope in the southern popular press. Almost always involving women as central characters, these stories made light of the devotion to oaths by making it clear that when faced with the everyday battle to make ends meet, former Confederates would, of course, swear to an oath, even if they made it clear that they were not in earnest.[36]

Treating oaths as a means to an end—an empty act of bureaucratic acquiescence that in no way represented the contrite capitulation they were intended to be—was a southern sentiment quickly picked up by northern papers. They connected the foot-dragging of southern oath-takers to a broader attempt to legislate African Americans back into slavery and made both a symbol of Confederate intransigence that threatened Presidential Reconstruction almost as soon as it started. The lenience of loyalty oaths and the open-ended freedom it permitted oath-takers to rejoin the Union as citizens so soon after the war had ended struck many northerners as too much, too soon. Newspapers like Horace Greeley's *New York Tribune* reported that while it was uncharitable for Unionists to "humiliate those already drinking the bitter cup of discomfiture," it was ludicrous to think that former Confederates could be allowed to explain away their treason to the nation. Postwar loyalty meant unflinching fealty to the federal government and the Union, and not "till it is settled that no State can release a citizen from his obligation of loyalty to the Union, can we feel that there is any validity or sense in swearing ex-Rebels back into citizens." Swearing an oath connected southerners to the Union; it made the nation-state the principal institution to which all Americans were bound in allegiance, and any attempt to obfuscate prior actions as anything less than treason made oaths hardly worth the effort to administer them. So long as "each citizen owes a divided allegiance" and was permitted to see the oath as little more than an empty pledge, the country could never be whole.[37]

The passing of Black Codes in states throughout the South also brought the issue of the loyalty of African Americans to a head. Worries about African Americans being forced back into slavery solidified public opinion that white southern legislators were making a mockery of the Union, but many of the arguments calling on Republicans to act more forcefully turned not on the question of preserving emancipation but on the depth of blacks' loyalty to the Union. The national government was bound "by the most solemn obligation to take care that the race which remained true to it when all around them were recreant" would not suffer for their allegiance to the republic now that the war was over. By the end of 1865, the growing sense that the depth of southern loyalty was only skin-deep had hardened into a stern northern conviction. Recounting the actions of southern constitutional conventions, an editorialist in the *New York Times* remarked that delegates had used the magnanimous terms of presidential amnesty "to give color to the pretense that, in the view of the government itself, no real crime had been committed," and that past acts of treason had been dissolved in a process of restoration that were "little else than a matter of form." The benevolence of amnesty should not be taken as proof that treason had been devalued, "nor is it a token of a disposition to humor a disloyal spirit in any of its forms." Former

Confederates had been offered humane, lenient terms. They were now required to accept defeat, recognize the Union and its federal government as the supreme power, and be grateful that their treason had been so gently set to one side.[38]

In this context Congress attempted to have their say on Andrew Johnson's Reconstruction by convening a joint committee in December to investigate the state of the occupied South. Pushed forward by Thaddeus Stevens, the purpose of the committee was to identify the key problems with Johnson's program of national reunification, a program that by then had resulted in Republicans in Congress blocking the admittance of southern members to both houses, while northern newspapers reported on southern legislatures passing Black Codes to legislate African Americans back into a social and economic position akin to what free blacks had experienced before the war. Given the growing rift between Johnson and Republican members of Congress, the committee was meant to pass judgment on Johnson and provide the pretext for broader, more radical action: in particular, a new constitutional amendment that protected the civil rights of freedpeople. Composed of twelve Republicans and three Democrats, the committee called 144 witnesses to testify. While the report wound up splitting the committee along party lines, the questions put to witnesses placed an inordinate emphasis on loyalty in all of its permutations. The purpose of this line of questioning was to effectively skewer Johnson and his Reconstruction plan, to show that the president's emphasis on loyalty as the key to reunification had been dodged, explained away, manipulated, or ignored outright by former Confederates. As the summary opinion made perfectly clear, it was a mockery "to contend that a people who have thrown off their allegiance, destroyed the local government which bound their States to the Union," defied federal authority and national law, "and abrogated every provision which gave" white southerners rights as citizens could still allow those same individuals rights as citizens in a postwar Union. "To admit such a principle for one moment would be to declare that treason is always master and loyalty a blunder." It was through this lens that the committee sought evidence of just how much loyalty had been so lightly cast aside and manipulated by Johnson and whites in the former Confederacy.[39]

Committee testimony made it clear that loyalty in the South was anything but secure. Witness after witness testified to the widespread refusal of former Confederates to accept their status in the republic as a defeated group, and there was even less acceptance of anything approaching African Americans rights. Some pointed to the fact that hatred of the Union and hatred of freed African Americans had combined into a complex hostility toward the nation-state, particularly among the white lower classes. Union officer Edward Hatch reported that despite the disposition of freedpeople to work in places like Mississippi, "the poorer classes of the white people have an intense dislike towards them" that infected their feelings about the nation that protected their freedom as well. It would have escaped no one's notice that an indictment of the loyalty of poorer whites exposed Andrew Johnson's support of their allegiance to the Union as little more than a sham. Other witnesses suggested that regardless of whites' pledges of loyalty, the practical effect of Reconstruction hinged on persistent military pressure, without which southern states would quickly devolve into anarchy. Ezra Hienstadt, a lawyer who had lived in New Orleans since the 1830s, believed that if the government removed federal troops from the city and state, "the Union men, as we call those who were loyal during the rebellion, would be driven from almost all the rural portions of the State at least, if not from the city of New Orleans," to say nothing of the status of the black population. The weight of testimony suggested that regardless of Andrew Johnson's view on loyalty, Union occupation of the South teetered on a crumbling precipice.[40]

The testimony also suggested that the lawlessness and broader disloyal sentiment in the occupied South were due to the lenience of Johnson's policies on loyalty. Several witnesses testified that while many white southerners were resigned to their fate following the surrender of Confederate forces in the spring of 1865, the terms of amnesty put in place by Johnson had only exacerbated a latent hatred of the government. W. A. P. Dillingham, a Treasury agent, testified that while a broad disposition to accept defeat permeated Mississippi society following the collapse of the Confederacy, "that feeling seemed to disappear; and after the policy of President Johnson was thoroughly inaugurated, the old bitterness seemed to develop," as expectations expanded and whites believed that they could once again take control of the affairs of state. Dillingham was quick to suggest that Johnson's lenience on southern amnesty was part of a broader attempt to knit a new national party together, with the president at its head. The cumulative effect of this interpretation of loyalty was to depict Johnson's Reconstruction as a narrow-minded, partisan bid for lasting political power. The committee also placed hastily reconstituted southern governments under intense scrutiny and found them wanting. Some suggested that truly loyal citizens had little trust in state legislators and congressmen who purported to be loyal, and even men appointed by Johnson doubted that Unionism could withstand the onslaught if the federal government retreated from its position of dominance. "If the power of the federal government and its influence were entirely withdrawn," claimed Georgia governor James Johnson, "I think a majority of the people would express a preference for a confederacy."[41]

The 800 pages of testimony laid blame directly at Andrew Johnson's feet for creating a program of reconciliation that one half of the country did not trust and the other half found ample room to dodge. Perhaps more fundamentally, though, loyalty as an idea and a political identity had begun to change shape. In the face of growing opposition to Johnson's plan, loyalty as a key to membership in the body politic was being replaced with a harder application of federal power that would reunify the nation by force. The first indications of just how much the idea of loyalty was undergoing a redefinition could be detected in the way that members of Congress dealt with the implications of slavery's abolition. By the end of 1865, Republicans had set out to sustain the military control of the South by giving the national government the power to intervene in the making of state law, by giving Congress oversight and the right to overturn legislation, without restriction. Massachusetts Republican Henry Wilson called for wartime powers to be ceded to Congress—not the executive—to annul laws deemed injurious to the Thirteenth Amendment in states that Wilson declared still in rebellion. While Wilson framed his legislation as merely an act of common humanity, to protect freedpeople from former slaveholders, the definition of loyalty laid out by Andrew Johnson was clearly in question and hung in the balance. As a stand-off between Johnson and Congress gathered momentum, it had become clear to many that the security of the republic depended upon making black and not white loyalty the cornerstone of a new political system. "The animating soul of the Rebellion was an assumption that 'This is a White man's government,' wherein Blacks and Browns had properly no rights but such as Whites chose to concede them," claimed a *New York Tribune* editorial in March 1866. "Whoever intelligently holds to that faith is at heart a Rebel to-day, no matter how many 'iron-clad' oaths he may have taken, or may be willing to take." The idea that the loyalty of African Americans carried more weight than the professions of whites worked in tandem with the sustained powers of a national government still at war to empty oaths of white allegiance and professions of white southern Unionism of much of their meaning.[42]

At issue were also the limits of national reconciliation. Even Unionists who had no concern for African Americans or their status in the republic could agree that less than one year after the end of the war, former Confederates were now testing the limits of forgiveness. In a long-winded digression on the history of the subject, Charles Sumner suggested that while the idea of clemency ought to be preached, it could not be held in perfect balance with simple justice. Speaking directly to Johnson, Sumner argued that no pardon "can be allowed to imperil the nation; nor can any pardon be allowed to imperil those who have a right to look to us for protection. There must be no vengeance upon enemies; but there must be no sacrifice of friends." In drawing a line under the kind of loyalty and oath-taking proffered by the president, Sumner called for the country to treat disloyal southerners according to a simple maxim: "*Nothing for vengeance; everything for justice.*"[43] As the case for the federal protection of African Americans gathered strength—as not only a moral duty but also an obligation to protect the only truly loyal part of a recalcitrant region—the underpinning had been knocked out from under Andrew Johnson's Reconstruction. Loyalty, ultimately, had to be measured as something more than mere words. Actions mattered more.

IF ANDREW JOHNSON REGISTERED ANY ALARM that his plans for the nation were falling to pieces in the later months of 1865, he did not put pen to paper. Even if the political rumblings of a growing opposition in Washington threatened his political future, a man who kept few friends around him lured few new ones into his confidence. One of the only indications of his inner thoughts lay in a letter he wrote in November 1865. Since his capture, former Confederate vice president Alexander Stephens had written the president repeatedly, asking for a pardon. Johnson had refused, even after Stephens had secured his reelection to Congress. With a cordiality that did not comport with his public comments about loyalty, Johnson stated firmly through an intermediary that while his relationship with Stephens remained warm, he stood "charged with Treason, and no disposition has been made of his case." All the same, Johnson allowed that the southern election of former disloyal Confederates to state and federal office had thrown a wrench into his Reconstruction plans: "There seems in many of the elections Something like defiance, which is all out of place at this time."[44]

In the span of only a few months, Johnson's hope that he could knit the country together again began to unravel, and with it, the idea of loyalty as a path to a new kind of national citizenship. The extent to which loyalty had been devalued—by office-seekers who saw an opportunity to do in politics and in law that which they could not do on the battlefield, by former Confederates who could only bring themselves to mouth the words, and by northerners who could not trust them— began to shape a national debate over a future redefinition of citizenship that had gathered steam in the nation's capital. Yet the group who continued to believe in the power of loyalty as a political tool and a path to power was the very group for whom Andrew Johnson had not accounted. On plantations, in cities, and in small towns throughout the Reconstruction South, African Americans were in the process of bringing their bid for a meaningful citizenship to fruition. From the moment the war ended, they had fought an ongoing struggle over the terms of their labor, the meaning of their freedom, and the future of their communities. They had used their loyalty both as a weapon and as the foundation of their bid for political power in the wake of their emancipation. While Andrew Johnson had attempted to build loyalty between white southerners and the federal government, freedpeople had willingly offered their loyalty and allegiance, with the hope that they might secure a meaningful emancipation. Though their efforts had not been without setbacks, they had convinced many of their veracity. The question that now faced the Union was whether the loyalty of blacks ought to entitle former slaves to rights over those of their former owners. In this, Mississippi would be one of the principal battlegrounds.

CHAPTER SIX

It Looks Much Like Abandoned Land

There was nothing remarkable about the church on the corner of State and Wall Streets. Prior to the Civil War it had stolidly stood for nearly a decade, home to one of the largest Baptist congregations in Natchez. Like many Baptist churches in parts of the American South where slavery reigned, the faithful who filed into Wall Street Baptist were of two races, though it was not long before blacks outnumbered whites each Sunday. At another moment, in another place, such a racial imbalance might not have been a worry. Religious services had, after all, served to reinforce white supremacy all over the South in the early to mid-nineteenth century. By the middle of the 1850s, however, propriety and sectionalism had pushed the white deacons of Wall Street Baptist to act. They divided the congregation along racial lines, and for their part, the black members of the church had eagerly supported the plan. With donations from black congregants, they built a new church a few blocks away, called Rose Hill. The new church—deeded to a black drayman and led by a black preacher—had revolutionary potential in a slaveholding center like Natchez. For this reason the Wall Street deacons ensured that Rose Hill was not an independent church in its own right. It was, instead, the product of genteel segregation, geographically separate but still tied to the original church and firmly under white authority. To ensure order, a few of the great and good among the white population of Natchez attended services at Rose Hill to ensure that the new church comported with denominational regulations and that black church leaders did not overstep the mark. Two buildings, two pieces of sanctified property, one congregation.[1]

War, military occupation, and emancipation turned Natchez upside down. In the upheaval, property of all kinds, including churches, took on new meaning. Perhaps out of a hardheaded fear of the trouble that was to follow, when the Civil War began, the white deacons of Wall Street shuttered their church rather than continue to hold services. As a result, the building lay dormant until Union forces occupied Natchez in early 1863. Once firmly in control, Union chaplains reopened the church to minister to soldiers stationed in the city, though according to the black congregants of Rose Hill, local whites had refused to attend. African Americans claimed that Confederate sympathizers, in a show of loyalty and an unsubtle act of resistance, would have rather heard "the Devil Preach than a Yankee." Whites kept the faith with the Confederate cause, choosing to leave their church to the occupiers. However, this abdication of control over the Wall Street church offered the opportunity for African Americans to act.[2]

By 1864, with whites still refusing to attend, missionaries threw open the doors of Wall Street Baptist to black congregants, and in response, African Americans flocked to the church. In a matter of months, they turned the church into a center for a growing and increasingly emboldened black community in Natchez. There, freedpeople schooled their children, held prayer meetings, learned more about Union plans for the occupied South, and in time, supported communal efforts to build a vibrant political culture of their own, using the Wall Street church as a base. For all of these reasons, when the war ended and white members began to organize to regain control of the property once more, black congregants blocked their path. They sought and secured recognition from the Southern Baptist Convention as an independent congregation, and in petitions they sent to the Freedmen's Bureau, they attempted to permanently wrest control of the church property from white hands. In their petitions, the black leaders of Wall Street showed how much loyalty had changed the political landscape in the former Confederacy and how much African Americans had learned. With an awareness of what the American state sought from the defeated South, they wrapped their claim to their church in the language of loyalty, in contrast to whites, whose allegiance was suspect. Black congregants were, the deacons claimed, "the only rightfull owners of the said Wall St. property, that has been abandoned by trators." Freedpeople ought to be given the deed to the property as, in the loaded language of the moment, the church "looks much like abandoned land." Aware of what the property represented to its former white congregants, African Americans pressed for control of the church and used their wartime loyalty to cement their claim.[3]

By the end of the Civil War, the language of loyalty mixed with the language of citizenship to saturate the emancipating South. Talk of loyalty was everywhere: in letters passed between friends and family, in newspapers all over the region, and in documents that made their way up and down the chain of American military command. War and the destruction of slavery had not only made loyalty to the American nation-state paramount to political access and power, but people professed their loyalty through the claims and counterclaims they made to property. In many respects, the language of loyalty deployed by white and black alike was forged from the directives of those atop the government in Washington. But it was not long before people creatively and persuasively bent this language to suit their own purposes.

Pledges of allegiance and professions of loyalty—in print or in public—became opportunities to claim membership in a body politic that was dramatically changing its shape. By turns, the importance of loyalty also turned expectations of what loyalty ought to win people into something concrete and profound. And in the South, where the war and constitutional amendments had together set the right of white people to own black people completely on its head, the language of loyalty and rights to property of all sorts quickly became fused. As an act of political alchemy, African Americans attempted to turn their loyalty into hard currency. Freedpeople learned to make use of their new relationship with the federal state, leveraging their loyalty in return for federal protection and civic rights. Claiming their loyalty to the Union as both more profound and all the more trustworthy when compared with that of former Confederates, African Americans deployed the politics of loyalty in a bid for citizenship, through the possessions they believed were rightfully theirs.[4]

Conflicts over loyalty and property laid bare two unexplained aspects of Reconstruction history. While scholars have made much of the efforts by the federal government to craft a meaningful peace in the former slave South, this work has, with some justification, focused on what was lacking in the federal response.[5] But if we focus not on what Washington failed to do in this period and instead on what Mississippians hoped Washington would do in the months that followed Confederate surrender, a picture emerges of a rural people whose demands for property became the basis of their relationship with the federal government. Reinforcing their wartime loyalty with postwar claims that freedpeople were the political key to stability and Unionism in a region where the allegiance of whites was anything but certain, African Americans pushed loyalty to its obvious conclusion. In so doing, they took active part in sketching the most radical possibilities of what could be in the postemancipation United States.

When the relationship between loyalty and citizenship was pushed to its limit, however, the struggle over property in Reconstruction Mississippi also brought about a slow diminution of the very thing in which so many African Americans had placed so much hope for change. If wartime loyalty and the obligations of national citizenship cracked open the door for African Americans to be counted as part of the body politic, claims of loyalty also began to slowly lose their salience as Americans all over the country stepped back from more dramatic change. As quickly as loyalty and citizenship had become fused, they slowly began to separate once more, in Congress, in popular culture, and in the contests over land, labor, and local power on which the success of freedpeople and the project of American emancipation depended.

ISAAC SHOEMAKER WAS A WITNESS to revolution in wartime Mississippi. Shoemaker was the northern lessee of a plantation five miles outside Vicksburg, and his diary contains a variety of impressions about emancipation. He wrote of black children who attended school, freedpeople who received religious instruction from missionaries, and former slaves who signed portentous contracts to work on abandoned plantations. For Shoemaker, all of these events were symptoms of the slaveholding South turning a page. But his shock at the scene he saw in March 1864 as he watched hundreds of freedpeople filing into Vicksburg spoke to the jarring depth of change. Shoemaker saw freedpeople, under armed escort, traveling in carriages and hacks loaded with a variety of goods and driven by mules and teams of oxen, the "remnants of Massa's property . . . All loaded with old Men, Women and Children of all ages." To Shoemaker, the hundreds of freedpeople who made their way into Vicksburg, their clothes covered in turnpike dust, were a forlorn sight. To freedpeople, however, the scene would have looked far different. Cut loose from slavery, African Americans did face an uncertain future. Many would find themselves mustered into U.S. regiments or working on plantations behind American lines, as they had done before the war started. But many did have those possessions that they took to be theirs, and in time, freedpeople would lay the groundwork to claim much more. It was the property in their hands, on their backs, or in their horse wagons—not to mention the children they carried or who marched with them into Vicksburg—that symbolized their freedom, as much as the distance that now separated them from the plantations they had called home.[6]

It is perhaps obvious to suggest that a war of emancipation made rights to property both deeply contentious and political. Too often, though, the point gets overlooked. Inasmuch as the destruction of slavery became one of the war's principal outcomes, emancipation was born of the belief that according to the laws of war, the demands of armies trumped private claims to property, particularly if it was coveted by an armed force in enemy territory. The slow liquidation of slave property knocked the legs out from under not only the plantation system but the very right to property itself. The ownership of people had been the hub around which southern society had revolved, and without it, all was thrown up in the air. As a result, property rights in Mississippi had undergone a thorough revolution from the moment the war began, and that revolution only intensified by the conflict's end. By the time large swathes of the state lay occupied by American forces, property or the lack of it became the common experience that united many if not most Mississippians by the end of the war. The general want of possessions, after armies had descended on counties like a plague, sharpened the criticism individuals leveled against their governments. After a Federal raid in northern Mississippi left a majority of whites without the means to survive an oncoming winter, citizens pressed the beleaguered state government not only for supplies but for answers. "Many being now, without even bedding, blankets or provisions of any kind," a colonel in the state militia warned in September 1864, loyal Confederates might be forced to trade with the enemy unless cotton could be freed up to pay for supplies.[7]

While the demands of the Union and the Confederacy to property would expand quickly and continue to grow in intensity by the war's final years, the one constant that ran through the conflict was the fusion of personal loyalty with the right to possessions. By the winter of 1865, officials like T. L. Bowers stated that which had become established fact all over the occupied South. Loyal individuals, including those who had been Confederate citizens but who now availed themselves of the benefits of Union amnesty, "should be permitted the same privileges in the rental of their property as if they resided in the Loyal States of the North." For those whose loyalty was suspect or who held out the hope of a Confederate resurgence, all bets were off. The property of disloyal persons "should be taken possession of and used or rented to the highest bidder for the benefit of Government." As the war ended and ideas about amnesty and loyalty became the hardened heart of Union Reconstruction policy, African Americans needed no primer in politics or the laws of occupation to understand what was in the offing. As loyalty had become currency in the former Confederacy, freedpeople could use their allegiance to the Union as leverage, to secure free property of all sorts from their former owners.[8]

The revolutionary implications of what the Civil War set in motion were underscored by the broader Atlantic history of emancipation that white and black southerners knew only too well. For slaveholders, the obvious corollary to what masters hoped was happening in the occupied South lay in their understanding of British emancipation three decades before. There, slaveholders had been compensated for their loss of property, a parliamentary decision that blunted the sharper, more radical possibilities of what emancipation could have wrought on Caribbean sugar islands. In the British case, emancipation had not come as a result of war, nullifying the possibility that former slaves could claim rights to property on the strength of their allegiance to warring parties. All the same, the persistent rumor that former slaveholders could pry concessions from Congress for their lost human property persisted well into 1865. By August of that year, Mississippi governor William Sharkey received a letter from North Carolina legislator Kenneth Rayner that suggested some form of coordinated strategy among newly constituted state governments in the South. Compensation could be secured less as a demand and more out of a sense of "justice, generosity, magnanimity, humanity, on the part of a victorious conqueror." Carl Schurz reported to Congress in December that in a variety of newspapers and in conversations he had with planters, former slaveholders were still angling for some form of recompense for emancipation.[9] Writing as Schurz was, as sketchy reports of the 1865 Morant Bay rebellion made their way from Jamaica and into American newspapers, the perils of a British emancipation that many white southerners had seen as moderate and controlled only added to the worries and the demands of former masters all over the South.[10]

For African Americans, the same history of Atlantic emancipation provided an inexorable story of freedom. The compelling example of revolution in Haiti had, for a half-century, provided slaves and abolitionists of every stripe with an inspiring example of what could come from a revolutionary war. No half-measures lay in that story, even if the decade's long civil war that followed revolution on that island would have given the keen observer pause for thought. Slaves attached their efforts to what an earlier generation had accomplished in Haiti. They formed regiments in the name of Toussaint L'Ouverture, looked to the history of that revolution as a moment when former slaves joined together to govern themselves, and saw in Haitian independence a republic that protected all slaves from bondage, no matter where they resided. If anything, what freedpeople saw as distinguishing them from their Haitian forebears was that while revolution on that island resulted in a weak state, without the means or the friendship of foreign governments to protect them, African Americans had cast their lot with an American nation-state of immense power. It was before that state that freedpeople had laid their hopes for the future, and armed with the argument that their loyalty should mean something, in a region of the United States where white loyalty was thin on the ground, African Americans pressed their claims for a freedom that included the land and possessions of their former owners.[11]

Emancipation in Mississippi had all but obliterated the most basic tenets of common property law. By May 1865, an official from the American adjutant general's office directed what was left of the state government of Mississippi to secure records of land titles, suggesting that these documents were anything but secure. Protecting something as basic as deeds to land was not the only concern of American officials. A superintendent of a contraband camp near the small town of Washington, near Natchez, wrote a rushed letter to his superiors asking about what to do with freedpeople who not only were making their way to his camp but were under the impression that "thear is Houses and Provisions hear for all who may come." By the end of July, Samuel Thomas, superintendent of the Freedmen's Bureau in the state, reflected that Mississippi had descended into perfect anarchy. Thomas stated that in many parts of the state, "neither civil nor military law exists. The state of all classes, white and black, has been, and is, deplorable." While he held out the hope that a lasting order could be established, Thomas made it clear that former slaveholders were determined to thwart emancipation at every turn. "Nothing will convert them till they see they can not stop the progress of events and that with them, or without them the negro will be free." It was a sign of just how much ideas about loyalty had saturated thinking among American officials that Thomas hoped that in addition to caring for themselves and their families as independent laborers, freedpeople might also become "an element of strength to the Government."[12]

In the gap created by the collapse of slavery and an inchoate free labor order, African Americans and their former owners laid claim to land and possessions as part of a struggle for resources that revolved around their allegiance. Federal policy laid out by Andrew Johnson set many of the terms of this battle, but the wartime experiences of both groups forced this particular conflict into uncharted territory. For their part, freedpeople pressed their case for the right not simply to be counted as free or to labor for a wage but to claim property as well. In contrast, white southerners made every effort to buttress their claims to land with professions of loyalty, with the hope that their previous status as citizens of the United States gave them the upper hand. What the efforts of both groups suggest is a multifaceted conflict over property that began during the war and intensified as both emancipation and loyalty became the twinned projects of the federal state. And in their attempts to anticipate or divine what the federal state might do in the midst of emancipation, both white and black Mississippians looked to bend new ideas about loyalty and citizenship to suit them.

Much like the letters and petitions that white southerners filed with the federal government to reclaim their rights as citizens, pleas for the return of property ownership leaned heavily on a painful history of divided allegiance. The task before white petitioners who sought the reclamation of property was to prove not only their loyalty but that they had not abandoned their homes or their possessions. What complicated this task was that abandoning property damaged or all but negated a pledge of allegiance to the federal state, no matter how earnest the pledge may have been. And as so much of Mississippi was a divided state during the war, claiming property and citizenship as a loyal American became a difficult task. This was certainly the case for white southerners like Alex P. McMillan. McMillan was a Natchez merchant who had owned a home in town that had been used by the American officers a few months after the city had been taken in the summer of 1863. In his petition to reclaim his property, McMillan made it clear that his loyalties and business interests had predisposed him to maintain his loyalty to the United States. What was at issue in his claim was that, in early 1864, he and his family left their Natchez home and retired to a plantation outside the city, owned by his wife. This decision, along with testimony from an enemy that he had left the city to join the Confederate Army, was enough to force McMillan to rhetorically prostrate himself before federal officials. Reaching for whatever shred of evidence he could to prove his loyalty in spite of his having abandoned his property, McMillan claimed that he had never abetted the Confederacy and had willfully broken Confederate law by paying his northern creditors in full during the war. In the organization of his claim, McMillan took no chances. He made sure to receive the endorsement of Mississippi governor William Sharkey as well as the favorable backing of bureau officials.[13]

If some petitioners, like Alex McMillan, accepted the complexities of loyalty and property abandonment, others confronted the problem more directly. One letter writer pressed Samuel Thomas for a clarification of what constituted abandoned land by suggesting that, given the circumstances in Mississippi in which homes had been seized and occupied by the U.S. Army, property owners had not necessarily abandoned their homes and land so much as their property had been seized. "The owners did not abandon, but were kept out of their property by orders which they could not refuse to obey." To abandon land implied a voluntary decision, much like McMillan's decision to leave Natchez. But in the main, land had been deemed abandoned by owners as the result of armed coercion rather than volition. As in most actions undertaken by an occupying nation-state, legal precedent and military regulations rarely squared all the complexities of life in a war zone. When druggist Morris Emanuel filed his application for the return of his Vicksburg home and business—which he had abandoned when he and his family evacuated Vicksburg in anticipation of a Union siege—the problems of claiming property while justifying difficult wartime decisions were rendered in sharp relief. There was nothing left of Emanuel's home or drugstore. Both had been reduced to rubble by the U.S. bombardment of the city. Leaving the city was, at least on the surface, a sound decision. Yet abandoning his property and the city behind placed him on the wrong side of the federal government. In the changed circumstances brought about by the federal state's fusion of loyalty and property, Emanuel's abandonment of his home made his case anything but straightforward. Though he took the oath to the United States at the first opportunity and professed that his "allegiance and loyalty, are as strong to the U.S. Government now, as they were before the war," Emanuel's actions still required several trips to bureau offices and a long, tortured letter detailing all of the U.S. officers who had trusted both him and his allegiances in the past. Regardless of the complexities, the abandonment of property was deemed a declaration of disloyalty, and it fell to petitioners like Emanuel to surmount this obstacle if they were to reclaim what had been theirs.[14]

The trouble that white Mississippians faced in claiming their property was compounded by the actions of federal officials. Reports that made their way up the chain of command at the Freedmen's Bureau testified to the ad hoc way in which loyalty was trusted in the heat of the moment. Some officials laid punitive measures before whites in response to the efforts made by former slaveholders to keep African Americans in servitude. Upon hearing that white landowners were resurrecting the practice of hiring out black workers and pocketing the proceeds in the summer of 1865, Stuart Eldridge, a high-ranking bureau official, called for a subordinate to determine the value of the transaction and force whites to pay freedpeople a wage for their labor, "by seizure of property if necessary." By the summer of 1865, cotton merchants took great interest in an illegal black market in cotton that had grown to become a clear threat to the authority of the Treasury Department in the Mississippi Valley. It did not escape the notice of southern whites that this cotton was making its way to market with the help, at least in part, of American officials who were out to make a personal profit. While not all bureau officials were as forthright about their intentions, many used their authority to secure property for freedpeople whenever the opportunity arose. One official, who wrote to his superiors about what to do with a former Confederate hospital located near Lauderdale Springs, offered a telling summation of his own view on the subject. Given that the property had been owned by the Confederate government, it was fitting justice "that these buildings should be appropriated for the benefit of that class of persons in the South that have been and are truly loyal to the Government." It was hardly surprising, then, that freedpeople glimpsed opportunities to claim property of their own. The war had created an environment in Mississippi where federal officials were left with the power to make all kinds of decisions about who ought to claim possessions. Often as not, wartime loyalty determined individual cases.[15]

The personal grudges of bureau officials against whites also resulted in a capricious application of federal power. W. R. Gilreath was a Natchez planter who had the misfortune to cross a high-ranking U.S. brigadier general. Whether warranted or not, the officer directed that a schoolhouse for African American children be built on Gilreath's land. In his letter, Gilreath objected not to the idea of a schoolhouse for freed black children but to the fact that his land had been singled out for divestment, despite his long-standing loyalty to the federal government. Gilreath pleaded for reprieve by underscoring his abiding Unionism: "Had your Petitioner been disloyal or Committed any act to Justify the Seizure of this property, I would not Complain." Given the circumstances, Gilreath faced an uphill struggle. As representatives of the state, Union officers possessed the power to define loyalty, determine what it would win white southerners, and by turns, decide whose loyalty could be trusted. With a schoolhouse on his land, Gilreath and his family were in the line of fire. A symbol of black freedom on his property would advertise his Unionism, toward which disgruntled former Confederates could direct their anger.[16]

By August 1865, Samuel Thomas, in a widely published circular, attempted to lay down some broad principles for both white and black Mississippians. Coming as it did as the reconstituted state legislature was meeting to push back at the introduction of free labor in the state, the document was unequivocal. Thomas argued that emancipation was now a fact of life in the state and federal representatives in Mississippi were determined to maintain this new status quo. Echoing the free labor rhetoric that had become established policy, he called on landowners and workers to work together. Sharing as they did a common interest, Thomas claimed that any community of whites that supposed "itself capable of managing its own government" ought to see the realities of free labor as plain fact. In the middle of his circular, Thomas addressed the question of African American claims to property. The possessions of former slaves, declared Thomas, were to "be recognized and respected by all" when legitimately acquired. What Thomas could not say, however, was that by the late summer of 1865, the Freedmen's Bureau was already fielding pointed letters and bold petitions from blacks and whites alike, which suggested that freedpeople were beginning to press their claims to property with more force. In a state where legitimately acquired property was determined at least in part by the loyalty of its owner, African Americans made it clear in word and deed that they had no intention of quietly accepting the professions of loyalty mouthed by their former masters.[17]

Regarding black petitions for property, the Freedmen's Bureau was a reluctant ally. Though bureau officials made decisions that countermanded the position of the federal government, the official line was that property rights were to be respected. Despite the fact that the bureau maintained jurisdiction over abandoned lands in Mississippi that amounted to more than 43,000 acres, Samuel Thomas believed that cementing emancipation and bringing free labor to the state was more than enough for his office to wrestle with.[18] According to Thomas, conflicts over property, let alone its distribution, fell well outside his remit. In a letter to the head of the Freedmen's Bureau in September, Thomas made it clear that while tremendous pressure was being placed on his office to adjudicate claims to property, it would "require a hero to execute it, and a military force to protect" the claims of freedpeople to any land the bureau might see fit to divest from white hands. With only fifty-eight bureau officials scattered across the state, the task of maintaining a grip over contracts was daunting enough. Moreover, white and black Mississippians alike seemed to believe that Thomas and his associates possessed the power "to return every house and every foot of land." To whites, Thomas made it plain that an honest reckoning with their allegiances to the Confederacy and a show of present and future loyalty to the United States was required before the bureau and the government it represented would act. Professions of loyalty by blacks, not to mention their claims to property, took a different shape and revealed a broader set of concerns.[19]

African American pledges were not as readily documented in letters and petitions. Rather than tortured written pleas for pardons, the professions of freedpeople were often more public and articulated at the point of conflict between laborers and landowners or in conflicts with white law enforcement. Like white pledges and pleas, black efforts centered on expectations, but what distinguished them was what black communities understood their loyalty to the federal state to entail. Freedpeople saw the war and its aftermath as a turning point of profound importance. But African Americans also understood the day of jubilee as just one part of a relationship between their community and the state that had a hand in securing their freedom. It was a state whose soldiers freedpeople could see but whose intentions were not always clear. Black pledges of allegiance took shape in an environment of contest and violence and without the rights and privileges of citizenship. Indeed, African Americans in Mississippi placed their trust in a Union that did not always serve their interests. What lay at the core of the pledges of freedpeople was the articulation of a particular kind of relationship between themselves and the Union: a state that possessed the power to act in their interest, a state that protected their hard-won gains in emancipation, and a state that, freedpeople hoped, possessed the knowledge of how important African Americans would be to securing the former Confederacy as a part of the republic again. In the months that followed the war, freedpeople conjured an imagined state that they believed would act as a bulwark to protect fledgling free black communities, even if that state did not always meet their expectations. Ultimately, the basic idea that loyalty in war would bring protection and preferential access to federal authority formed the core of black pledges and pleas during Reconstruction. It would also become the idea around which black definitions of citizenship would revolve.

The pledges of loyalty that freedpeople made as part of their claims to property also took on an added importance, given that so many African Americans sought not only a claim to possessions but the protection of their families. For many freedpeople, the opportunities to prove their loyalty came about as part of their efforts as parents to claim children as their own. When a Works Progress Administration interviewer asked Anna Baker in the 1930s about what she remembered of her moment of freedom, the former Monroe County slave recounted a scene involving her former master, a mother she did not know, and the papers her mother received from a Union state official. "After de war was over my ma got some papers from de Progro Marshall and come to de place and tell de marster she wants her children," remembered Baker. When Baker's master claimed that her mother could have all of her children except Anna, Baker's mother immediately sought out federal officials for more documents to prove her claim to her daughter. Baker remembered that her initial reaction to seeing her mother for the first time was one of trepidation. "She came out of de house to get us and at fust I was scared of her case I didden know who she was," Baker recounted. "But she put me in her lap and loved me and I knowed den I love her too."[20]

Baker's remembrances were recounted in similar scenes all over the South in the months following the war. Together they make up some of the most heart-rending stories of Reconstruction, as African Americans attempted to reconstitute families torn to pieces by slavery and the slave trade. Typically, historians have interpreted these stories as part of the emancipation process, as former slaves attempted to achieve some measure of social stability within their communities and families. For mothers and fathers, however, preventing their children from remaining the property of whites was not just a claim to liberty. It was also a battle over property rights in people. The specter of re-enslavement and the threats made to the sanctity of freed families were constant, as white Mississippians attempted to find new ways to maintain control over their former human possessions. Moreover, Union policies intended to jump-start the southern cotton economy placed added strain on an already tenuous black freedom. As one historian has remarked, emancipation brought about a "revolution in property." But in the months after the war, the issue of whether whites in the postemancipation South would continue to count people as property remained an open question.[21]

The legal basis for the continued enslavement of black children was created from a bundle of policy directives that dealt with the wartime care of African American women and children. By the middle stages of the war, the U.S. Army and charity organizations like the American Missionary Association had taken on a duty of care to thousands of freedpeople in camps along the Mississippi River and in the conquered northern portion of the state. It was a system that fell under the aegis of the Freedmen's Bureau, but at the war's end, local courts and local law enforcement allowed apprenticeship as part of an effort to keep black families bound to their former owners. By the end of 1865, the apprenticeship of young freedpeople amounted to little more than bondage with a contract.[22]

For freedpeople, the apprenticeship of children was a battle in which state and federal policies were arrayed against them. As early as the summer of 1865, Freedmen's Bureau officials detected a will among former slaveholders to create "a system of apprenticeship, or some manner of involuntary servitude" to replace slavery. Given this broad determination, it was hardly an accident that at the heart of the state legislature's Black Code, passed in late November, was an apprentice law. The law gave incredible latitude to both local courts and law enforcement to bind minors who were either orphans or children "whose parent or parents have not the means or who refuse to provide for" them. So long as there was no clear case of cruel mistreatment, which was never fully defined, the language and effect of the law made it plain that the masters or mistresses of apprentices could expect a relationship akin to slavery for their terms of service.[23] Moreover, while the Freedmen's Bureau worked to curtail the more egregious forms of enslavement that apprentice laws allowed, many officials struggled to see the connection between black property claims and claims to freed children.[24] In a single letter, John L. Critchfield expressed alarm at armed squads of whites who searched the homes of freedpeople for arms while at the same time updating superiors on the progress of indenturing orphaned children. "I am satisified," wrote Critchfield, "that this will save considerable suffering" among African American communities.[25] Among the freed children that Critchfield apprenticed was six-year-old Rosanna Charles. According to her apprenticeship papers, the young girl from Canton had "voluntarily expressed a willingness to live and be bound" to a white family until her eighteenth birthday. While the indenture claimed that she was to be treated fairly—educated and schooled in "the art to be a house servant"—the apprenticeship was predicated not only on a young girl understanding the finer points of law but also on her mother's inability to care for her.[26]

Even among bureau officials with more self-awareness than Critchfield, apprenticeship presented what many saw as the clearest threat to emancipation. It also proved to be one of the biggest challenges African Americans faced as they attempted to turn ideas about loyal citizenship into practice. Freedmen's Bureau officials received complaints from African Americans attesting to the outright enslavement of their children who were bonded into labor without cause. One subassistant commissioner revealed that by "Binding out children . . . in direct opposition to the wishes of either Parent or Child," local judges all over his district were apprenticing children, removing them from families who easily satisfied the basic requirements of the child's welfare. White landowners were also not above using black children as pawns to compel their parents to work under whatever conditions they deemed appropriate. Jane Fitzgerald and "Mary" had both been slaves to a man named Archie Fitzgerald, who offered contracts to both women to work in his home at the beginning of 1866. When the women refused to sign, Fitzgerald claimed rights over Jane's and Mary's children until they reached the age of twenty-one. When the freed women refused to relent, Fitzgerald made quick use of local law enforcement to compel them to continue in his employ. Both Mary and Jane were clapped in prison, with their former slaveholder threatening to sell them both to the highest bidder. When they were released and Jane found work with another landowner, Fitzgerald refused to relinquish control over her children.[27]

Faced with a determined effort on the part of their former owners to legislate their children back into slavery, freedpeople had few weapons at their disposal. It was a measure of the challenge arrayed against African Americans that while the Constitution provided some broad protections for citizens and their rights to property, the more practical, more specific provisions that ensured the safety of property lay with local and state government. This mismatch—between the state that freedpeople appealed to and those parts of the federal system where real power over property lay—would be addressed by African Americans as they made a bolder attempt to lay claim to the political process. In the interim, however, black communities found that their loyalty was often a blunt instrument.

Since government power worked against African Americans, their claims to children or possessions they believed to be rightfully theirs developed in a politically charged atmosphere. If even a fraction of the cases of larceny and petit larceny that were brought against African Americans in late 1865 and early 1866 stood on solid evidence, many freedpeople took every opportunity to claim property by any means necessary. In places like Warren County and the city of Vicksburg, property crime doubled in the four years after the end of the war.[28] Moreover, cases that found their way to county or circuit courts often revolved around property in dispute. James W. Davis, a Vicksburg solicitor, noted that many African Americans had taken property in the honest belief that they could do so "under the rigid rules of evidence," and that persons were being charged with having property in their possession merely "claimed by the owner as stolen."[29]

County courts all over the state also extracted harsh penalties on freedpeople found guilty of stealing property, well in excess of precedent. The court in Noxubee County, in the state's eastern black prairie, dealt with several cases involving freedpeople charged with property crimes. Lewis Connor pleaded not guilty to the charge of larceny, but as a result of his trial, he was sentenced to three years' hard labor. Eliza Davis was sentenced to five years' hard labor after she pleaded guilty to larceny and burglary. Peter Shaw received a six-month prison sentence for larceny. After Shaw's release, the court ordered that he pay the costs incurred by the county for both his trial and imprisonment.[30] Courts also dealt with cases that made it plain that African Americans were still being counted as property in disputes between whites, even after the war. In a dispute over the refusal to pay the value of a slave who had been sold before the war, the court in the northern county of Pontotoc brought former slave-traders to testify as expert witnesses in 1867 to verify how much the freed slave would have fetched in the open market. In 1869, a case involving two widows in the Delta county of Bolivar whose husbands had agreed to a sale of slaves worth $50,000 was brought before the court for failure to fulfill the contract. Melinda Williams had sold the slaves in question and pocketed the proceeds without paying Julia Claggett for the human property. While Williams prevailed upon the court for mercy, claiming that she hadn't the money to pay, the court ruled that all her lands were forfeit and were to be sold at public auction. Taken together, the machinations of county law throughout the state made it clear to freedpeople that not only was the state government ready to stand against any attempts made by African Americans to claim property, but county courts stood equally ready to dispense harsh justice on freedpeople, whom many judges still counted as property in law.[31]

Union officials worried at length about these abuses taking place throughout the state. Threats to the children of freedpeople struck a chord with northern audiences reared on affective antislavery literature and harrowing tales of families torn apart. State and local governments, not to mention local courts that defended the right of whites to treat blacks as property, made a mockery of emancipation itself. Attending these moral concerns were political ones as well. By the end of 1865, it had become clear to many Republicans that the success of Reconstruction depended upon protecting the rights of freedpeople. The problem reached a critical point as rumors of both black insurrection and the widespread seizure of property took shape in the summer and fall of 1865. Initial reports described armed bands of freedpeople acting in localities independent of one another. By the end of that year, talk of blacks operating in concert and with the help of the Union state across Mississippi spread throughout the region.

What lay at the heart of the white rumors of black actions (real or imagined) were not only fears of an outright war over property rights. In truth, struggles over property had been raging for several years. Rather, what signaled a turning point was the frustration among freedpeople that loyalty to the Union had not brought about a stable claim to either their families or citizenship. When mixed with whites' worries about the very idea of black Unionism, pitched battles over property took on a deeper and more ominous meaning by late 1865. As early as October, letters sent to officials suggested that unless black troops were removed from the state, they would set a "universal Massacre" in motion that would turn "this fair land into another Haiti," while other reports from Freedmen's Bureau field offices recounted stories of armed whites seizing blacks' property with impunity. Newspapers also fanned the flames. An article in the *Natchez Daily Courier* in October dismissed the talk of property seizure as idle and vicious rumor, but the paper printed the accounts from other reports all the same. Southern newspapers began to carry these rumors as fact, whipping whites into a frenzy about the prospect of a potentially violent overthrow of the status quo.[32]

Though officials in the Freedmen's Bureau attempted to correct it, the logic at the heart of what would become known as the Christmas Day insurrection scare of 1865 was the determination of freedpeople that their loyalty should guide the division of southern property.[33] "The freedmen are generally unwilling to enter into any contract that extends longer than Christmas," wrote R. S. Donaldson to his superiors, "as some of them have the erroneous idea that their former master's lands and stock are to be divided among them at that time. I have used every available means in my power to disabuse their minds of this idea, and at the places where I have been able to send agents of the Bureau, I think that they have given up the false hope that they had at one time of having property given to them by the Government."[34]

By the end of October, letters from around the state reported the broad expectations of freedpeople that the redistribution of land was just around the corner. Marion Shields, a Noxubee County planter, wrote a letter to President Andrew Johnson detailing the rumors among blacks in his county who hoped that the federal government would reward its loyal constituency with property, homes, mules, and horses. "They even believe that they will own all & we will have to emigrate else where. The most of them will not work. They Seem to be entirely out of their element . . . waiting [for] their supposed joyful day of Christmas, when they will be blessed with the fat of the land. They seem to think all will come by & from you they will not believ any thing else." Governor Sharkey felt compelled to write a letter that month asking the Freedmen's Bureau to send agents around the state to make sure freedpeople understood that freedom did not entail the property of former owners. In his letter, Sharkey painted a grim picture of what would happen if the federal government did not act. "It is very certain that the negroes are expecting a distribution of property this winter," wrote Sharkey, "and it is also certain that we have many reasons to believe that a general revolt is contemplated unless the property is divided. . . . Most of the Negroes in the country have arms, procured from soldiers or officers, which it is supposed they are producing for the purpose of carrying out their diabolical scheme."[35]

Sharkey need not have worried about a coming battle between white landowners and black laborers. In reality, the fear of insurrection created opportunities for state and local governments to hammer black communities and consolidate their control over freedpeople. The confiscation of weapons and provisions from the homes of freedpeople indicated not only that Reconstruction would not bring about the dramatic division of land but also that with the use of force it would be black, not white, property that was under threat. What these attacks amounted to was not just an attempt to diminish the claims of freedpeople to defend themselves. They were a political statement by whites who intended to show freedpeople just what their loyalty to the Union amounted to. Local governments and local law enforcement, disregarding black rights to property, administered a stinging rebuke of the federal state in the Reconstruction South. They showed what whites could do, regardless of federal law, and freedpeople were made to appreciate the limits of their loyalty.[36]

Yet the seizure of property only substantiated something that had been merely inchoate a few months before. By the end of 1865, the ownership of property had become symbolic of a relationship to the Union state. It was a relationship that did not treat former slaves and former Confederates on equal terms. Whites had to prove their loyalty. African Americans did not. This fact would create problems for freedpeople. Even before the state government called for the raising of white militia companies to protect communities throughout the region, freedmen expressed pessimism about the future for African Americans in Mississippi. "The more intelligent freedmen . . . seemed to be very much discouraged indeed at their future prospects in this state, and some of them having means were preparing to emigrate to some more favored locality where they would be protected in their rights of person and property." According to many whites in the state, the sentiment was an accurate reflection of what lay ahead.[37]

By January 1866, testimony in a complaint made by a Pike County freedman about his being beaten by a gang of whites for his two horses clarified the new parameters of loyalty and property. When the freedman presented a bill of sale for the horses, the self-styled lieutenant of the armed band informed him that "Negroes were not allowed any property larger than a Chicken." The bureau official who issued a report about the occurrence claimed that most of the witnesses to the event perjured themselves rather than give testimony against the assailants. "All or nearly all, have subscribed to the Amnesty Oath, and have sworn to refrain from the very acts, they are performing . . . while at the same time it should be remembered that this same . . . country is continually reporting negro insurrections being on foot, a perfect 'Hot-bed' for originating insurrection canards."[38]

Attacks by whites may have dampened the aggressiveness of freedpeople in claiming property, but they also dared federal officials to act. Reports of unreconstructed former Confederates vying for control of local and state government and an intensifying battle between President Johnson and the Republican Congress over the scope of Reconstruction itself left little doubt in the minds of legislators in Washington that Mississippi's future in the Union would depend upon the continued loyalty of former slaves. The relationship between state and constituency was anything but perfect. Radical Republicans believed that dependent slaves, lacking the most rudimentary tools necessary to becoming good citizens, would have to learn the value of frugality, respectability, and rugged independence. Yet inasmuch as the presumption of black loyalty reflected white racial assumptions about the fitness of African Americans to become citizens in good standing, loyalty to the state remained the best weapon in the arsenal of freedpeople. A political relationship between African Americans and the Union state, which had developed during the war, now opened the door to freedpeople to create their own political structures, vie for their own place in state and local government, and make a bid for citizenship in a postwar United States as among the most loyal Americans.

At the first session of the Fortieth Congress, held in the spring of 1867, Thaddeus Stevens presented a bill on the floor of the Senate proposing changes to the Confiscation Act of 1862 that placed African American loyalty front and center. The bill, titled Claims to Loyalists for Damages, stipulated that as punishment for the disloyal who had cast their lot with the Confederacy, all public lands "belonging to the ten States that formed the government of the so-called 'confederate states of America' shall be forfeited by said States and become forthwith vested in the United States." The land would be distributed to freedpeople in much the same way that General Sherman had allotted Low Country Georgia land to former slaves in the war's final months: forty acres to each male or widowed female head of the household. "The punishment of traitors has been wholly ignored by a treacherous Executive and by a sluggish Congress," declared Stevens, and a bill intended to place loyal African Americans on a social and economic footing as independent producers would do more than any other measure to ensure the stability of a postwar South. "Nothing is so likely to make a man a good citizen," argued Stevens, "as to make him a freeholder." Ultimately, Stevens's bill would never become law. The use of loyalty as a weapon to beat white southerners into submission proved too aggressive, too unsparing for congressmen who did not want to push past public opinion on such bold action. All the same, it is telling that the bill's language echoed the aspirations of freedpeople. By 1867, "loyalty" in a state like Mississippi had become synonymous with freedpeople and the small but significant pockets of white Unionists who made a lie of unified white opposition to Radical Reconstruction. Black political allegiance and black loyalty would form the skeleton of a postwar political culture of former slaves turned freeholders, creating a political bulwark to the disloyalty of former Confederates who would be left on the periphery.[39]

EVEN IF EVENTS AT THE CLOSE OF 1865 foreclosed some of the more radical possibilities of black loyalty to the Union, few white Mississippians could ignore the continued problems that they faced. "There is a word that we never heard or saw used, in connection with American politics or patriotism, until this late war of the 'so-called' Rebellion," argued an editorial in the *Panola Star* in the spring of 1866. "But now it is the standard word of the republic. It is used to measure the relation of every man to the United States Government." The word in question was "loyalty," and while the editorial fumed that it belonged in wartime courts-martial and military commissions, it had no place in the American nation: "It is only the measure of our degradation and subserviency to false ideas and false standards. Its true and legitimate meaning is fidelity to prince or sovereign." Since "loyalty" was cast as an antiquated term emptied of meaning in a country that claimed to be modern, white southerners made the case with increasing ferocity that in a nation constituted by, of, and for its people, what institution was "there in a Republican Constitutional Government to be loyal to?"[40]

The age-old problem of Americans seeing their nation-state with any clarity notwithstanding, what the discussion of loyalty among whites in Mississippi missed was that despite their early bid for dominance over their former slaves in the first months of Reconstruction, former Confederates now faced the national government as outsiders. Particularly as Congress wrested control of Reconstruction policy from Andrew Johnson and trained the force of the national government on the South, white Mississippians looked for any opportunity to make sense of their newly marginal place in the republic. A report from Jones County, gleefully taken up in a Vicksburg newspaper, recounted that during the war, many white citizens of Jones had counted themselves as the most radical dissenters in the Confederacy, "a refuge of deserters." Now, however, that allegiance to the Union mattered above all, and where loyalty "now means, to let negroes do any sort of devilment without retribution in kind," whites in the county had dealt with a recalcitrant freedman in 1868 by taking matters into their own hands and reportedly skinning him alive. Making light of a dark act of violence might have given readers the quiet satisfaction that their loyalty to a failed Confederate nation had been warranted. What it did not do was foment anything more than quiet grumbling about a broader state of affairs over which white Mississippians had little control. With African Americans registering to vote in droves by the end of 1867, and with constitutional protections of black rights in the offing, emancipation, it seemed, had set in train an unprecedented political revolution.[41]

Yet even if the battle over property and loyalty exposed the limits of the political imagination at the heart of Reconstruction, the fusion of these two ideas persisted all the same. In the 1870s, as the federal government sought to settle issues of property claimed during the war, the Southern Claims Commission once again made loyalty a key hurdle that claimants had to surmount if they were to receive compensation. Nearly all of the eighty questions that claimants were required to answer as part of their application revolved around loyalty: the decisions or sympathies of individuals before, during, and after the war; the aid offered to the Confederacy; and the support provided to the Union. Moreover, even among claims that were approved by the commission, the old problems of loyalty among former Confederates persisted. John W. Austin received $257 for lost property seized by the Union, though he sought much more. While he emphasized his Unionism throughout his application, he could not hide the fact that two of his sons had served in the Confederate Army. William Lewis filed a claim for three mules and horses seized by the Union in 1864 from his now-deceased father. While his father's Unionist credentials were without blemish, the same could not be said of William Lewis or his family. In the end, Lewis was awarded only half of his claim, as the allegiances of his mother and siblings to the Union were found wanting. Even though John Kirk's home in Bolivar County had been threatened by the U.S. Army and occupied as early as 1863, his claim for more than $10,000 in lost property was denied, not because he did not profess what the commission took to be genuine Unionist sympathies during the war. Rather, the fact that Kirk was forced to live in a war zone "between the two armies" had "obliged him at times to play neutral." For his decision to sit on the fence rather than pick the winning side, Kirk received only $1,663.34.[42]

In sharp contrast, African Americans who made claims to the Southern Claims Commission found federal officials more sympathetic to their cause. As they had done a decade before, African Americans showed a keen awareness of the politics of loyalty and an equally keen understanding of what loyalty could secure them. Lorenzo Grant, a carriage maker and blacksmith who resided in Pontotoc County, secured a claim for horses, corn, hogs, flour, and bacon taken by Union troops in 1863. When he had been a slave, Grant had hired out his time and had accumulated property of his own. He had also maintained friendly relations with his master, D. B. Grant, who resided in Lorenzo's home in the weeks before his death in 1876. During the war, when Lorenzo Grant pressed for compensation to his property, he had been harassed by American troops. He had been stripped of his clothing by enlisted men before an officer had stopped them. He left undoubtedly enraged, believing that "no one but myself" had any interest in his claim. Perhaps because of his ill treatment, when Grant was asked about his wartime sympathies, he responded, "I done but little for the Union cause, short some of the horses of the soldiers, belonging to the Union Army." Aware, perhaps, of his ambivalent feelings and testimony, Grant made sure that at his commission hearing, he came armed with witnesses. One of them, Mississippi state senator J. A. McNeil, testified that African Americans like Grant "were all loyal to the Union case, and evinced so far as they dared to. No loyal man was allowed to express his sentiments during the rebellion."[43]

Other freedpeople needed no such support. When former slave and Vicksburg hack driver Henry Banks was asked about his sympathies, he made it clear that from the outset, his loyalties were with the Union. "I felt its cause to be right and I told other colored people that should the Yankees succeed, we could go when & how we pleased, and our children would no longer be sold and that negro trading would be played out." Banks supported his claim with a witness, Alston Mygatt, who, when asked whether Banks had been for the Union during the war, replied that Banks had been a member of the Vicksburg Loyal League. Some African Americans were even more blunt. Martha Berry was a midwife and the widow of an American soldier. She had lost everything. When asked about her loyalty, she replied, "I never took any amnesty oath. I was never pardoned by the President. I did not need it. . . . I was always a good Union woman to the bone."[44]

All over Mississippi and the nation, African Americans kept up the attack on white southerners by emphasizing their traitorous actions and, by turns, the closeness of former slaves to the American state. "On the dispersal of the Confederate armies, the people were again made subjects of the Government of the United States," wrote one black pamphleteer in 1868. The power of the federal government over the government of individual states during Reconstruction had extinguished the idea of individual state sovereignty. The federal state remained supreme, "or at any rate the scope of the power it has attained is sufficient to secure compliance in every case where the general interests of the country may require it." But the part that African Americans would play in this consolidation of federal power depended upon Americans remaining aware of how much national stability depended upon keeping loyal freedpeople in power at the expense of disloyal whites. Loyalty, the writer argued, was "the grave question, and on its solution the stability of the Republic will depend."[45]

The urgency evinced by calls to place loyalty at the civic center of the nation was more than hyperbole. By 1871, Congress was already beginning the process of detaching loyalty from citizenship. That body rewrote the Ironclad Oath so that it only bound individuals to be loyal and pledge their allegiance in the future, rather than holding their actions to the same high standard retrospectively. It was a measure of just how riddled with division the idea of loyalty had become that despite President Ulysses S. Grant's attempt to keep the bill from becoming law, it was still passed by Congress over his veto.[46] In addition, in the debate over the Fourteenth and Fifteenth Amendments to the Constitution, Congress ultimately looked upon loyalty as something less than a stable foundation for citizenship. After all the letting of blood and all the conflict over which African Americans had staked their future, they received constitutional guarantees of their rights as citizens of the United States at the same moment that the republic began to slowly dismantle the framework of loyalty that had supported their claim. Whereas former slaves had used their loyalty as a crowbar to pry open the door of the state for access and meaningful power—and as a weapon to beat back white southerners—by the early 1870s that same tool was quickly losing its effectiveness. This left African Americans with a legal claim to the title of citizen, not a historical argument rooted in the nation's common experience in the civil war that was fast becoming the crucible of the modern republic. The question of why Congress and a broader American public refused to include any measure of loyalty or test of allegiance in the Constitution would become one of the most unusual issues in the history of the republic.

epilogue

At the end of 1866, Frederick Douglass penned a rousing call for Congress to act on the question of Reconstruction. With many of the issues for which the Civil War had been fought still unresolved, Douglass argued that the future of the republic hung by a thread. The question that mattered most, he argued, was whether the American national government would permit the introduction of southern states back into the Union, states "into which no loyal man from the North may safely enter," or whether, "as the rightful reward of victory over treason," Americans could build a new republic in which loyalty, liberty, and equality were sacrosanct. Steps that Congress had taken earlier that spring to craft a national definition of citizenship were a start, but for Douglass, more was required. An act of Congress that legislated universal birthright citizenship left the door open to treasonous white southerners to return unimpeded into the civic life of the nation. More disquieting for Douglass was the lack of attention paid by Congress to the wartime sacrifice of African Americans. A refusal to rivet loyalty to citizenship in the nation's founding document ran the risk of devaluing the wartime loyalty of African Americans, while at the same time leaving no room for an activist national government to exert its power over a region that had torn the Union to pieces. Only the upending of American governance could cement the American victory in war: "one law, one government, one administration of justice"; equality between the races in the exercise of the franchise; and a single citizenship for all, "as will protect loyal men."[1]

By the time Douglass published his plea that wartime loyalty ought to continue to matter, congressional debate over citizenship had made it clear that the oppsite was taking place. Older arguments about citizenship would not die. When

Michigan Republican Jacob M. Howard introduced the constitutional amendment that would become the Fourteenth Amendment, the text was barely uttered before many of the same antebellum questions were aired once more. Some critics, like Pennsylvania Republican Edgar Cowan, asked how the title "citizen of the United States" had been defined. "Is it simply to put a man in a condition that he may be an elector in one of the States? Is it to put him in a condition to have the right to enter the United States courts and sue?" Or, Cowan argued, was this attempt to craft a national citizen merely an effort to "set him upon some pedestal, some position, to put him out of the reach of State legislation and State power?" While Cowan's worries turned on his concern that foreigners might claim rights that white citizens of Pennsylvania might object to, the debate exposed the old ambiguities all over again. In the Senate floor debate, members spent the bulk of their time deliberating over whether the new amendment would permit Native Americans to become citizens in good standing.[2]

The architects of the Fourteenth Amendment felt confident that their intervention in the nation's founding document put an end to debate over black citizenship and white southern treason, though Senate deliberations should have given them some cause for concern. The debate over the amendment exposed some deeper sea change in the way that Congress was defining loyalty itself. Though the wartime debate over the idea had been expansive, there was an inexorable narrowing of loyalty in the way that the Senate scrutinized the amendment in question. Its third section focused specifically on former members of the government and the nation's military who had joined the Confederacy. The amendment barred them from holding similar positions in a postwar Union if they had "engaged in insurrection or rebellion against the same, or given aid or comfort to the enemies thereof," save a two-thirds majority vote in Congress, which could overturn the ban. The introduction of this section was designed to soothe the worries of Unionists who, by then, had become enraged at former secessionists taking their place in power so easily and so soon after the Civil War had ended. But the language reflected a sharp turn from how loyalty had been defined in and out of Washington during the war and Presidential Reconstruction. Having expanded the remit of the national government in the Civil Rights Act only a month before—giving it the power to reach past federalist checks and balances to protect the rights of citizens—members of Congress expressed some disquiet over whether barring former traitors from holding office was a bridge too far. Some, like West Virginia's Peter Van Winkle, made the case that oaths taken to hold office ought to govern the actions of individuals only while they served and nothing more. While some high-ranking Confederates had joined legislatures in state governments once the fighting had stopped, their wartime actions were not perforce acts of treason over which the national government ought to have any control. Others, like Kentucky Democrat James Guthrie, warned that barring a generation of southern leaders from office would damage the future unity of the republic. What conciliation and national feeling there was in the South was at best fragile, and upsetting a tense and tender peace might tip the country back into conflict. Former secessionists had flirted with nationhood and lost, claimed Guthrie. They were now ready "to join in the Government heart and hand, and carry forward its flag." Past transgressions ought to matter less than future national harmony. Legislating loyalty as a test of whether someone ought to enjoy the rights of citizenship would drive a wedge between the loyal and the disloyal in southern communities. The most basic obligation of citizenship—that individuals protected by the national government should not endeavor to do that government harm—ought to lie beyond the amendment.[3]

There are many reasons why the Fourteenth Amendment stepped back from a clear renunciation of postwar citizenship as a price for wartime disloyalty. Certainly by the time Congress wrested control of Reconstruction from Andrew Johnson's administration, a good many legislators, not to mention the broader public, had come to view loyalty as tarnished or, at the very least, devalued. Johnson's obsession had become discredited, and in the rush to knock him off his presidential pedestal, the mere mention of loyalty brought forth a frustrated collective reaction from Johnson's opponents. Even while supporters of Congressional Reconstruction made it clear that due respect would be paid to loyalty, the hope that allegiance to the Union would be respected—that a volitional definition of citizenship would maintain pride of place—was balanced with worry that national reunification was a long way off. A Republican mouthpiece like the *New York Tribune* expressed the hope that the Reconstruction Acts could lay out a blueprint for national prosperity in which military rule over the defeated South could stabilize the region and would be followed by a process in which "the army would hold but a subordinate place, and of which loyalty and impartiality would form the basis" of civil governance. But even here, a republic that might shun the membership of those who had broken the country in the first place—with freedpeople given equal powers in the body politic—seemed a rosy prognostication that supporters could see only if they squinted at the horizon. What replaced the optimistic vision of a more loyal, volitional citizenship was instead a quick resolution in which the country could establish an impartial definition, stripped of wartime concerns about loyalty and treason.[4]

Whether Americans began to uncouple citizenship from loyalty out of fear or frustration, the inability to reckon with the ambiguities of both had consequences. For one, white southern tactics to thwart Reconstruction began to eat away at the foundations of wartime ideals about political equality. The principle of universal suffrage, one of the hallmarks of Radical thinking about a Reconstruction South, began to take a beating in the press almost as soon as it was put forward by Republicans. According to a writer in the *North American Review*, "the principle of universal suffrage, and the more general doctrines that the governed have a right to a voice in the administration of public affairs," was more an ideal than a hard reality. Citizens who regarded political equality as a fundamental right had to face the truth that Americans "have never attained to that dignity in the practical workings of our political institutions." This pragmatism, when conjoined with the steady drumbeat of a narrative that would become the Lost Cause, also put newly enfranchised African Americans on the defensive. They continued to wield loyalty as a political weapon, but it became more and more of a blunt instrument. The release of a seemingly innocuous history of the Civil War for young Americans written by R. G. Horton for a New York publishing house in 1867 directed young readers to the idea of emancipation as a sad chapter in the nation's history, which ought to be overcome with sober reflection. Horton—whose bona fides as a Democrat had been highlighted before the war with the publication of an election-year biography of James Buchanan—sounded the familiar refrain of Republican opposition. In a volume intended for children, however, Horton's interpretation of the Emancipation Proclamation as having bestowed freedom upon a race who were now allowed "to be as lazy and useless as they pleased" struck a particularly ominous chord. "Future ages," he wrote, "will scarcely be able to believe that such madness could have existed among otherwise sane people." Without the faith that the republic could be set on a durable foundation, ideas about national citizenship also absorbed a blow, at the same moment as constitutional amendments clarified the title.[5]

For those like Frederick Douglass who still held out the hope that the obligation of loyalty ought to be central to postwar citizenship, the problem was plain. As an editorial published in 1869 on the moral significance of Reconstruction made clear, the paradox that the nation faced was that securing a lasting peace required that Americans set racial prejudice to one side. Circumstances demanded that the country accede to African American demands and give former slaves rights as citizens, over those of former Confederates. To do otherwise would ensure that the "class on whose loyalty the government could depend would be practically sacrificed to the classes whose loyalty the government had the best reason to distrust." But if Radical Reconstruction was a plan of Republican congressmen and senators, "it was really the plan of the government of the country," and in this, calls for a more loyal republic had to square with the power of the federal state placed squarely behind a plan that most white southerners detested and about which many more Americans across the country were ambivalent. Even if the course of Congressional Reconstruction was best for the future of the country, supporters of the plan would come to see it as a bitter pill, a plan whereby much of the country "was not so much ruled as overruled." Whereas loyalty had been one of the key elements that sharpened Reconstruction to a fine point in 1865, the ebbing of the idea from any discussion of the nation's future only allowed what support there was for punishing the South to melt away. All that was left was the raw, coercive power of the federal state in the emancipated South, and while African Americans may have cheered at the result, few people in the rest of the country would have honestly yearned to live in its midst.[6]

In spite of the challenges they now faced, African Americans continued to emphasize that loyalty to the state ought to be venerated. In the years that followed, African Americans built viable and often strong political organizations that cemented their hold on political power in counties and regions all over the South. Firmly tethered to the Union, freedpeople crafted bases of power for themselves and their communities that were progressive and, where possible, racially inclusive. In impressive numbers, African Americans voted, took active part in local politics, and joined political associations like Union Leagues that required members to affirm and reaffirm their loyalty to the republic and the party that acted as a guarantor of their emancipation. A Union League manual printed for members in Alabama and Tennessee called on new members to gather before an altar draped with a Union flag on top of which sat a Bible, copies of the republic's founding documents, a sword, a gavel, and a ballot box, as well as a sickle, shuttle, anvil, and "other emblems of industry." Members swore oaths at the beginning of every meeting to uphold the Union and all that it stood for and to "protect, defend and strengthen all loyal men and members," as well as to instruct all people in "the duties of American citizenship, and for the inculcation of sentiments of true charity and brotherly affection among the members of our order."[7]

Yet the claims of loyalty and all the public displays of black allegiance that had propped open the door to the body politic were not strong enough to withstand the pressure of white southern opposition or growing national ambivalence. In states like Mississippi, it became clear by the early 1870s that a grassroots paramilitary movement was gathering strength, and despite the efforts of many in the federal government, neither black political organizations or the nation-state could stop it. As a white Republican from Lee County explained to Mississippi governor Ridgley Powers in the summer of 1872, the combination of white terror and the inaction of sympathetic local government officials had made it impossible to protect black citizens and white Republicans from harm. "A citizen here is not safe," he wrote. "My life would not be worth two cents if it was known here I had written you." C. H. Green, an African American from Noxubee County who had been duly elected as a county judge, was forced to write a letter in November 1875 in which he pleaded with Republican governor Adelbert Ames for help. Penning his note as he hid out in the forest on the edges of his home, Green recounted that armed whites had threatened him with death if he did not resign from his office and leave the county. "I have offered no resistance," wrote Green, "knowing that There Is a Law in the United States and in the State of Mississippi under which Every Citizen is promised Protection." With help not forthcoming, Green eventually surrendered to a white mob more than fifty strong. He and his family left the county for points unknown, the armed insurgency having apparently paid for their one-way ticket.[8]

What lay behind the hurried missives of Green and other black political figures was an argument about one of the most basic obligations of a state to citizens: that law-abiding individuals ought to be protected from harm. With their wartime support of the Union devalued, African Americans had to make as much of their political circumstances as they might, even as armed forces gathered around them to shove them out of power. Historians have written a good deal about the hard-headed alliances that black Americans forged late in Reconstruction to thwart white attempts to deny them a meaningful place in southern politics. Scholars have also pointed to federal efforts to arrest and prosecute, with some success, white supremacist groups like the Ku Klux Klan in the 1870s. But these attempts at biracial alliance and organization barely touched the bigger problem. By 1873, G. Wiley Wells, attorney general for Mississippi's northern district, reported to his superiors that federal officials had arrested more than 670 Klan members. The group, Wells argued, had been cut off at the knees, though letters that Wells received made it clear that much more action was needed. "The great trouble with us now has come out of the great mildness of the Government in the treatment of Such leaders of the Rebellion," wrote J. D. Barton. "They will leave nothing undone." Barton's reference to the war cut to the heart of the issue. Since the federal government had stepped back from protecting persons who had been loyal during the war, federal safeguards of postwar citizenship could never fully deal with what had become a white terrorist insurgency in the South by the middle of the 1870s.[9]

Nothing underscored the incapacity of federal power or the ambivalence of the nation more than the Democratic takeover of Mississippi's state government in 1875. Building on the strength of a coordinated terror campaign, Democratic leaders attempted to thwart Republican government in the state with rapid-response pamphlet campaigns, pitched battles with African Americans, and widespread vote tampering that amounted to one of the most fraudulent elections in the nation's history. Ballot boxes from staunchly Republican precincts in the state were lost, damaged, or destroyed. A prominent politician from the Delta remembered that favorite tactics of whites in his county included mixing bills of lading in with votes, shipping ballot boxes to other parts of the country, emptying ballots from the windows of trains bound for the capital, or any trick "that seemed to promise a chance of success." With such a primal right of citizenship so thoroughly disregarded, the federal government could only convene congressional committees to investigate. More direct and forceful action on the part of the nation-state was no longer a palatable option.[10]

As the obligations of citizenship receded, loyalty in all of its forms contracted to such an extent that it left room in the popular consciousness for histories of the war in which there seemed to have been little reason for the conflict in the first place. The Lost Cause became a narrative of such power precisely because it allowed white southerners to venerate their connection to a failed state to the point of obsession, while at the same time permitting them to take active part in governing the nation that had defeated them. Ironies abounded in the project, but the clever omission of the acts that had propelled the nation to war—secession, southern independence, renunciation of American citizenship—once again clouded that which had been all too clear when the war was at its height. If Americans ultimately stepped back from making loyalty a prerequisite for membership in the nation, the wartime attempt to do so tells us a great deal. Americans grappled with the breakup of their nation and the rapid expansion of modern states in ways that complicate the history of the war. Loyalty—as a language and a political tactic—clarified, however brutally but for the first time, the obligations of American citizenship. It also represented one of the most powerful means through which Americans attempted to make sense of the dramatic growth of states in their day-to-day lives. Perhaps most important, the history of wartime loyalty helps us to understand not simply why African Americans sought rights as citizens, but how they secured a place for themselves in the political life of the nation. Though it would be emptied of much of its meaning in time, the most powerful argument that African Americans could make in their bid for citizenship was not the moral case that the nation needed to square their republic with its highest ideals. Rather, it was that black Americans were the most loyal population in a region that had torn the Union in two. By emphasizing their obligations to the nation at a time of peril, African Americans acted on that which their former owners worked so hard to explain away.

If loyalty vanished from serious political discussion by the end of Reconstruction, the basic worry that had prompted its explosion in debate a few decades before never went away. It merely became folded into vague debates over the

Schoolchildren pledging allegiance to the flag, 8th Division, ca 1899. Photograph by Frances Benjamin Johnston. Courtesy of the Library of Congress Prints and Photographs Division, LC-USZ62-14693.

future of the nation and the place of foreigners in it. It would retain some loose relation to questions of citizenship, though it was not until the turn of the twentieth century that it emerged again, with a different tenor and pitch. In 1892, *The Youth's Companion*, a popular children's magazine, published instructions for a flag ceremony with a pledge that editors hoped teachers and schoolchildren would recite to commemorate the 400th anniversary of Christopher Columbus setting foot in the New World. Written by Christian socialist minister Francis Bellamy, the ceremony directed readers to unfurl an American flag and recite a one-sentence oath: to "pledge allegiance to my Flag and the Republic for which it stands, one nation, indivisible, with liberty and justice for all." Bellamy hoped that his pledge would instruct newly minted Americans, who flooded the country in ever-greater numbers from all over the world by the end of the nineteenth century. Yet even as the Pledge of Allegiance ascended to the status of a childhood rite of passage by the early decades of the twentieth century, the story of the Civil War that children learned in their history lessons had been stripped of the loyalties and obligations that had given that conflict so much of its meaning.

As Americans continue to wrestle with the memory of the Civil War, the power of the national government, and what it means to be a citizen of the republic, the older questions still go unanswered. As with the infinitely regressive argument that never seems to be untangled, Americans continue to struggle to sharpen or clarify their obligations to the national government, even if to push that government at arm's length from their lives. For a republic founded on the principle of personal liberty, reckoning with a nation-state is perhaps the one argument that might never be settled. But during the Civil War, at a moment when the country changed in profound ways, Americans who lived through the carnage attempted to refine this hazy relationship. While a burden for some and an opportunity for others, loyalty to a modern America emerged as a political bludgeon. Though it possessed revolutionary potential to reshape the republic and set the nation on a very different course, volitional citizenship would be set to one side. The parameters of citizenship would be narrowed; birthright and not individual action would matter. But in a revolutionary moment, loyalty held out the possibility of far-reaching change. Out of that struggle—to claim rights as loyal citizens or explain away treasonous acts—would come many of the tensions of modern American citizenship.

notes

Asst. Comm-MS   Records of the Assistant Commissioner for the State of Mississippi (M826), RG 105

BRFAL   Bureau of Refugees, Freedmen, and Abandoned Lands

DU   Rubenstein Rare Book and Manuscript Library, Duke University, Durham, N.C.

LC   Library of Congress, Washington, D.C.

MDAH   Mississippi Department of Archives and History, Jackson

NA   National Archives, Washington, D.C.

OR   *The War of the Rebellion: A Compilation of the Official Records of the Union and Confederate Armies.* Washington, D.C.: GPO, 1880–1901.

OR   citations take the following form: volume number(part number):page number(s)—e.g., *OR* 38(3):66–67. Unless otherwise cited, all references are to series 1.

SHC   Southern Historical Collection, University of North Carolina at Chapel Hill

INTRODUCTION

1. G. G. Lorry et al. to Gov. Clark, Bolivar Co., Miss., 20 February 1864, folder 4, box 949, ser. 768, Governor Charles Clark, Correspondence and Papers, 1863–1865, MDAH.

2. Though political philosophers have not, of late, spent much time on the subject, loyalty has long been a topic of concern in the work of political philosophers ranging from Immanuel Kant to Jeremy Bentham to Adam Smith. For a recent study on the more modern dimensions of loyalty, see George P. Fletcher, *Loyalty: An Essay on the Morality of Relationships* (New York: Oxford University Press, 1993), esp. 61–77.

3. Some of the best work in this field has included Georgia Lee Tatum, *Disloyalty in the Confederacy* (Chapel Hill: University of North Carolina Press, 1934); Harold M. Hyman, *Era of the Oath: Northern Loyalty Tests during the Civil War and Reconstruction* (Philadelphia: University of Pennsylvania Press, 1954); Harold M. Hyman, *To Try Men's Souls: Loyalty Tests in American History* (Berkeley: University of California Press, 1960); Daniel E. Sutherland, *Seasons of War: The Ordeal of a Confederate Community, 1861–1865* (New York: Free Press, 1995); Margaret M. Storey, *Loyalty and Loss: Alabama's Unionists in the Civil War and Reconstruction* (Baton Rouge: Louisiana State University Press, 2004); Gordon B. McKinney, "Layers of Loyalty: Confederate Nationalism and Amnesty Letters from Western North Carolina," *Civil War History* 51, no. 1 (2005): 5–22; Jarret Ruminski, "'Tradyville': The Contraband Trade and the Problem of Loyalty in Civil War Mississippi," *Journal of the Civil War Era* 2, no. 4 (2012): 511–37; William A. Blair, *With Malice toward Some: Treason and Loyalty in the Civil War Era* (Chapel Hill: University of North Carolina Press, 2014); and Susanna Michelle Lee, *Claiming the Union: Citizenship in the Post–Civil War South* (Cambridge: Cambridge University Press, 2014).

4. On the early history of American citizenship, see James H. Kettner, *The Development of American Citizenship, 1608–1870* (Chapel Hill: Published for the Omohundro Institute of Early American History and Culture by the University of North Carolina Press, 1978), 173–209, 287–333; Joan R. Gundersen, "Independence, Citizenship, and the American Revolution," *Signs* 13, no. 1 (1987): 59–77; Linda K. Kerber, *Women of the Republic: Intellect and Ideology in Revolutionary America* (New York: Norton, 1986); Linda K. Kerber, "The Paradox of Women's Citizenship in the Early Republic: The Case of *Martin vs. Massachusetts*, 1805," *American Historical Review* 97, no. 2 (1992): 349–78; Rogers M. Smith, *Civic Ideals: Conflicting Visions of Citizenship in U.S. History* (New Haven: Yale University Press, 1997), 70–196; Catherine A. Holland, *The Body Politic: Foundings, Citizenship, and Difference in the American Political Imagination* (New York: Routledge, 2001); Barbara Young Welke, "Law, Personhood, and Citizenship in the Long Nineteenth Century: The Borders of Belonging," in *The Cambridge History of Law in America*, vol. 2, *The Long Nineteenth Century (1789–1920)*, ed. Christopher Tomlins and Michael Grossberg (Cambridge: Cambridge University Press, 2008), 345–86; Douglas Bradburn, *The Citizenship Revolution: Politics and the Creation of the American Union, 1774–1804* (Charlottesville: University of Virginia Press, 2009); and Douglas Bradburn, "'The Great Field of Human Concerns': The States, the Union, and the Problem of Citizenship in the Era of the American Revolution," in *State and Citizen: British America and the Early United States*, ed. Peter Thompson and Peter S. Onuf (Charlottesville: University of Virginia Press, 2013), 77–112.

5. On nationalism in the early republic and the social and political associations that helped to give American ideas of citizenship their meaning, see David Waldstreicher, *In the Midst of Perpetual Fetes: The Making of American Nationalism, 1776–1820* (Chapel Hill: Published for the Omohundro Institute of Early American History and Culture by the University of North Carolina Press, 1997); Reeve Huston, *Land and Freedom: Rural Society, Popular Protest, and Party Politics in Antebellum New York* (New York: Oxford University Press, 2000); Andrew W. Robertson, "'Look on This Picture . . . And on This!' Nationalism, Localism, and Partisan Images of Otherness in the United States, 1787–1820," *American Historical Review* 106, no. 4 (2001): 1263–80; William J. Novak, "The American

Law of Association: The Legal-Political Construction of Civil Society," *Studies in American Political Development* 15, no. 2 (2002): 163–88; Johann N. Neem, *Creating a Nation of Joiners: Democracy and Civil Society in Early National Massachusetts* (Cambridge, Mass.: Harvard University Press, 2008); John L. Brooke, *Columbia Rising: Civil Life on the Upper Hudson from the Revolution to the Age of Jackson* (Chapel Hill: University of North Carolina Press, 2010); and Barbara Young Welke, *Law and the Borders of Belonging in the Long Nineteenth Century United States* (New York: Cambridge University Press, 2010).

6. The literature on the history of American citizenship is immense, though some of the most formative work in the field includes Kettner, *Development of American Citizenship*; Eric Foner, *Reconstruction: America's Unfinished Revolution, 1863–1877* (New York: Harper and Row, 1988); Judith N. Shklar, *American Citizenship: The Quest for Inclusion* (Cambridge, Mass.: Harvard University Press, 1991); Smith, *Civic Ideals*; Linda K. Kerber, "The Meanings of Citizenship," *Journal of American History* 84, no. 3 (1997): 833–54; Linda K. Kerber, *No Constitutional Right to Be Ladies: Women and the Obligations of Citizenship* (New York: Hill and Wang, 1998); Nancy F. Cott, "Marriage and Women's Citizenship in the United States, 1830–1934," *American Historical Review* 103, no. 5 (1998): 1440–74; Nancy Isenberg, *Sex and Citizenship in Antebellum America* (Chapel Hill: University of North Carolina Press, 1998); Candace Bredbenner, *A Nationality of Her Own: Women, Marriage, and the Law of Citizenship* (Berkeley: University of California Press, 1998); William J. Novak, "The Legal Transformation of Citizenship in Nineteenth-Century America," in *The Democratic Experiment: New Directions in American Political History*, ed. Meg Jacobs and Julian E. Zelizer (Princeton: Princeton University Press, 2003), 85–119; Bradburn, *Citizenship Revolution*; Hannah Rosen, *Terror in the Heart of Freedom: Citizenship, Sexual Violence, and the Meaning of Race in the Postemancipation South* (Chapel Hill: University of North Carolina Press, 2009); Stephen Kantrowitz, *More Than Freedom: Fighting for Black Citizenship in a White Republic, 1829–1889* (New York: Penguin, 2012); and Carole Emberton, *Beyond Redemption: Race, Violence, and the American South after the Civil War* (Chicago: University of Chicago Press, 2013).

7. American citizenship, as both an area of study and a broader narrative theme, also remains an important part of twentieth-century historiography. See, for example, Lizabeth Cohen, *A Consumer's Republic: The Politics of Mass Consumption in Postwar America* (New York: Knopf, 2003); Margot Canaday, *The Straight State: Sexuality and Citizenship in Twentieth-Century America* (Princeton: Princeton University Press, 2009); and Thomas J. Sugrue, *Sweet Land of Liberty: The Forgotten Struggle for Civil Rights in the North* (New York: Random House, 2009). For a book that places due attention on the relationship between obligation and citizenship in the United States in the lead-up to the country's entry into World War I, see Christopher Capozzola, *Uncle Sam Wants You: World War I and the Making of the Modern American Citizen* (New York: Oxford University Press, 2008).

8. Carole Pateman, *The Problem of Political Obligation: A Critical Analysis of Liberal Theory* (New York: John Wiley and Sons, 1979). Following Pateman's intervention, gender historians have deftly dealt with the legal and political implications of obligation for women in wars. See, for example, Kerber, *No Constitutional Right to Be Ladies*, and Stephanie McCurry, "Citizens, Soldiers' Wives, and 'Hiley Hope Up' Slaves: The Problem of Political Obligation in the Civil War South," in *Gender and the Southern Body Politic*, ed. Nancy Bercaw (Jackson: University Press of Mississippi, 2000), 95–124.

9. The foundational literature on the history of the American state includes Stephen Skowronek, *Building a New American State: The Expansion of National Administrative Capacities, 1877–1920* (Cambridge: Cambridge University Press, 1982); Theda Skocpol, Dietrich Rueschmeyer, and Peter B. Evans, eds., *Bringing the State Back In* (Cambridge: Cambridge University Press, 1985); Richard F. Bensel, *Yankee Leviathan: The Origins of Central State Authority in America, 1859–1877* (New York: Cambridge University Press, 1990); Theda Skocpol, *Protecting Soldiers and Mothers: The Political Origins of Social Policy in the United States* (Cambridge, Mass.: Belknap Press of Harvard University Press, 1992); Richard R. John, *Spreading the News: The American Postal System from Franklin to Morse* (Cambridge, Mass.: Harvard University Press, 1995); and William J. Novak, *The People's Welfare: Law and Regulation in Nineteenth-Century America* (Chapel Hill: University of North Carolina Press, 1996).

10. The importance of seeing the development of states through a visual reorientation comes from James C. Scott's *Seeing Like a State: How Certain Schemes to Improve the Human Condition Have Failed* (New Haven: Yale University Press, 1998). For the more recent literature on American state formation, see Richard John, "Governmental Institutions as Agents of Change: Rethinking American Political Development in the Early Republic, 1787–1835," *Studies in American Political Development* 11, no. 2 (1997): 347–80; Novak, *People's Welfare*; Max M. Edling, *A Revolution in Favor of Government: Origins of the U.S. Constitution and the Making of the American State* (New York: Oxford University Press, 2003); Robin L. Einhorn, *American Taxation, American Slavery* (Chicago: University of Chicago Press, 2006); William J. Novak, "The Myth of the 'Weak' American State," *American Historical Review* 113, no. 3 (2008): 752–72; Brian Balogh, *A Government out of Sight: The Mystery of National Authority in Nineteenth-Century America* (Cambridge: Cambridge University Press, 2009); Max M. Edling, *A Hercules in the Cradle: War, Money, and the American State, 1783–1867* (Chicago: University of Chicago Press, 2014); and Gary Gerstle, *Liberty and Coercion: The Paradox of American Government from the Founding to the Present* (Princeton: Princeton University Press, 2015). For a recent collection that foregrounds the Civil War and its aftermath as a key battleground between Native Americans and the American state, see Adam Arenson and Andrew R. Graybill, eds., *Civil War Wests: Testing the Limits of the United States* (Berkeley: University of California Press, 2015). A book that calls for a reformulation of the thinking on American state formation is Steven Hahn, *A Nation without Borders: The United States and Its World in an Age of Civil Wars, 1830–1910* (New York: Penguin, 2016).

11. Despite being one of the most important battlegrounds of the Civil War, Mississippi has not received the same attention that other southern states have garnered. While a significant literature has examined the antebellum and postbellum periods in the state, only a handful of recent studies have attempted to survey the region's wartime history, and an even smaller number have followed the history of the state through the war, from both the American and Confederate sides of the conflict. The best work in this field includes William Barney, *The Secessionist Impulse: Alabama and Mississippi in 1860* (Princeton: Princeton University Press, 1974); William C. Harris, *The Day of the Carpetbagger: Republican Reconstruction in Mississippi* (Baton Rouge: Louisiana State University Press, 1979); Michael Wayne, *The Reshaping of Plantation Society: The*

Natchez District, 1860–1880 (Baton Rouge: Louisiana State University Press, 1983); Charles C. Bolton, *Poor Whites of the Antebellum South: Tenants and Laborers in Central North Carolina and Northeast Mississippi* (Durham: Duke University Press, 1994); Bradley G. Bond, *Political Culture in the Nineteenth-Century South: Mississippi, 1830–1900* (Baton Rouge: Louisiana State University Press, 1995); Christopher Morris, *Becoming Southern: The Evolution of a Way of Life, Warren County and Vicksburg, Mississippi, 1770–1860* (New York: Oxford University Press, 1995); Christopher J. Olsen, *Political Culture and Secession in Mississippi: Masculinity, Honor, and the Antiparty Tradition, 1830–1860* (New York: Oxford University Press, 2000); Nancy Bercaw, *Gendered Freedoms: Race, Rights, and the Politics of Household in the Delta, 1861–1875* (Gainesville: University Press of Florida, 2003); Thomas C. Buchanan, *Black Life on the Mississippi: Slaves, Free Blacks, and the Western Steamboat World* (Chapel Hill: University of North Carolina Press, 2004); Armstead L. Robinson, *Bitter Fruits of Bondage: The Demise of Slavery and the Collapse of the Confederacy, 1861–1865* (Charlottesville: University of Virginia Press, 2005); Anthony E. Kaye, *Joining Places: Slave Neighborhoods in the Old South* (Chapel Hill: University of North Carolina Press, 2007); Walter Johnson, *River of Dark Dreams: Slavery and Empire in the Cotton Kingdom* (Cambridge, Mass.: Harvard University Press, 2013); and Justin Behrend, *Reconstructing Democracy: Grassroots Black Politics in the Deep South after the Civil War* (Athens: University of Georgia Press, 2015).

12. While American historians have been slow to take the political expressions of unlettered people seriously—particularly when those expressions do not square with the overarching sense of Americans as self-conscious liberal individualists—a start has certainly been made in the work of Steven Hahn, *A Nation under Our Feet: Black Political Struggles in the Rural South from Slavery to the Great Migration* (Cambridge, Mass.: Harvard University Press, 2003); Dylan C. Penningroth, *The Claims of Kinfolk: African American Property and Community in the Nineteenth-Century South* (Chapel Hill: University of North Carolina Press, 2003); Laura F. Edwards, "Status without Rights: African Americans and the Tangled History of Law and Governance in the Nineteen-Century U.S. South," *American Historical Review* 112, no. 2 (2007): 365–93; Kaye, *Joining Places*; Laura F. Edwards, *The People and Their Peace: Legal Culture and the Transformation of Inequality in the Post-Revolutionary South* (Chapel Hill: University of North Carolina Press, 2009); and Gregory Downs, *Declarations of Dependence: The Long Reconstruction of Popular Politics in the South, 1861–1908* (Chapel Hill: University of North Carolina Press, 2011). This literature builds on the insights of scholars in other fields who have fruitfully excavated the political ideas of people at a distance from power. This work, which has influenced my own, includes Shahid Amin, "Gandhi as Mahatma: Gorakhpur District, Eastern UP, 1921–22," in *Selected Subaltern Studies*, ed. Gayatri Chakravorty Spivak and Ranajit Guha (New York: Oxford University Press, 1988), 288–348; James C. Scott, *Domination and the Arts of Resistance: Hidden Transcripts* (New Haven: Yale University Press, 1990); Ranajit Guha, *Elementary Aspects of Peasant Insurgency in Colonial India* (1983; Durham: Duke University Press, 1999); and Partha Chatterjee, *The Politics of the Governed: Reflections on Popular Politics in Most of the World* (New York: Columbia University Press, 2004).

13. *U.S. Const.* amend. XIV, § 1 and 2.

1. The metaphor is elaborated in Brian Balogh, *A Government out of Sight: The Mystery of National Authority in Nineteenth-Century America* (Cambridge: Cambridge University Press, 2009), 1–53.

2. The idea of the American state as a bundle of contradictions, albeit one with the means to change its shape in all sorts of creative ways, has been best expressed by Gary Gerstle in *Liberty and Coercion: The Paradox of American Government from the Founding to the Present* (Princeton: Princeton University Press, 2015), 17–54, 89–123. For a work that focuses on American governance on its imperial margins, see Steven Hahn, *A Nation without Borders: The United States and Its World in an Age of Civil Wars, 1830–1910* (New York: Penguin, 2016), 12–42, 115–91.

3. William Novak's point about the presentism tied up with the history of American citizenship is well taken. Atomistic understandings of the rights-bearing individual, in relation to a broader society, are certainly products of a more modern era. The focus in this chapter, however, has less to do with a concern over the struggle for rights and more to do with the concern Americans had about the personal bond they shared with the nation-state. See William J. Novak, "The Legal Transformation of Citizenship in Nineteenth-Century America," in *The Democratic Experiment: New Directions in American Political History*, ed. Meg Jacobs and Julian E. Zelizer (Princeton: Princeton University Press, 2003), 85–119, esp. 88–89, 95–97.

4. The best of this work, for the early to mid-nineteenth century, includes James H. Kettner, *The Development of American Citizenship, 1608–1870* (Chapel Hill: Published for the Omohundro Institute of Early American History and Culture by the University of North Carolina Press, 1978); Joan R. Gundersen, "Independence, Citizenship, and the American Revolution," *Signs* 13, no. 1 (1987): 59–77; Judith N. Shklar, *American Citizenship: The Quest for Inclusion* (Cambridge, Mass.: Harvard University Press, 1991); Linda K. Kerber, "The Meanings of Citizenship," *Journal of American History* 84, no. 3 (1997): 833–54; Rogers M. Smith, *Civic Ideals: Conflicting Visions of Citizenship in U.S. History* (New Haven: Yale University Press, 1997), 70–196; Linda K. Kerber, *No Constitutional Right to Be Ladies: Women and the Obligations of Citizenship* (New York: Hill and Wang, 1998); Nancy Isenberg, *Sex and Citizenship in Antebellum America* (Chapel Hill: University of North Carolina Press, 1998); and Barbara Young Welke, *Law and the Borders of Belonging in the Long Nineteenth Century United States* (New York: Cambridge University Press, 2010).

5. *Journals of the Conventions of the People of South Carolina, Held in 1832, 1833, and 1852* (Columbia: R. W. Gibbes, 1860), 50–51, 97. For the history of the Nullification Crisis, the classic works include William W. Freehling, *Prelude to Civil War: The Nullification Controversy in South Carolina, 1816–1836* (1965; New York: Oxford University Press, 1992); William W. Freehling, *The Road to Disunion*, vol. 1, *Secessionists at Bay, 1776–1854* (New York: Oxford University Press, 1990), 213–86; Lacy K. Ford, *Origins of Southern Radicalism: The South Carolina Upcountry, 1800–1860* (New York: Oxford University Press, 1988), 99–144; Stephanie McCurry, *Masters of Small Worlds: Yeoman Households, Gender Relations, and the Political Culture of the Antebellum South Carolina Low Country* (New York: Oxford University Press, 1995), 239–76; Manisha Sinha, *The Counterrevolution of Slavery: Politics and Ideology in Antebellum South Carolina* (Chapel Hill: University of

North Carolina Press, 2000), 33–61; and Sean Wilentz, *The Rise of American Democracy: Jefferson to Lincoln* (New York: Norton, 2005), 374–90.

6. On this question, see Edmund S. Morgan, *Inventing the People: The Rise of Popular Sovereignty in England and America* (New York: Norton, 1988).

7. For more on the McCready and McDonald case and its importance, see Harold M. Hyman, *To Try Men's Souls: Loyalty Tests in American History* (Berkeley: University of California Press, 1960), 118–38; Kettner, *Development of American Citizenship*, 265–67; and Freehling, *Prelude to Civil War*, 314–18.

8. *The Book of Allegiance; or A Report of the Arguments of Counsel and Opinions of the Court of Appeals of South Carolina, on the Oath of Allegiance* (Columbia: The Telescope, 1834), 45, 59, 70–71.

9. Ibid., 103, 125.

10. 9 Reg. Deb. 543 (1833).

11. David Ramsay, *A Dissertation on the Manner of Acquiring the Character and Privileges of a Citizen of the United States* (1789), 3, 5–6, 8. On the problem of defining the relationship between Americans and their national government in the manner Ramsay envisioned, see Benjamin H. Irvin, *Clothed in the Robes of Sovereignty: The Continental Congress and the People out of Doors* (New York: Oxford University Press, 2011). On the distinction between subjecthood and citizenship, see T. H. Breen, "Subjecthood and Citizenship: The Context of James Otis's Radical Critique of John Locke," *New England Quarterly* 71, no. 3 (1998): 378–403. For more on the religious background of subjecthood and the long-standing colonial argument that Ramsay was speaking to, see Holly Brewer, "Subjects by Allegiance to the King? Debating Status and Power for Subjects—and Slaves—through the Religious Debates of the Early British Atlantic," in *State and Citizen: British America and the Early United States*, ed. Peter Thompson and Peter S. Onuf (Charlottesville: University of Virginia Press, 2013), 25–51.

12. On the fiction of popular sovereignty, see Morgan, *Inventing the People*, 122–73. On citizenship and the framing of the Constitution, see Kettner, *Development of American Citizenship*, 173–209; Smith, *Civic Ideals*, 115–36; Douglas Bradburn, *The Citizenship Revolution: Politics and the Creation of the American Union, 1774-1804* (Charlottesville: University of Virginia Press, 2009); and Douglas Bradburn, "'The Great Field of Human Concerns': The States, the Union, and the Problem of Citizenship in the Era of the American Revolution," in Thompson and Onuf, *State and Citizen*, 77–112.

13. Act of 29 January 1795, ch. 19, *Stat.* 414–15; Act of 14 April 1802, ch. 28, *Stat.* 153–55; Act of 26 May 1824, ch. 186, *Stat.* 69. On citizenship, laws of coverture, and the hereditary title to civic rights that excluded women, see Linda K. Kerber, "The Paradox of Women's Citizenship in the Early Republic: The Case of *Martin vs. Massachusetts*, 1805," *American Historical Review* 97, no. 2 (1992): 349–78, and Kerber, *No Constitutional Right to Be Ladies*, 3–46. On the naturalization debate, see Kettner, *Development of American Citizenship*, 65–128, 213–47, and Gerstle, *Liberty and Coercion*, 29–33.

14. Noah Webster, *An American Dictionary of the English Language* (New York: S. Converse, 1828), 1:387. For the nationalism of early republican America, see Michael Warner, *The Letters of the Republic: Publication and the Public Sphere in Eighteenth-Century America* (Cambridge, Mass.: Harvard University Press, 1990); David Waldstreicher, *In the Midst of Perpetual Fetes: The Making of American Nationalism, 1776-1820* (Chapel Hill:

Published for the Omohundro Institute of Early American History and Culture by the University of North Carolina Press, 1997), 108–245; Jeffrey L. Pasley, *The Tyranny of Printers: Newspaper Politics in the Early American Republic* (Charlottesville: University of Virginia Press, 2001); Andrew W. Robertson, "'Look on This Picture . . . And on This!' Nationalism, Localism, and Partisan Images of Otherness in the United States, 1787–1820," *American Historical Review* 106, no. 4 (2001): 1263–80; Jeffrey L. Pasley, Andrew Robertson, and David Waldstreicher, eds., *Beyond the Founders: New Approaches to the Political History of the Early American Republic* (Chapel Hill: University of North Carolina Press, 2004); John L. Brooke, "Cultures of Nationalism, Movements of Reform, and the Composite–Federal Polity: From Revolutionary Settlement to Antebellum Crisis," *Journal of the Early Republic* 29, no. 1 (2009): 1–33; Carolyn Eastman, *A Nation of Speechifiers: Making an American Public after the Revolution* (Chicago: University of Chicago Press, 2010); and Nicole Eustace, *1812: War and the Passions of Patriotism* (Philadelphia: University of Pennsylvania Press, 2012).

15. For free blacks in the post-Revolutionary period as well as northern emancipation more generally, see Steven Hahn, *The Political Worlds of Slavery and Freedom* (Cambridge, Mass.: Harvard University Press, 2009), 1–54, and Manisha Sinha, *The Slave's Cause: A History of Abolition* (New Haven: Yale University Press, 2016), 65–96. My thinking about civil society and the early republic has been informed by John L. Brooke, *Columbia Rising: Civil Life on the Upper Hudson from the Revolution to the Age of Jackson* (Chapel Hill: University of North Carolina Press, 2010), 13–167. For the battle over citizenship in Haiti, see Carolyn E. Fick, *The Making of Haiti: The Saint Domingue Revolution from Below* (Knoxville: University of Tennessee Press, 1990); Laurent Dubois, *A Colony of Citizens: Revolution and Slave Emancipation in the French Caribbean, 1787–1804* (Chapel Hill: Published for the Omohundro Institute of Early American History and Culture by the University of North Carolina Press, 2004), 171–314; and Ada Ferrer, *Freedom's Mirror: Cuba and Haiti in the Age of Revolution* (Cambridge: Cambridge University Press, 2014). The classic study of revolution and democratic politics in the Atlantic remains Robert R. Palmer, *The Age of the Democratic Revolution: A Political History of Europe and America, 1760–1800* (1959; 1964; Princeton: Princeton University Press, 2014).

16. A point made by Alan Taylor, *The Civil War of 1812: American Citizens, British Subjects, Irish Rebels, and Indian Allies* (New York: Knopf, 2010), 101–23, and Eustace, *1812*, 88–92. An excellent study of the War Department has placed due attention on the power of the federal state's military capacity in the early republican period. See William D. Adler, "State Capacity and Bureaucratic Autonomy in the Early United States: The Case of the Army Corps of Topographical Engineers," *Studies in American Political Development* 26, no. 2 (2012): 107–24.

17. Benjamin L. Oliver, *The Rights of an American Citizen, with a Commentary on States Rights, and on the Constitution and Policy of the United States* (Boston: Marsh, Capen and Lyon, 1832), 65–73 (quote on 71). Like that of many of his generation, Oliver's understanding of citizenship lay with a particular sense that Americans shared a collective past that informed their connection to the nation. This idea of citizenship as a shared sense of belonging has been picked up on by several historians who have influenced my thinking, including Welke in *Law and the Borders of Belonging*.

18. *American Whig Review* 2, no. 6 (December 1845): 614–22 (quote on 620). The literature on the development of mass democracy is immense, but recent key texts include

Alexander Keyssar, *The Right to Vote: The Contested History of Democracy in the United States* (New York: Basic Books, 2000); Glenn C. Altschuler and Stuart M. Blumin, *Rude Republic: Americans and Their Politics in the Nineteenth Century* (Princeton: Princeton University Press, 2000); Pasley, Robertson, and Waldstreicher, *Beyond the Founders*; Wilentz, *Rise of American Democracy*; Johann N. Neem, *Creating a Nation of Joiners: Democracy and Civil Society in Early National Massachusetts* (Cambridge, Mass.: Harvard University Press, 2008); and Brooke, *Columbia Rising*. For a view that challenges the prevailing idea of mass democracy as being so closely wedded to the so-called Age of Jackson, see Donald Ratcliffe, "The Right to Vote and the Rise of Democracy, 1787–1828," *Journal of the Early Republic* 33, no. 2 (2013): 219–54.

19. Cong. Globe, 24th Cong., 1st Sess. 607 (1836); Cong. Globe, 26th Cong., 2nd Sess. 143 (1841).

20. Cong. Globe, 25th Cong., 2nd Sess. 307 (1838). There is a desperate need for more work to be done on the relationship between geography and citizenship in the American republic, though studies that pay closer attention to this issue include Mae M. Ngai, *Impossible Subjects: Illegal Aliens and the Making of Modern America* (Princeton: Princeton University Press, 2004); Linda K. Kerber, "The Stateless as the Citizen's Other: A View from the United States," *American Historical Review* 112, no. 1 (2007): 1–34; Barbara Young Welke, "Law, Personhood, and Citizenship in the Long Nineteenth Century: The Borders of Belonging," in *The Cambridge History of Law in America*, vol. 2, *The Long Nineteenth Century (1789–1920)*, ed. Christopher Tomlins and Michael Grossberg (Cambridge: Cambridge University Press, 2008), 345–86; and Lisa Maria Perez, "Citizenship Denied: The 'Insular Cases' and the Fourteenth Amendment," *Virginia Law Review* 94, no. 4 (2008): 1029–81.

21. *Freedom's Journal*, 16 March 1827; David Walker, *Walker's Appeal in Four Articles, Together With A Preamble to the Coloured Citizens of the World* (Boston: Priv. Printed, 1830). On women and the struggle for citizenship, see Kerber, "Paradox of Women's Citizenship"; Candace Bredbenner, *A Nationality of Her Own: Women, Marriage, and the Law of Citizenship* (Berkeley: University of California Press, 1998); Kerber, *No Constitutional Right to Be Ladies*; Elizabeth R. Varon, *We Mean to Be Counted: White Women and Politics in Antebellum Virginia* (Chapel Hill: University of North Carolina Press, 1998); and Nancy Cott, *Public Vows: A History of Marriage and the Nation* (Cambridge, Mass.: Harvard University Press, 2000). For more on Walker and the abolitionist circles out of which he emerged, see Peter P. Hinks, *To Awaken My Afflicted Brethren: David Walker and the Problem of Antebellum Slave Resistance* (University Park: Pennsylvania State University Press, 1997); Stephen Kantrowitz, *More Than Freedom: Fighting for Black Citizenship in a White Republic, 1829–1889* (New York: Penguin, 2012), 28–40; and Sinha, *Slave's Cause*, 195–227. On the work of black abolitionists who pressed for equality of citizenship, see Sinha, *Slave's Cause*, 316–30. For an important reminder of the gap between the racial rhetoric that surrounded citizenship and the more complex reality, particularly in the antebellum South, see Ariela J. Gross, "Litigating Whiteness: Trials of Racial Determination in the Nineteenth-Century South," *Yale Law Journal* 108 (1998): 109–88.

22. *Report of the Debates of the Convention of California on the Formation of the State Constitution, in September and October, 1849* (Washington, D.C.: John T. Towers, 1850), 4; Cong. Globe, 31st Cong., 1st Sess. 774 (1850). The study of territorial citizenship remains another misunderstood and largely untouched topic in the literature on citizenship. A start

has been made, though, with Kunal M. Parker, "State, Citizenship, and Territory: The Legal Construction of Immigrants in Antebellum Massachusetts," *Law and History Review* 19, no. 3 (2001): 583–643; Eric Biber, "The Price of Admission: Causes, Effects, and Patterns of Conditions Imposed on States Entering the Union," *American Journal of Legal History* 46, no. 2 (2004): 119–208; and Kunal M. Parker, "Citizenship and Immigration Law, 1800–1924: Resolutions of Membership and Territory," in Tomlins and Grossberg, *Cambridge History of Law*, 2:168–203.

23. *Report of the Debates of the Convention of California*, 11, 22.

24. Ibid., 34–35. The relationship between Native Americans and national citizenship is particularly important to the debate in the early national period. Federal treaties and later court opinions effectively turned Natives into protected persons: restricted from holding rights as citizens of a given state but given a position in American law akin to national subjects, or at least persons theoretically protected as dependent persons by the federal government. See Kettner, *Development of American Citizenship*, 288–300, and Smith, *Civic Ideals*, 181–85, 235–42. On slavery in California, see Stacey L. Smith, *Freedom's Frontier: California and the Struggle over Unfree Labor, Emancipation, and Reconstruction* (Chapel Hill: University of North Carolina Press, 2013), esp. 47–89.

25. *Report of the Debates of the Convention of California*, 63–73 (quote on 71–72).

26. Cong. Globe, 31st Cong., 1st Sess. App. 891–92 (1850); Cong. Globe, 31st Cong., 1st Sess. 1843 (1850).

27. Cong. Globe, 31st Cong., 1st Sess. 1145–46 (1850). Works that make the case for the imperial vision of the republic in this period include Hahn, *Nation without Borders*, and Matthew Karp, *This Vast Southern Empire: Slaveholders at the Helm of American Foreign Policy* (Cambridge, Mass.: Harvard University Press, 2016). An interesting study that examines more deeply the figuring of the state as female can be found in Joseph S. Bonica, "'The Motherly Office of the State': Cultural Struggle and Comprehensive Administration before the Civil War," *Studies in American Political Development* 22, no. 1 (2008): 97–110.

28. Cong. Globe, 31st Cong., 1st Sess. 451–55 (1850). For the best examination on the Compromise and its meaning for American national politics, see David M. Potter, *The Impending Crisis, 1848–1861* (New York: Harper and Row, 1976), 63–120. Potter's focus on an enduring American nationalism in the middle decades of the nineteenth century is well taken, though a focus on citizenship and the connections between Americans and the national government underscores the need to complicate the traditional narrative of this period, with its preoccupation with sectionalist and nationalist sentiment.

29. *American Whig Review* 13, no. 76 (April 1851): 289–301 (quote on 289); *DeBow's Review* 9, no. 3 (1850): 257–71 (quote on 260).

30. For more on the reaction to the Fugitive Slave Act, see William A. Link, *Roots of Secession: Slavery and Politics in Antebellum Virginia* (Chapel Hill: University of North Carolina Press, 2003), and Stanley Harrold, *Border War: Fighting over Slavery before the Civil War* (Chapel Hill: University of North Carolina Press, 2010).

31. Cong. Globe, 31st Cong., 1st Sess. 399–400 (1850). For more on the question of citizenship on the high seas, see Denver Brunsman, "Subjects vs. Citizens: Impressment and Identity in the Anglo-American Atlantic," *Journal of the Early Republic* 30, no. 4 (2010): 557–86, and Nathan Perl-Rosenthal, *Citizen Sailors: Becoming American in the Age of Revolution* (Cambridge, Mass.: Harvard University Press, 2015).

32. William Hosmer, *The Higher Law, in its Relations to Civil Government: With Particular Reference to Slavery, and the Fugitive Slave Law* (Auburn: Derby and Miller, 1852), 66, 77. Gautham Rao argues that in the context of American state formation, the Fugitive Slave Act represented an important turning point: a moment in which the latent connections between slavery and federal power were laid bare. In many respects, one can see the reactions of northern abolitionists, and the distance they sought between themselves and national citizenship, as a reaction to this development. See Gautham Rao, "The Federal *Posse Comitatus* Doctrine: Slavery, Compulsion, and Statecraft in Mid-Nineteenth-Century America," *Law and History Review* 26, no. 1 (2008): 1–56.

33. John M. Krebs, *The American Citizen: A Discourse on the Nature and Extent of our Religious Subjection to the Government Under Which We Live* (New York: Scribner, 1851), 22–23, 25; John Henry Hopkins, *The American Citizen: His Rights and Duties, According to the Spirit of the Constitution of the United States* (New York: Pudney and Russell, 1857), 119. For more on the abolitionist reaction to the Fugitive Slave Act and the Compromise of 1850, see Sinha, *Slave's Cause*, 461–99, esp. 490–99.

34. *DeBow's Review* 24, no. 2 (1858): 136–46 (quotes on 136, 138, 145).

35. For the early history of the case, see Walter Ehrlich, "The Origins of the Dred Scott Case," *Journal of Negro History* 59, no. 2 (1974): 132–42, and Don E. Fehrenbacher, *The Dred Scott Case: Its Significance in American Law and Politics* (1978; New York: Oxford University Press, 2001), 250–65. For an excellent study of Harriet Scott, see Lea VanderVelde, *Mrs. Dred Scott: A Life on Slavery's Frontier* (New York: Oxford University Press, 2009).

36. *Scott v. Sandford*, 60 U.S. 393 (1858), 407. The best, most complete study remains Fehrenbacher, *Dred Scott Case*, though recent work has complicated the picture historians have drawn of the case, Taney, and the implications of the ruling. See John S. Vishneski, "What the Court Decided in *Dred Scott v. Sandford*," *American Journal of Legal History* 32, no. 4 (1988): 373–90; Lea VanderVelde and Sandhya Subramanian, "Mrs. Dred Scott," *Yale Law Journal* 106, no. 4 (1997): 1033–1122; Smith, *Civic Ideals*, 263–71; Dennis K. Boman, "The Dred Scott Case Reconsidered: The Legal and Political Context in Missouri," *American Journal of Legal History* 44, no. 4 (2000): 405–28; Keith E. Whittington, "The Road Not Taken: Dred Scott, Judicial Authority, and Political Questions," *Journal of Politics* 63, no. 2 (2001): 365–91; Timothy S. Huebner, "Roger B. Taney and the Slavery Issue: Looking Beyond—and Before—Dred Scott," *Journal of American History* 97, no. 1 (2010): 17–38; and Michael A. Schoeppner, "Status across Borders: Roger Taney, Black British Subjects, and a Diplomatic Antecedent to the Dred Scott Decision," *Journal of American History* 100, no. 1 (2013): 46–67. For two recent studies that situate the case in a broader national context, see Elizabeth R. Varon, *Disunion! The Coming of the American Civil War, 1789–1859* (Chapel Hill: University of North Carolina Press, 2008), 295–304, and James Oakes, *Freedom National: The Destruction of Slavery in the United States, 1861–1865* (New York: Norton, 2013), 1–48.

37. Fehrenbacher, *Dred Scott Case*, 64–73, 295–96.

38. *Scott v. Sandford*, 60 U.S. 393 (1858), 405, 406, 410. On this point, see Fehrenbacher, *Dred Scott Case*, 335–64, esp. 345–46, and Gerstle, *Liberty and Coercion*, 72. Given the political context in which it was offered, it is worth setting Taney's opinion alongside the arguments of Republican Party leaders, who (in contrast to Taney) interpreted the

Constitution as a document that bestowed broad powers in the national government to abolish slavery. For more on this idea, see Oakes, *Freedom National*, 34–42.

39. *Scott v. Sandford*, 60 U.S. 393 (1858), 509–17 (quote on 516–17).

40. Cong. Globe, 35th Cong., 2nd Sess. 982–83 (1859). On nativism and the Republican Party, see Potter, *Impending Crisis*, 225–66; William E. Gienapp, *The Origins of the Republican Party, 1852–1856* (New York: Oxford University Press, 1987); Tyler Anbinder, *Nativism and Slavery: The Northern Know-Nothings and the Politics of the 1850s* (New York: Oxford University Press, 1992); and Bruce Levine, "Conservatism, Nativism, and Slavery: Thomas R. Whitney and the Origins of the Know-Nothing Party," *Journal of American History* 88, no. 2 (2001): 455–88.

41. *Oxford Intelligencer*, 14 November 1860.

42. On secession and Confederate nationalism, see Drew Gilpin Faust, *The Creation of Confederate Nationalism: Ideology and Identity in the Civil War South* (Baton Rouge: Louisiana State University Press, 1988); Anne Sarah Rubin, *A Shattered Nation: The Rise and Fall of the Confederacy, 1861–1868* (Chapel Hill: University of North Carolina Press, 2005); Stephanie McCurry, *Confederate Reckoning: Power and Politics in the Civil War South* (Cambridge, Mass.: Harvard University Press, 2010); and Paul Quigley, *Shifting Grounds: Nationalism and the American South, 1848–1865* (New York: Oxford University Press, 2012).

43. *Journal of the Convention of the People of South Carolina* (Columbia: R. W. Gibbes, 1862), 52, 249.

44. William R. Smith, ed., *The History and Debates of the Convention of the People of Alabama* (Atlanta: Wood, Hanleiter, Rice and Co., 1861), 29, 53, 55, 68–74 (quotes on 29, 68–69). On secession in Alabama, see William Barney, *The Secessionist Impulse: Alabama and Mississippi in 1860* (Princeton: Princeton University Press, 1974); William W. Freehling, *The Road to Disunion*, vol. 2, *Secessionists Triumphant, 1854–1861* (New York: Oxford University Press, 2007), 492–95; and McCurry, *Confederate Reckoning*, 60–63.

45. *Journal of the Proceedings of the Convention of the People of Florida* (Tallahassee: Dyke and Carlisle, 1861), 103–4. On secession in Florida, see Ralph A. Wooster, "The Florida Secession Convention," *Florida Historical Quarterly* 36, no. 4 (1958): 373–85; Potter, *Impending Crisis*, 572–80; and McCurry, *Confederate Reckoning*, 53–55.

46. Smith, *History and Debates*, 223–25; *Journal of the Public and Secret Proceedings of the Convention of the People of Georgia* (Milledgeville: Boughton, Nisbet and Barnes, 1861), 72–73. For more on the gendered implications of secession, see McCurry, *Confederate Reckoning*, 38–84.

47. *Atlantic Monthly* 7, no. 40 (February 1861): 235–46 (quotes on 237, 239, 246).

48. The best biography of Davis remains William J. Cooper, *Jefferson Davis, American* (New York: Knopf, 2001).

49. Cong. Globe, 36th Cong., 2nd Sess. 487 (1861).

50. Cooper, *Jefferson Davis*, 349–50; *Natchez Daily Courier*, 10 January 1861.

CHAPTER TWO

1. An Abolitionist to Gov. Pettus, Vicksburg, Miss., 30 November 1859, folder 1, box 930 (roll 1), ser. 757, Governor John Jones Pettus, Correspondence and Papers, 1859–1863 and Undated, MDAH. On slave insurrection in Mississippi and elsewhere, see Herbert

Aptheker, *American Negro Slave Revolts* (1943; New York: International Publishers, 1968); Winthrop D. Jordan, *Tumult and Silence at Second Creek: An Inquiry into a Civil War Slave Conspiracy* (Baton Rouge: Louisiana State University Press, 1993); Justin Behrend, "Rebellious Talk and Conspiratorial Plots: The Making of a Slave Insurrection in Civil War Natchez," *Journal of Southern History* 77, no. 1 (2011): 17–52; and Walter Johnson, *River of Dark Dreams: Slavery and Empire in the Cotton Kingdom* (Cambridge, Mass.: Harvard University Press, 2013), 46–72.

2. Robert W. Dubay, *John Jones Pettus, Mississippi Fire-Eater: His Life and Times, 1813–1867* (Jackson: University Press of Mississippi, 1975), 3–37; *Mississippi Free Trader*, 15 July 1859; Gov. J. J. Pettus to Gov. William H. Gist, 7 April 1860, Jackson, Miss., vol. 44 (reel 4287), ser. 758, Executive Journals, John Jones Pettus, MDAH. For more on the Nashville Convention, see William W. Freehling, *The Road to Disunion*, vol. 1, *Secessionists at Bay, 1776–1854* (New York: Oxford University Press, 1990), 481–86. On Mississippi politics in the 1850s, see Bradley G. Bond, *Political Culture in the Nineteenth-Century South: Mississippi, 1830–1900* (Baton Rouge: Louisiana State University Press, 1995), 81–114, and Christopher J. Olsen, *Political Culture and Secession in Mississippi: Masculinity, Honor, and the Antiparty Tradition, 1830–1860* (New York: Oxford University Press, 2000), 71–95.

3. See William W. Freehling, *The South vs. The South: How Anti-Confederate Southerners Shaped the Course of the Civil War* (New York: Oxford University Press, 2001); William W. Freehling, *The Road to Disunion*, vol. 2, *Secessionists Triumphant, 1854–1861* (New York: Oxford University Press, 2007); and Stephanie McCurry, *Confederate Reckoning: Power and Politics in the Civil War South* (Cambridge, Mass.: Harvard University Press, 2010), 38–84, on the problems inherent in the secessionist project. The influence of planters over the nonslaveholding majority was dissected by Eugene Genovese in his often forgotten but powerfully argued article, "Yeoman Farmers in a Slaveholder's Democracy," *Agricultural History* 49, no. 2 (1975): 331–42. For a more recent and quite different view that emphasizes the imperial ambition of planters and the brutal cost accounting of cotton monoculture in the Mississippi Valley, see Johnson, *River of Dark Dreams*, 303–420.

4. The representative work on secession includes Avery O. Craven, *The Growth of Southern Nationalism, 1848–1861* (Baton Rouge: Louisiana State University Press, 1953); David M. Potter, *The South and the Sectional Conflict* (Baton Rouge: Louisiana State University Press, 1968); Steven A. Channing, *Crisis of Fear: Secession in South Carolina* (New York: Simon and Schuster, 1970); Emory M. Thomas, *The Confederacy as a Revolutionary Experience* (Englewood Cliffs, N.J.: Prentice-Hall, 1971); William Barney, *The Secessionist Impulse: Alabama and Mississippi in 1860* (Princeton: Princeton University Press, 1974); Michael Johnson, *Toward a Patriarchal Republic: The Secession of Georgia* (Baton Rouge: Louisiana State University Press, 1977); John McCardell, *The Idea of a Southern Nation: Southern Nationalists and Southern Nationalism, 1830–1860* (New York: Norton, 1979); Drew Gilpin Faust, *The Creation of Confederate Nationalism: Ideology and Identity in the Civil War South* (Baton Rouge: Louisiana State University Press, 1988); Daniel W. Crofts, *Reluctant Confederates: Upper South Unionists in the Secession Crisis* (Chapel Hill: University of North Carolina Press, 19888); George C. Rable, *The Confederate Republic: A Revolution against Politics* (Chapel Hill: University of North Carolina Press, 1994); William A. Link, *Roots of Secession: Slavery and Politics in Antebellum Virginia* (Chapel Hill: University of North Carolina Press, 2003); Anne Sarah Rubin, *A Shattered Nation:*

The Rise and Fall of the Confederacy, 1861–1868 (Chapel Hill: University of North Carolina Press, 2005); Freehling, *Road to Disunion*, vol. 2; Elizabeth R. Varon, *Disunion! The Coming of the American Civil War, 1789–1859* (Chapel Hill: University of North Carolina Press, 2008); and Paul Quigley, *Shifting Grounds: Nationalism and the American South, 1848–1865* (New York: Oxford University Press, 2012).

5. The focus of this chapter, on the formation of states as well as the Confederacy, builds on the work of scholars like Gary Gerstle, who has made a strong case for understanding American states as a powerful part of the federalist picture. See Gerstle, *Liberty and Coercion: The Paradox of American Government from the Founding to the Present* (Princeton: Princeton University Press, 2015), 55–86.

6. For the 1832 constitution, see Francis Newton Thorpe, ed., *The Federal and State Constitutions, Colonial Charters and Other Organic Laws of the States, Territories and Colonies Now or Heretofore Forming the United States of America* (Washington, D.C.: GPO, 1909), 4:2049–63.

7. For population data, see National Historical Geographic Information System (NHGIS), University of Minnesota, https://www.nhgis.org (21 February 2017). On this early national history of Mississippi, see Charles S. Sydnor, *Slavery in Mississippi* (New York: D. Appleton-Century, 1933); Percy Lee Rainwater, *Mississippi: Storm Center of Secession, 1856–1861* (Baton Rouge: Otto Claitor, 1938); Winbourne Magruder Drake, "The Mississippi Constitutional Convention of 1832," *Journal of Southern History* 23, no. 3 (1957): 354–70; Edwin A. Miles, *Jacksonian Democracy in Mississippi* (New York: Da Capo Press, 1970); John Hebron Moore, *The Emergence of the Cotton Kingdom in the Old Southwest: Mississippi, 1770–1860* (Baton Rouge: Louisiana State University Press, 1988); Charles C. Bolton, *Poor Whites of the Antebellum South: Tenants and Laborers in Central North Carolina and Northeast Mississippi* (Durham: Duke University Press, 1994); Bond, *Political Culture in the Nineteenth-Century South*; Christopher Morris, *Becoming Southern: The Evolution of a Way of Life, Warren County and Vicksburg, Mississippi, 1770–1860* (New York: Oxford University Press, 1995); Daniel H. Usner, "Frontier Exchange and Cotton Production: The Slave Economy in Mississippi, 1798–1836," *Slavery and Abolition* 20, no. 1 (1999): 24–37; David J. Libby, *Slavery and Frontier Mississippi, 1720–1835* (Jackson: University Press of Mississippi, 2004); Adam Rothman, *Slave Country: American Expansion and the Origins of the Deep South* (Cambridge, Mass.: Harvard University Press, 2005); Anthony E. Kaye, *Joining Places: Slave Neighborhoods in the Old South* (Chapel Hill: University of North Carolina Press, 2007); Johnson, *River of Dark Dreams*; and Erik Mathisen, "'Know All Men by These Presents': Bonds, Localism, and Politics in Early Republican Mississippi," *Journal of the Early Republic* 33, no. 4 (2013): 727–50.

8. Lewis C. Gray, *History of Agriculture in the Southern United States to 1860* (Washington, D.C.: Carnegie Institution of Washington, 1933), 2:697 (fig. 8); National Historical Geographic Information System (NHGIS), University of Minnesota, https://www.nhgis.org (21 February 2017); *Vicksburg Sun*, 9 April 1860. See also Moore, *Emergence of the Cotton Kingdom*; Bond, *Political Culture in the Nineteenth-Century South*; Joshua D. Rothman, *Flush Times and Fever Dreams: A Story of Capitalism and Slavery in the Age of Jackson* (Athens: University of Georgia Press, 2012), 157–206; Johnson, *River of Dark Dreams*, esp. 151–302; and Sven Beckert, *Empire of Cotton: A New History of Global Capitalism* (London: Allen Lane, 2014), 98–135.

9. Dantzler to Susan Dantzler, 27 November 1860, Jackson, Miss., and Dantzler to his Brother, 7 December 1860, Macon, Miss., folder 3, box 1, Dantzler Papers, DU.

10. *New York Times,* 10 December 1860; *Proceedings of the Mississippi State Convention, Held January 7th to 26th, A.D. 1861* (Jackson, Miss.: Power and Caldwater, 1861), 110–11.

11. *Proceedings of the Mississippi State Convention,* 10–14, 16.

12. Ibid., 14, 72–74.

13. Dantzler to Susan, Jackson, Miss., 17 January 1861, folder 3, box 1, Dantzler Papers, DU; *Journal of the House of Representatives of the State of Mississippi* (Jackson: E. Barksdale, 1861); *Laws of the State of Mississippi, Passed at a Called Session of the State Legislature, Held in the City of Jackson, July 1861* (Jackson: E. Barksdale, 1861), 3–7.

14. A. B. Dilworth to Gov. Pettus, Danville, Miss., 24 January 1861, folder 3, box 931 (roll 2); Citizens of Hair River to Gov. J. J. Pettus, Hair River, Miss., 18 May 1861, folder 4, box 932 (roll 3); and L. Lyles to His Excellency Gov. Pettus, Mobile, Ala., 5 May 1861, folder 1, box 932 (roll 3), Pettus Correspondence, MDAH. Secession in places like South Carolina confirm that popular military mobilization was hardly an aberration. See Stephen A. West, "Minute Men, Yeomen, and the Mobilization for Secession in the South Carolina Upcountry," *Journal of Southern History* 71, no. 1 (2005): 75–104.

15. C. B. Neut to His Excellency, J. J. Pettus, Rodney, Miss., 14 January 1861, folder 3, box 931 (roll 2), and Howard Hines to Gov. J. J. Pettus, Jefferson Co., Miss., 14 May 1861, folder 4, box 932 (roll 3), Pettus Correspondence, MDAH; *Natchez Daily Courier,* 30 October 1861. On the problem of slave loyalty from the slaveholder's perspective, the most perceptive interpretation remains Eugene D. Genovese, *Roll, Jordan, Roll: The World the Slaves Made* (New York: Pantheon, 1974), 87–97.

16. *Journal of the House of Representatives of the State of Mississippi* (1861), 8, 26–27. The state legislature would pass a law in August 1861 that placed a minimum ten-year jail term on any white inhabitant in the state who aided or abetted a slave rebellion. Punishments for slaves who took part in a similar action were not mentioned. See Act of 6 August 1861, ch. 48, *Laws of the State of Mississippi* (1861), 67–68.

17. *Natchez Daily Courier,* 22 January 1861.

18. Thorpe, *Federal and State Constitutions,* 4:2062. For more on the legal and political power rooted in southern counties, see Wooster, *People in Power,* 81–106; John Hebron Moore, "Local and State Governments in Antebellum Mississippi," *Journal of Mississippi History* 44, no. 2 (1982): 104–34; Stephanie McCurry, *Masters of Small Worlds: Yeoman Households, Gender Relations, and the Political Culture of the Antebellum South Carolina Low Country* (New York: Oxford University Press, 1995), 92–129; Gautham Rao, "The Federal *Posse Comitatus* Doctrine: Slavery, Compulsion, and Statecraft in Mid-Nineteenth-Century America," *Law and History Review* 26, no. 1 (2008): 1–56; Laura F. Edwards, *The People and Their Peace: Legal Culture and the Transformation of Inequality in the Post-Revolutionary South* (Chapel Hill: University of North Carolina Press, 2009); and Mathisen, "'Know All Men by These Presents.'"

19. *Annual Report of the Adjutant General of the State of Mississippi* (Jackson: Mississippian Book and Job Printing Office, 1861), 6; *Proceedings of the Mississippi State Convention,* 49–55, 64.

20. For regulations governing officer elections in the state, see Report of the Board (1861), Jackson, Miss., 20 February 1861, folder 1, box 416, Military Board of Mississippi

Minutes, ser. 394, Papers of the Military Board, 1861–1863, MDAH; William B. Trotter to Hon. John J. Pettus, Quitman, Miss., 12 April 1861, folder 9, box 931 (roll 2), and John C. Higgins to Hon. J. J. Pettus, Meridian, Miss., 18 January 1861, folder 3, box 931 (roll 2), Pettus Correspondence, MDAH. On the importance of militias, see John Hope Franklin, *The Militant South, 1800–1861* (Cambridge, Mass.: Belknap Press of Harvard University Press, 1956), 171–92; Mark Pitcavage, "An Equitable Burden: The Decline of the State Militias, 1783–1858" (Ph.D. diss., Ohio State University, 1995); McCurry, *Masters of Small Worlds*, 92–129; Sally E. Hadden, *Slave Patrols: Law and Violence in Virginia and the Carolinas* (Cambridge, Mass.: Harvard University Press, 2001), 47–104; Ira Katznelson, "Flexible Capacity: The Military and Early American Statebuilding," in *Shaped by War and Trade: International Influences on American Political Development*, ed. Martin Shefter (Princeton: Princeton University Press, 2002), 82–110; and Rao, "Federal *Posse Comitatus* Doctrine."

21. Robert Dubay, Pettus's biographer, lays much of the blame for this tug-of-war over the military at the feet of the state legislature, though the evidence suggests that this was a small concern when compared with the broader forces in Mississippi politics that Pettus would have had to face, to wrest control of the military from the hands of localities. See Dubay, *John Jones Pettus*, 92–117.

22. James R. Gates to Gov. Pettus, Charleston, Miss., 8 June 1861, folder 7, box 932 (roll 3), Pettus Correspondence, MDAH.

23. For more on the language of supplication in Civil War letters to government officials, see Gregory Downs, *Declarations of Dependence: The Long Reconstruction of Popular Politics in the South, 1861–1908* (Chapel Hill: University of North Carolina Press, 2011), 15–41. This point raises questions posed by Christopher Olsen, who argued that at least in Mississippi, local allegiances trumped party loyalty. See Olsen, *Political Culture and Secession in Mississippi*, 71–119. For the ways in which women bent this language in wartime to suit their own ends, see McCurry, *Confederate Reckoning*, 85–177. On the other dimensions of fictive kin, both white and black, see Herbert G. Gutman, *The Black Family in Slavery and Freedom, 1750–1925* (New York: Pantheon, 1976), 185–256; Orville Vernon Burton, *In My Father's House Are Many Mansions: Family and Community in Edgefield, South Carolina* (Chapel Hill: University of North Carolina Press, 1985), 47–103; Robert C. Kenzer, *Kinship and Neighborhood in a Southern Community: Orange County, North Carolina, 1849–1881* (Knoxville: University of Tennessee Press, 1987), and Dylan C. Penningroth, *The Claims of Kinfolk: African American Property and Community in the Nineteenth-Century South* (Chapel Hill: University of North Carolina Press, 2003), 79–109.

24. G. W. Gill to His Honor, J. J. Pettus, Marshall Co., Miss., 24 April 1861, folder 11, box 931 (roll 2); Friends of the Soldiers to Gov. J. J. Pettus, Rodney, Miss., 19 August 1861, folder 4, box 939 (roll 4); J. G. Love, M.D., to Governor Pettus, Carroll Co., Miss., 22 November 1861, folder 7, box 940 (roll 5); D. N. Cooper to His Excellency John Jones Pettus, Guntown, Miss., 23 May 1861, folder 5, box 932 (roll 3), Pettus Correspondence, MDAH.

25. *American Citizen*, 10 August 1861; Dubay, *John Jones Pettus*, 110–16; B. C. E. Estes to Gov. Pettus, Marion Station, Miss., 6 September 1861, folder 6, box 939 (roll 4), Pettus Correspondence, MDAH. The legislature's attempt to push the Confederacy to absorb state troops can be found in the Act of 6 August 1861, ch. 22, *Laws of the State of Mississippi* (1861), 45–46. The Confederate reply can be found in Jefferson Davis to Gen. L. Polk,

Richmond, Va., 15 September 1861, in *OR* 4:188. For the tally of Pettus's election victory, see *Journal of the Senate of the State of Mississippi* (Jackson: Cooper and Kimball, 1862), 29–30.

26. *Journal of the House of Representatives of the State of Mississippi, at a Regular Session thereof, held in the City of Jackson, November and December 1861, and January 1862* (Jackson: Cooper and Kimball, 1862), 10–16.

27. *Militia Law of the State of Mississippi* (Jackson: Cooper and Kimball, 1862); *Natchez Daily Courier*, 22 February 1862.

28. Thomas, *Confederacy as a Revolutionary Experience*; Richard Bensel, "Southern Leviathan: The Development of Central State Authority in the Confederate States of America," *Studies in American Political Development* 2 (1987): 68–136; Richard F. Bensel, *Yankee Leviathan: The Origins of Central State Authority in America, 1859–1877* (New York: Cambridge University Press, 1990); Armstead L. Robinson, *Bitter Fruits of Bondage: The Demise of Slavery and the Collapse of the Confederacy, 1861–1865* (Charlottesville: University of Virginia Press, 2005).

29. W. J. Reeves to Gov. Pettus, Baldwin, Miss., 5 January 1862, folder 1, box 941 (roll 6); D. L. Smythe to Gov. Pettus, Kosciusko, Miss., 4 March 1862, folder 4, box 941 (roll 6); John G. Battiff to Gov. Pettus, Verona, Miss., February 1862, folder 4, box 941 (roll 6), Pettus Correspondence, MDAH; *Daily Mississippian*, 21 July 1862.

30. W. R. Stewart to Gov. Pettus, Bolivar Co., Miss., 20 July 1862, folder 5, box 942 (roll 7), Pettus Correspondence, MDAH. For the importance of a culture of sacrifice in the development of Confederate nationalism, see Faust, *Creation of Confederate Nationalism*, 22–57; Rubin, *Shattered Nation*, 50–79; and Quigley, *Shifting Grounds*, 171–213.

31. For the order, see Gen. Order No. 9 (Adjut. Gen. Maj. M. M. Kimmell), Vicksburg, Miss., 4 July 1862, *OR* 15:772, and Charles F. Howell to Gov. Pettus, Jackson Co., Miss., 23 August 1862, folder 7, box 942 (roll 7), Pettus Correspondence, MDAH.

32. E. R. Brown to Gov. Pettus, Mount Hope, Miss., 11 November 1862, folder 2, box 943 (roll 8); Judge Scarborough to Gov. Pettus, Kosciusko, Miss., 5 November 1862, folder 1, box 943 (roll 8); and Sheriff J. H. Jones to Gov. Pettus, Panola Co., Miss., 12 November 1862, folder 2, box 943 (roll 8), all in Pettus Correspondence, MDAH; *Journal of the House of Representatives of the State of Mississippi, December Session of 1862, and November Session of 1863* (Jackson: Cooper and Kimball, 1864), 12–13, 15–23. For more on the deprivations that placed added strain on state and Confederate governments alike, see the literature that includes Mary E. Massey, *Ersatz in the Confederacy* (Columbia: University of South Carolina Press, 1952); Paul D. Escott, "The Cry of the Sufferers: The Problem of Welfare in the Confederacy," *Civil War History* 23 (1977): 228–40; Stephen V. Ash, *When the Yankees Came: Conflict and Chaos in the Occupied South, 1861–1865* (Chapel Hill: University of North Carolina Press, 1995); William A. Blair, *Virginia's Private War: Feeding Body and Soul in the Confederacy, 1861–1865* (New York: Oxford University Press, 1998), 81–107, 134–52; Robinson, *Bitter Fruits of Bondage*, 104–88; and McCurry, *Confederate Reckoning*, 178–217.

33. *American Citizen*, 27 March 1863; Maj. Gen. S. J. Gholson to Col. James S. Hamilton, Adjut. Gen., Tibber, Miss., 14 August 1863, folder 10, box 392, ser. 400, Adjutants-General Correspondence, 1861–1864, MDAH.

34. *Laws of the State of Mississippi, Passed at a Called and Regular Session of the Mississippi Legislature, Held in Jackson and Columbus, Dec. 1862 and Nov. 1863* (Selma:

Cooper and Kimball, 1864), 108–9; *Journal of the House of Representatives of the State of Mississippi, 1862 and 1863*, 112–13, 117, 119, 122 (quote on 119).

35. *Journal of the House of Representatives of the State of Mississippi, 1862 and 1863*, 271–75 (quotes on 271, 275).

36. William Delay to His Excellency, Gov. Charles Clark, Oxford, Miss., 27 November 1863, folder 1, box 949; Clark to Delay, Columbus, Miss., 6 December 1863, folder 1, box 949; N. M. Thompson to Gov. Clark, Yazoo City, Miss., 21 January 1864, folder 3, box 949, ser. 768, Governor Charles Clark, Correspondence and Papers, 1863–1865, MDAH. On slave impressments and the demands of the Confederacy, see, for example, Gov. Charles Clark to Maj. J. C. Dunnis, Macon, Miss., 11 January 1864, vol. 44 (reel 4287), ser. 758, Executive Journals, 1817–1887, Charles Clark, 1864–1865, MDAH. On Clark, see John Coleman Wade, "Charles Clark: Confederate General and Mississippi Governor" (M.A. thesis, University of Mississippi, 1949). On contraband trading in Mississippi, see Jarret Ruminski, "'Tradyville': The Contraband Trade and the Problem of Loyalty in Civil War Mississippi," *Journal of the Civil War Era* 2, no. 4 (2012): 511–37

37. Sheriff D. W. Bradley to Gov. Clark, Augusta, Miss., 8 February 1864, and W. H. Horner to His Excellency, Gov. Charles Clark, Smith Co., Miss., 8 February 1864, folder 4, box 949, Clark Correspondence, MDAH. The literature on disloyalty in the Confederacy has long been a vibrant area of research. For the best of this work, see Albert B. Moore, *Conscription and Conflict in the Confederacy* (New York: Macmillan, 1924); Ella Lonn, *Desertion during the Civil War* (New York: Century, 1928); Georgia Lee Tatum, *Disloyalty in the Confederacy* (Chapel Hill: University of North Carolina Press, 1934); Charles W. Ramsdell, *Behind the Lines in the Southern Confederacy* (New York: Greenwood, 1969); and Victoria E. Bynum, *The Free State of Jones: Mississippi's Longest Civil War* (Chapel Hill: University of North Carolina Press, 2001). Scholars like Bynum have often connected this disaffection to the nation, not individual state governments and their collapse. In the case of Mississippi, the timing of real threats—most notably in places like Jones County— suggests that it was the disintegration of state authority that contributed as much, if not more, to the spread of dissent.

38. Though more focused on the measurement of state power at the national level, see Bensel, *Yankee Leviathan*.

39. *Journal of the House of Representatives of the State of Mississippi, 1862 and 1863*, 89–90; *Natchez Daily Courier*, 20 October 1863.

40. For the legislation of the Confederate Congress relating to the seizure of property, see Act of 17 March 1862, ch. 5, *Statutes at Large of the Confederate States of America* [1862] (Richmond: R. M. Smith, 1862), 2. For the regulation of impressment, see Act of 26 March 1863, ch. 10, *Statutes at Large of the Confederate States of America* [1863] (Richmond: R. M. Smith, 1863), 102–4. For the state debate over impressment of slaves, see *Journal of the House of Representatives of the State of Mississippi, 1862 and 1863*, 6, 38, 40, 177, 187, and Gen. Order No. 138 (24 October 1863), ser. 390 (reel 2), RG 94, The Negro in the Military Service of the United States, 1639–1886 (M858), NA. The best literature on Confederate impressment and confiscation includes Bensel, *Yankee Leviathan*, 156–60; Brian R. Dirck, "Posterity's Blush: Civil Liberties, Property Rights, and Property Confiscation in the Confederacy," *Civil War History* 48, no. 3 (2002): 237–56; Daniel W. Hamilton, "The Confederate Sequestration Act," *Civil War History* 52, no. 4 (2006): 373–408; and Daniel W. Hamilton, *The Limits of*

Sovereignty: Property Confiscation in the Union and the Confederacy during the Civil War (Chicago: University of Chicago Press, 2007).

41. Gov. Charles Clark to Col. F. S. Blount, Macon, Miss., 1 April 1864, and Gov. Charles Clark to Maj. J. C. Dunnis, Macon, Miss., 11 January 1864, vol. 44 (reel 4287), Executive Journals, Charles Clark, MDAH; Gov. Charles Clark to J. W. C. Watson, Macon, Miss., 21 December 1863, folder 2, box 949, Clark Correspondence, MDAH.

42. *Journal of the House of Representatives of the State of Mississippi, Called Session at Columbus, February and March, 1865* (Meridian: J. J. Shannon and Co., 1865), 12–13.

43. Ibid., 61, 95.

CHAPTER THREE

1. *Army Regulations Adopted for the use of the Army of the Confederate States, In Accordance with the Late Act of Congress* (Atlanta: Gaulding and Whitaker, 1861), 24–26, 62–66, 71–75 (quote on 7); John P. Curry, *Volunteers' Camp and Field Book* (Richmond: West and Johnston, 1862), 75–77, 83, 86, 89, 100–101 (quote on 96). The best work on life in the Confederate camp remains Bell Irvin Wiley, *The Life of Johnny Reb: The Common Soldier in the Confederacy* (Baton Rouge: Louisiana State University Press, 1943), but see also J. Tracy Power, *Lee's Miserables: Life in the Army of Northern Virginia from the Wilderness to Appomattox* (Chapel Hill: University of North Carolina Press, 1998), and Chandra Manning, *What This Cruel War Was Over: Soldiers, Slavery, and the Civil War* (New York: Knopf, 2007).

2. As Stephanie McCurry has argued, individuals not counted as citizens by the Confederacy had their own bruising experience of citizenship. See McCurry, *Confederate Reckoning: Power and Politics in the Civil War South* (Cambridge, Mass.: Harvard University Press, 2010), 133–77, 263–357.

3. The most important work on the Confederate state was taken up by Richard Bensel in his *Yankee Leviathan: The Origins of Central State Authority in America, 1859–1877* (New York: Cambridge University Press, 1990), 94–237, though other work that pays due attention to state formation includes Emory M. Thomas, *The Confederacy as a Revolutionary Experience* (Englewood Cliffs, N.J.: Prentice-Hall, 1971); Paul D. Escott, *After Secession: Jefferson Davis and the Failure of Confederate Nationalism* (Baton Rouge: Louisiana State University Press, 1978); Emory M. Thomas, *The Confederate Nation, 1861–1865* (New York: Harper and Row, 1979); George C. Rable, *The Confederate Republic: A Revolution against Politics* (Chapel Hill: University of North Carolina Press, 1994); Armstead L. Robinson, *Bitter Fruits of Bondage: The Demise of Slavery and the Collapse of the Confederacy, 1861–1865* (Charlottesville: University of Virginia Press, 2005); John Majewski, *Modernizing a Slave Economy: The Economic Vision of the Confederate Nation* (Chapel Hill: University of North Carolina Press, 2009); McCurry, *Confederate Reckoning*; and Paul Quigley, "State, Nation, and Citizen in the Confederate Crucible of War," in *State and Citizen: British America and the Early United States*, ed. Peter Thompson and Peter S. Onuf (Charlottesville: University of Virginia Press, 2013), 242–70.

4. The emphasis on the Confederacy as a bold gamble emerges most clearly in Stephanie McCurry's *Confederate Reckoning*, though in much of the literature, the emphasis remains wedded to explaining the state's collapse, rather than in taking stock of what Confederates

accomplished. The creativity of the Confederate project is evident in the literature on southern nationalism, most especially in Drew Gilpin Faust, *The Creation of Confederate Nationalism: Ideology and Identity in the Civil War South* (Baton Rouge: Louisiana State University Press, 1988); Anne Sarah Rubin, *A Shattered Nation: The Rise and Fall of the Confederacy, 1861–1868* (Chapel Hill: University of North Carolina Press, 2005); Paul Quigley, *Shifting Grounds: Nationalism and the American South, 1848–1865* (New York: Oxford University Press, 2012); and Enrico Dal Lago, "The Nineteenth-Century 'Other Souths,' Modernization, and Nation-Building: Expanding the Comparative Perspective," in *New Directions in Slavery Studies: Commodification, Community, and Comparison*, ed. Jeff Forret and Christina E. Sears (Baton Rouge: Louisiana State University Press, 2015), 219–38. Though scholars of transnational history have worked hard to explain away the importance of states, more recent work has focused on how much the middle decades of the nineteenth century were a hothouse moment for state-building all over the globe. See particularly C. A. Bayly, *The Birth of the Modern World, 1780–1914* (Oxford: Blackwell, 2004), 247–83; Jürgen Osterhammel, *The Transformation of the World: A Global History of the Nineteenth Century* (Princeton: Princeton University Press, 2014), 572–633; and Charles S. Maier, *Leviathan 2.0: Inventing Modern Statehood* (Cambridge, Mass.: Harvard University Press, 2014).

5. The idea of the military as an institution of political socialization draws on the work of Eugen Weber in his study of the French state. See Weber, *Peasants into Frenchmen: The Modernization of Rural France, 1870–1914* (Stanford: Stanford University Press, 1976), 241–77. For the rationalization of state control and the lasting mark it can leave in space, as well as on a populace, see James C. Scott, *Seeing Like a State: How Certain Schemes to Improve the Human Condition Have Failed* (New Haven: Yale University Press, 1998).

6. *Journal of the Congress of the Confederate States of America* (Washington, D.C.: GPO, 1904), 1:3–31.

7. *Confederate Const.* art. 2 §1; art. 4 §2, Avalon Project, Documents in Law, History and Diplomacy, Yale University Law School http://avalon.law.yale.edu (21 February 2017). See also James H. Kettner, *The Development of American Citizenship, 1608–1870* (Chapel Hill: Published for the Omohundro Institute of Early American History and Culture by the University of North Carolina Press, 1978), 334–38, and Thomas, *Confederate Nation*, 37–66.

8. *Journal of the Congress*, 1:37.

9. *Confederate Const.* art. 1 §2; art. 2 §1; art. 3 §2, Avalon Project. For Davis's message, see *Journal of the Congress*, 1:273. See also McCurry, *Confederate Reckoning*, 79–81.

10. For Stephens's famous "Cornerstone Speech," see *Alexander H. Stephens, in Public and Private: With Letters and Speeches, Before, During, and Since the War*, ed. Henry Cleveland (Philadelphia: National Publishing Co., 1866), 717–29. For an even more unequivocal reiteration of the basic racial tenets of the Confederate nation, see Stephens's address to the Virginia Secession Convention in late April 1861, in ibid., 729–45.

11. On nationalism in the broader context, see Eric Hobsbawm, *The Age of Revolution, 1789–1848* (1962; New York: Vintage Books, 1996), 132–45, and Benedict R. Anderson, *Imagined Communities: Reflections on the Origin and Spread of Nationalism* (London and New York: Verso, 1991). More specifically for the Confederacy, see Faust, *Creation of Confederate Nationalism*, and Quigley, *Shifting Grounds*. On the relationship between the Civil War and the revolutions of 1848, see Patrick J. Kelly, "The European Revolutions of 1848 and the Transnational Turn in Civil War History," *Journal of the Civil War Era* 4, no.

3 (2014): 431–43. On the broader international context within which Confederates made sense of their nation, see Andre M. Fleche, *The Revolution of 1861: The American Civil War in the Age of Nationalist Conflict* (Chapel Hill: University of North Carolina Press, 2012), and Don H. Doyle, *The Cause of All Nations: An International History of the American Civil War* (New York: Basic Books, 2015).

12. *Journal of the Congress*, 1:56, 217. For the text of the bill, see Act of 22 August 1861, ch. 37, *Confed. Stat.* 189–90.

13. *Journal of the Congress*, 1:288, 291, 302–3, 319–320. For the text of the law, see Act of 8 August 1861, ch. 19, *Confed. Stat.* 174.

14. For more on this in the American Revolutionary context, see Charles Royster, *A Revolutionary People at War: The Continental Army and American Character, 1775–1783* (New York: Norton, 1981), 127–254.

15. Maj. P. Tracy to Sec. of War, Yorktown, Va., 19 August 1861 (roll 7), Letters Received by the Confederate Secretary of War (M437), War Department Collection of Confederate Records, RG 109, NA.

16. Maj. Gen. Braxton Bragg to Maj. Gen. Mansfield Lovell, Richmond, Va., 23 December 1861, in *OR* 6:785; Maj. Gen. Braxton Bragg to Adjut. and Inspect. Gen. S. Cooper, Tupelo, Miss., 16 July 1862, in *OR* 17(2):647; Sec. of War J. P. Benjamin to Maj. Gen. R. E. Lee, Richmond, Va., 8 December 1861, in *OR* 6:340; Members of the Culpepper Minute Men to Col. A. P. Hill, Camp near Centerville, Va., 16 November 1861 (roll 17), Letters Received by the Confederate Secretary of War (M437), RG 109, NA.

17. There is an interesting literature on Confederate conscription, though in the main, historians have not really addressed the timing of such a sweeping measure. If we set it against the national government's difficulties in securing control of its own military, we might better see something of the thinking behind it. For the literature on conscription, see Albert B. Moore, *Conscription and Conflict in the Confederacy* (New York: Macmillan, 1924), 12–113; Escott, *After Secession*, 54–93; Thomas, *Confederate Nation*, 145–66; James M. McPherson, *Battle Cry of Freedom: The Civil War Era* (New York: Oxford University Press, 1988), 429–33; Bensel, *Yankee Leviathan*, 135–39; Robinson, *Bitter Fruits of Bondage*, 134–62; and Quigley, "State, Nation, and Citizen," 248–51.

18. *Journal of the Congress*, 2:22.

19. Ibid., 2:123, 128, 137.

20. Ibid., 2:140–42, 146, 153–54. For the Conscript Act, see Act of 16 April 1862, ch. 31, *Confed. Stat.* 29–32. On habeas corpus, see Act of 27 February 1862, ch. 2, *Confed. Stat.* 1. On the state's control over property and its destruction, see Act of 17 March 1862, ch. 5, *Confed. Stat.* 2. See also Bensel, *Yankee Leviathan*, 139–44, 146–61; Brian R. Dirck, "Posterity's Blush: Civil Liberties, Property Rights, and Property Confiscation in the Confederacy," *Civil War History* 48, no. 3 (2002): 237–56; Daniel W. Hamilton, "The Confederate Sequestration Act," *Civil War History* 52, no. 4 (2006): 373–408; and Daniel W. Hamilton, *The Limits of Sovereignty: Property Confiscation in the Union and the Confederacy during the Civil War* (Chicago: University of Chicago Press, 2007).

21. Furniaful to Sister, Savannah, Ga., 27 February 1862, George Furniaful Papers, Special Collections, DU.

22. J. L. Pugh to Hon. G. W. Randolph, Eufaula, Ala., 27 May 1862 (roll 68), and F. S. Hayward to Hon. G. W. Randolph, Richmond, Va., 11 October 1862 (roll 53), Letters

Received by the Confederate Secretary of War (M437), RG 109, NA. On the influence of exemptions and conscription on Confederate communities, see John K. Bettersworth, *Confederate Mississippi: The People and Policies of a Cotton State in Wartime* (Baton Rouge: Louisiana State University Press, 1943), 188–212, and William A. Blair, *Virginia's Private War: Feeding Body and Soul in the Confederacy, 1861–1865* (New York: Oxford University Press, 1998), 81–107.

23. Thomas H. Watts to Hon. George W. Randolph, Richmond, Va., May 1862 (roll 77), Letters Received by the Confederate Secretary of War (M437), RG 109, NA; *Richmond Examiner,* 18 September 1862. The issue of foreign persons in the Confederacy, as well as maturing ideas within the Confederacy regarding citizenship, is a point made especially well by Paul Quigley in "Civil War Conscription and the International Boundaries of Citizenship," *Journal of the Civil War Era* 4, no. 3 (2014): 373–97.

24. Report of Col. William P. Johnston, Richmond, Va., 15 July 1862, *OR* 10(1):780–81.

25. J. W. Reid, *History of the Fourth Regiment S.C. Volunteers, from the Commencement of the War until Lee's Surrender* (Greenville: Shannon and Co, 1892), 76.

26. J. R. Baird to J. H. Richards, Bethany, Va., 27 December 1860, folder 7, box 1, and J. W. Baird to "My Dear Lost Boy," Sunflower Co., Miss., 17 June 1861, folder 9, box 1, J. R. Baird Collection, Charles W. Capps Jr. Archives and Museum, Delta State University, Cleveland, Miss. For Baird's service record, see Civil War Soldiers and Sailors Database, National Parks Service https://www.nps.gov/civilwar/soldiers-and-sailors-database.htm (21 February 2017).

27. J. R. Baird to J. M. Baird, Shelbyville, Tenn., 18 March 1863, folder 12, box 1, and J. R. Baird to J. M. Baird, Camp Hindman, near Chattanooga, Tenn., 28 August 1863, folder 14, box 1, Baird Collection, Delta State University.

28. *Army Regulations Adopted for the use of the Army of the Confederate States,* 3–4, 175. One of the most grounded studies that helps to explain a growing veracity for the Confederate cause among soldiers is Aaron Sheehan-Dean, *Why Confederates Fought: Family and Nation in Civil War Virginia* (Chapel Hill: University of North Carolina Press, 2007).

29. L. V. Buckholtz, *Tactics for Officers of Infantry, Cavalry and Artillery* (Richmond: J. W. Randolph, 1861), 7–8. As John Fabian Witt makes clear, a similar process was taking place in the American Army as well. See Witt, *Lincoln's Code: The Laws of War in American History* (New York: Free Press, 2012), 197–249.

30. Isaac Alexander to his Mother and Sister, near Corinth, Miss., 22 May 1862, Isaac Alexander Papers, SHC; *American Citizen,* 18 January 1862. The best study on the idle life of the soldier is Wiley, *Life of Johnny Reb,* 36–58, 90–107, 151–73. See also Manning, *What This Cruel War Was Over.*

31. On politics and the Confederate Army, see David Donald, "The Confederate as Fighting Man," *Journal of Southern History* 25, no. 2 (1959): 178–93; James M. McPherson, *For Cause and Comrades: Why Men Fought in the Civil War* (New York: Oxford University Press, 1997); and Manning, *What This Cruel War Was Over.*

32. On the importance of religion to Confederate soldiers—and a growing literature that views the Civil War as a key moment of revivalism in the nineteenth century—see Drew Gilpin Faust, "Christian Soldiers: The Meaning of Revivalism in the Confederate Army," *Journal of Southern History* 53, no. 1 (1987): 63–90; Randall L. Miller, Harry S. Stout,

and Charles Reagan Wilson, eds., *Religion and the American Civil War* (New York: Oxford University Press, 1998); Steven E. Woodworth, *While God Is Marching On: The Religious World of Civil War Soldiers* (Lawrence: University Press of Kansas, 2001); George C. Rable, *God's Almost Chosen Peoples: A Religious History of the American Civil War* (Chapel Hill: University of North Carolina Press, 2010); and Timothy L. Wesley, *The Politics of Faith during the Civil War* (Baton Rouge: Louisiana State University Press, 2013).

33. Harry Lewis to His Mother, Camp Clark, 26 June 1861, folder 1, Harry Lewis Papers, SHC.

34. *Confederate Baptist,* 22 October, 4 November, 17 December 1862, 7 January 1863. For revivalism, see Faust, "Christian Soldiers," and Rable, *God's Almost Chosen Peoples,* 90–106, 127–46. On soldiers' religious newspapers, see Kurt O. Berends, "'Wholesome Reading Purifies and Elevates the Man': The Religious Military Press in the Confederacy," in Miller, Stout, and Wilson, *Religion and the American Civil War,* 131–66.

35. *Confederate Baptist,* 20 May 1863; Rev. J. H. Thornwell, *Our Danger and Our Duty* (Columbia: Southern Guardian Steam-Power Press, 1862), 5, 8.

36. As George Rable has recently made clear, religious organizations became key to the policing of loyalty in both North and South by the middle stages of the war. See Rable, *God's Almost Chosen Peoples,* 335–52. More recently, scholars have taken an increasingly dim view of this development, laying blame at the feet of the clergy on both sides of the battlefield for their toxic rhetoric that pushed the country into the war. See David Goldfield, *America Aflame: How the Civil War Created a Nation* (New York: Bloomsbury, 2011). On the importance of religion to Confederate nationalism, see Faust, *Creation of Confederate Nationalism,* 22–40.

37. Rev. John Paris, *A Sermon: Preached before Brig. Gen. Hoke's Brigade, at Kinston, N.C., on the 28th of February, 1864, by Rev. John Paris, Chaplain Fifty-Fourth Regiment N.C. Troops, upon the Death of Twenty-Two Men, Who Had Been Executed in the Presence of the Brigade for the Crime of Desertion* (Greensborough, N.C.: A. W. Ingold and Co., 1864), 7, 12.

38. The best estimates suggest that by the middle of 1863, between 50,000 and 136,000 Confederate soldiers were absent without leave, and that just over 100,000 had deserted the army by the Civil War's end. See Ella Lonn, *Desertion during the Civil War* (New York: Century, 1928), 21–37.

39. The best study on desertion has long been Ella Lonn's *Desertion during the Civil War,* though her work has been augmented by Mark Weitz in *More Damning Than Slaughter: Desertion in the Confederate Army* (Lincoln: University of Nebraska Press, 2005). See also Wiley, *Life of Johnny Reb,* 123–50; Reid Mitchell, *Civil War Soldiers* (New York: Simon and Schuster, 1988), 148–73; Richard Bardolph, "Confederate Dilemma: North Carolina Troops and the Deserter Problem," *North Carolina Historical Review* 66, no. 1 and 2 (1989): 61–86, 179–210; Gary W. Gallagher, *The Confederate War* (Cambridge, Mass.: Harvard University Press, 1997), 31–33; Rubin, *Shattered Nation,* 68–79; McCurry, *Confederate Reckoning,* 116–32; Scott King-Owen, "Conditional Confederates: Absenteeism among Western North Carolina Soldiers, 1861–1865," *Civil War History* 57, no. 4 (2011): 349–79; and Patrick Doyle, "Understanding the Desertion of South Carolinian Soldiers during the Final Years of the Confederacy," *Historical Journal* 56 (2013): 657–79.

40. Rev. Basil Manly, *The Young Deserter* (n.p., n.d.), 1, 3, 4–5.

41. Ibid., 6; *Report of the Adjutant and Inspector General*, Richmond, Va., 31 January 1863, and Lewis to his Mother, near Fredericksburg, Va., 7 January 1862, folder 1, Harry Lewis Papers, SHC.

42. Capt. W. M. Butt to White, camp near Rappadan, Va., 20 August 1862, folder 1, Andrew White Papers, DU.

43. Sentence of Capt. Jonathan Becker, 38th Ala. Regt., 17 June 1862; Sentence of Lieut. P. C. Harper, 25th La. Vols., 18 February 1863; Sentence of Jonathan Florrit, Lewis Ferrimen, and John Shorting, 1 December 1862, chap. 1, vol. 195, Records of Courts-Martial, 1861–1865, Records of the Adjutant and Inspector General's Department, RG 109, War Department Collection of Confederate Records, 1861–1865, NA.

44. *Daily Mississippian* (from the *Atlanta Confederacy*), 11 April 1863.

45. Circular No. 5, Richmond, Va., 29 January 1864, chap. 1, vol. 258, Circulars Issued by the Bureau of Conscription (1864), Records of the Adjutant and Inspector General's Department, RG 109, War Department Collection of Confederate Records, NA; *Army and Navy Herald*, 23 March 1865.

46. Cousin to Eliza Caldwell, Duck Hill, Miss., 15 March 1865, Eliza F. Caldwell Papers, DU; S. H. Melcher to Col. Samuel Thomas, La Grange, Tenn., 6 February 1865, roll 15 (Letters Received), Asst. Comm-MS, BRFAL, NA.

47. William McDonald, *The Two Rebellions; or Treason Unmasked* (Richmond: Smith, Bailey and Co., 1865), 7.

48. Ibid., 13–36, 64–72, 79–87 (quotes on 115, 117, 124).

49. On the tensions of loyalty that white Confederates carried with them into the postwar period, see James J. Broomall, "Personal Reconstructions: Confederates as Citizens in the Post-War South," in *Creating Citizenship in the Nineteenth Century South*, ed. William A. Link et al. (Gainesville: University Press of Florida, 2013), 111–33, and David T. Ballantyne, "'Whenever the Yankees Were Gone, I Was a Confederate': Loyalty and Dissent in Civil War–Era Rapides Parish, Louisiana," *Civil War History* 63, no. 1 (2017): 36–67.

CHAPTER FOUR

1. *Harper's New Monthly Magazine* 23, no. 138 (November 1861): 721–32 (quote on 730).

2. *New York Tribune*, 1 July 1861, 7 August 1862. By the middle stages of the war, Horace Greeley had come to see disloyalty within the Union as a threat equal to that of the Confederacy. In an open letter intended for publication in Minnesota, the *Tribune* editor expressed the fear that "disloyalty at the North would complete the ruin [set in motion by] treason at the South" (Greeley to John H. Stevens, New York, N.Y., 16 August 1863, box 1 [reel 1], Horace Greeley Papers, New York Public Library, New York, N.Y.).

3. On loyalty during the Civil War, see Harold M. Hyman, *Era of the Oath: Northern Loyalty Tests during the Civil War and Reconstruction* (Philadelphia: University of Pennsylvania Press, 1954); Harold M. Hyman, *To Try Men's Souls: Loyalty Tests in American History* (Berkeley: University of California Press, 1960); and William A. Blair, *With Malice toward Some: Treason and Loyalty in the Civil War Era* (Chapel Hill: University of North Carolina Press, 2014). On the impact of the war dead on American culture, see Drew Gilpin Faust, *The Republic of Suffering: Death and the American Civil War* (New York: Knopf, 2008).

4. On the redefinition of treason during the Civil War, see Blair, *With Malice toward Some*, 36–65.

5. Proclamation of Amnesty and Reconstruction, 8 December 1863, in *The Collected Works of Abraham Lincoln* https://quod.lib.umich.edu/cgi/t/text/text-idx?page=browse&c=lincoln (21 February 2017). As William Blair makes clear, wartime definitions of loyalty leaned heavily on popular understandings of the crime, which often bore little relation to the legal definition of treason. See Blair, *With Malice toward Some*, 36–65, 100–159.

6. The literature on the African American experience during the Civil War is massive, but the most influential work in this field includes Joseph T. Wilson, *The Black Phalanx: A History of the Negro Soldiers of the United States in the Wars of 1775–1812, 1861–65* (1888; New York: Arno Press, 1968); Benjamin Quarles, *The Negro in the Civil War* (Boston: Little, Brown, 1953); Dudley Taylor Cornish, *The Sable Arm: Black Troops in the Union Army, 1861–1865* (1956; Lawrence: University of Kansas Press, 1987); James M. McPherson, *The Negro's Civil War: How American Negroes Felt and Acted during the War for the Union* (1965; Urbana: University of Illinois Press, 1982); Leon F. Litwack, *Been in the Storm So Long: The Aftermath of Slavery* (New York: Knopf, 1979); Ira Berlin, Joseph P. Reidy, and Leslie S. Rowland, eds., *Freedom: A Documentary History of Emancipation, 1861–1867: The Black Military Experience*, ser. 2 (Cambridge: Cambridge University Press, 1982); John David Smith, ed., *Black Soldiers in Blue: African American Troops in the Civil War Era* (Chapel Hill: University of North Carolina Press, 2002); Keith P. Wilson, *Campfires of Freedom: The Camp Life of Black Soldiers during the Civil War* (Kent, Ohio: Kent State University Press, 2002); Donald R. Shaffer, *After the Glory: The Struggles of Black Civil War Veterans* (Lawrence: University Press of Kansas, 2004); Michael J. Bennett, *Union Jacks: Yankee Sailors in the Civil War* (Chapel Hill: University of North Carolina Press, 2004); Richard M. Reid, *Freedom for Themselves: North Carolina's Black Soldiers in the Civil War Era* (Chapel Hill: University of North Carolina Press, 2008); Carole Emberton, "'Only Murder Makes Men': Reconsidering the Black Military Experience," *Journal of the Civil War Era* 2, no. 3 (2012): 369–93; Chandra Manning, "Working for Citizenship in Civil War Contraband Camps," *Journal of the Civil War Era* 4, no. 2 (2014): 172–204; and Jonathan Lande, "Trials of Freedom: African American Deserters during the U.S. Civil War," *Journal of Social History* 49, no. 3 (2015): 693–709.

7. On Wigfall, see Alvy L. King, *Louis T. Wigfall: Southern Fire-eater* (Baton Rouge: Louisiana State University Press, 1970), and Edward S. Cooper, *Louis Trezevant Wigfall: The Disintegration of the Union and Collapse of the Confederacy* (Madison, N.J.: Fairleigh Dickinson University Press, 2012).

8. Cong. Globe, 36th Cong., Spec. Sess. 1447–48, 1449–50 (1861).

9. On Carroll's life, see Sarah Ellen Blackwell, *A Military Genius: Life of Anna Ella Carroll of Maryland* (Washington, D.C.: Judd and Detweiler, 1891), and Janet L. Coryell, *Neither Heroine nor Fool: Anna Ella Carroll of Maryland* (Kent, Ohio: Kent State University Press, 1990).

10. Anna Ella Carroll, *The War Powers of the General Government* (Washington, D.C.: Henry Polkinhorn, 1861), 2.

11. Ibid., 6, 8.

12. Ibid., 23. Carroll's discussion of slavery, which so presciently foreshadowed Union thinking on emancipation, echoes in the history examined by James Oakes in *Freedom*

National: The Destruction of Slavery in the United States, 1861–1865 (New York: Norton, 2013), 49–83. For a brilliant study on the history of the American laws of war, see John Fabian Witt, *Lincoln's Code: The Laws of War in American History* (New York: Free Press, 2012), 197–219. As Max Edling has persuasively argued, Carroll's imagining of a federal state could be seen less as a wartime innovation than as the culmination of a state that had long been imbued with enormous potential capacity. See Max M. Edling, *A Hercules in the Cradle: War, Money, and the American State, 1783–1867* (Chicago: University of Chicago Press, 2014), 178–221.

13. Cong. Globe, 37th Cong., 2nd Sess. 869 (1862).

14. Cong. Globe, 37th Cong., 2nd Sess. 1263–64 (1862).

15. For the oath, see Act of 6 August 1861, ch. 64, *Stat.* 326–27. The best examination of the problem of Civil War loyalty and the Select Committee on the Loyalty of Clerks remains Hyman, *To Try Men's Souls*, 157–65.

16. Select Comm. on the Loyalty of Clerks and Other Persons Employed by Government, H.R. Rep. No. 16 (1862), 2, 3, 5.

17. H.R. Rep. No. 16 (1862), 9–10, 16–21, 33.

18. On Seward, see Hyman, *To Try Men's Souls*, 141–44, and Glyndon G. Van Deusen, *William Henry Seward* (New York: Oxford University Press, 1967), 288–91. See also *North American Review* 94, no. 194 (January 1862), 153–74 (quotes on 154). For the growth of the federal state, see James M. McPherson, *Battle Cry of Freedom: The Civil War Era* (New York: Oxford University Press, 1988); Richard F. Bensel, *Yankee Leviathan: The Origins of Central State Authority in America, 1859–1877* (New York: Cambridge University Press, 1990); Philip S. Paludan, *A People's Contest: The Union and the Civil War, 1861–65* (Lawrence: University Press of Kansas, 1996); and Williamjames Hull Hoffer, *To Enlarge the Machinery of Government: Congressional Debates and the Growth of the American State, 1858–1891* (Baltimore: Johns Hopkins University Press, 2007). For suffrage restrictions subject to loyalty in the District of Columbia, see Act of 20 May 1862, ch. 78, *Stat.* 403. For petit or grand jurors oath, see Act of 17 June 1862, ch. 103, *Stat.* 430–31. For oaths of loyalty for all persons connected to government, see Act of 2 July 1862, ch. 128, *Stat.* 502–3. For an indication of the scope and speed at which the federal state expanded its powers to detain the disloyal, see *OR*, ser. 2, vol. 2.

19. *Atlantic Monthly* 9, no. 54 (April 1862): 469–74 (quote on 471).

20. Ibid., 474.

21. Ibid.; *Continental Monthly* 2, no. 1 (July 1862): 1–5 (quote on 5). Except for William Blair's recent book on the subject, few scholars have connected the harsher Union policies toward the South to the broader ideas about loyalty that gave the turn to "hard war" its key justification. See Mark Grimsley, *The Hard Hand of War: Union Military Policy towards Southern Civilians, 1861–1865* (Cambridge: Cambridge University Press, 1995); Stephen V. Ash, *When the Yankees Came: Conflict and Chaos in the Occupied South, 1861–1865* (Chapel Hill: University of North Carolina Press, 1995); and Blair, *With Malice toward Some*. The concern among opinion makers and politicians about the chronic instability of the nation in the wake of the war is a point picked up by Gregory Downs in "The Mexicanization of American Politics: The United States' Transnational Path from Civil War to Stabilization," *American Historical Review* 117, no. 2 (2012): 387–409.

22. *Opinion of Attorney General Bates on Citizenship* (Washington, D.C.: GPO, 1862), 17. See also James P. McClure et al., "Circumventing the Dred Scott Decision: Edward Bates, Salmon P. Chase, and the Citizenship of African Americans," *Civil War History* 43, no. 4 (1997): 279–309, and Oakes, *Freedom National*, 353–60.

23. Cong. Globe, 37th Cong., 2nd Sess. 2242, 2997 (1862).

24. Act of 17 July 1862, ch. 195, *Stat.* 589–92. William Blair argues that the Second Confiscation Act was a half-measure, watered down by moderates. While there is room to believe that harsher measures could have been implemented, it is difficult to read the text of the act and see it as lacking teeth. See William A. Blair, "Friend or Foe: Treason and the Second Confiscation Act," in *Wars within a War: Controversy and Conflict over the American Civil War*, ed. Joan Waugh and Gary W. Gallagher (Chapel Hill: University of North Carolina Press, 2009), 27–51, and Blair, *With Malice toward Some*, 81–90. For more on the literature surrounding this act, see Silvana R. Siddali, *From Property to Person: Slavery and the Confiscation Acts, 1861–1862* (Baton Rouge: Louisiana State University Press, 2005); John Syrett, *The Civil War Confiscation Acts: Failing to Reconstruct the South* (New York: Fordham University Press, 2005); Daniel W. Hamilton, *The Limits of Sovereignty: Property Confiscation in the Union and the Confederacy during the Civil War* (Chicago: University of Chicago Press, 2007); and Oakes, *Freedom National*, 224–55.

25. Though Oakes does not develop the point more fully, the insight into what the Second Confiscation Act meant to African Americans is discussed in his *Freedom National*, 244–45.

26. Narrative of Barney Alford, in *The American Slave: A Composite Autobiography*, ed. George P. Rawick, Jan Hillegas, and Ken Lawrence (Westport, Conn.: Greenwood, 1977), ser. 1, vol. 6, pt. 1, pp. 23–49 (quote on 28).

27. The best work on rumor in the Civil War includes Steven Hahn, *A Nation under Our Feet: Black Political Struggles in the Rural South from Slavery to the Great Migration* (Cambridge, Mass.: Harvard University Press, 2003), 13–61, 116–59, and Jason Phillips, "The Grape Vine Telegraph: Rumors and Confederate Persistence," *Journal of Southern History* 72, no. 4 (2006): 753–88. This literature draws on the work of Atlantic World scholars like Julius Scott, but also on literature of subaltern studies, which privileged rumor as a means through which illiterate peoples could pass news and protect themselves from harm. See, in particular, Julius S. Scott, "The Common Wind: Currents of Afro-American Communication in the Era of the Haitian Revolution" (Ph.D. diss., Duke University, 1986), 59–113; Ranajit Guha, *Elementary Aspects of Peasant Insurgency in Colonial India* (1983; Durham: Duke University Press, 1999), 220–77; and Shahid Amin, "Gandhi as Mahatma: Gorakhpur District, Eastern UP, 1921–22," in *Selected Subaltern Studies*, ed. Gayatri Chakravorty Spivak and Ranajit Guha (New York: Oxford University Press, 1988), 288–348.

28. Narrative of Louis Davis, in Rawick, Hillegas, and Lawrence, *American Slave*, ser. 1, vol. 7, pt. 2, pp. 577–89 (quote on 581).

29. Narrative of George Washington Albright, ser. 1, vol. 6, pt. 1, pp. 8–19 (quote on 11–12); narrative of Adeline Hodge, supp., ser. 1, vol. 1, pp. 182–83; and narrative of Berry Smith, supp., ser. 1, vol. 10, pt. 5, p. 1986, all in Rawick, Hillegas, and Lawrence, *American Slave*.

30. The best survey of this history remains Ira Berlin et al., eds., *Freedom: A Documentary History of Emancipation, 1861–1867: The Destruction of Slavery*, ser. 1

(Cambridge: Cambridge University Press, 1985), 1:249–69, and McPherson, *Battle Cry of Freedom*, 392–427. For 1860 census data, see National Historical Geographic Information System (NHGIS), University of Minnesota, https://www.nhgis.org (21 February 2017). On slaves passing news to the Union, see Brig. Gen. O. M. Mitchell to E. M. Stanton, 4 May 1862, in Berlin et al., *Freedom: Destruction of Slavery*, 1:275–76.

31. Brig. Gen. I. F. Quinby to Maj. Gen. U. S. Grant, Crossing of the Pigeon Roost and M. and C. Railroad, 6 January 1862, *OR* 17(2):542.

32. Hyman, *To Try Men's Souls*, 167–98 (quote on 168). On paper money and the problem of trust at the heart of American capitalism, see Stephen Mihm, *A Nation of Counterfeiters: Capitalists, Con Men, and the Making of the United States* (Cambridge, Mass.: Harvard University Press, 2007), esp. 209–59.

33. Though Thomas lacks a biographer, Michael T. Meier does an excellent job of illuminating his contribution in the Mississippi Valley. See Meier, "Lorenzo Thomas and the Recruitment of Blacks in the Mississippi Valley, 1863–1865," in Smith, *Black Soldiers in Blue*, 249–75. See also Cornish, *Sable Arm*, 112–31. For the efforts made by Thomas's enemies to discredit him, see *OR* 39(2):350–54.

34. Brig. Gen. L. Thomas, Adjut. Gen., to Maj. Gen. N. P. Banks, New Orleans, La., 12 February 1863 (reel 2), ser. 390, The Negro in the Military Service of the United States, 1639–1886 (M858), Records of the Adjutant General's Office, RG 94, NA; *Daily Mississippian* (from the *Chicago Times*), 28 April 1863; C. A. Dana to Hon. E. M. Stanton, Milliken's Bend, La., 20 April 1863 (reel 2), ser. 390 (M858), RG 94, NA.

35. *New York Times*, 7 June 1863. See also an account of the speech in John Eaton to Rev. S. S. Jocelyn, Memphis, Tenn., 18 May 1863, in Ira Berlin et al., eds., *Freedom: A Documentary History of Emancipation, 1861–1867: The Wartime Genesis of Free Labor, the Lower South*, ser. 1 (Cambridge: Cambridge University Press, 1990), 3:703–6.

36. For more on emancipation more broadly conceived, see Laurent Dubois, *A Colony of Citizens: Revolution and Slave Emancipation in the French Caribbean, 1787–1804* (Chapel Hill: Published for the Omohundro Institute of Early American History and Culture by the University of North Carolina Press, 2004); Philip D. Morgan and Christopher Leslie Brown, eds., *Arming Slaves: From Classical Times to the Modern Age* (New Haven: Yale University Press, 2006); and Robin Blackburn, *The American Crucible: Slavery, Emancipation, and Human Rights* (London: Verso, 2011).

37. Capt. Mark Hathaway to Asst. Adjut. Gen. T. W. Taggard, Vicksburg, Miss., 28 November 1864; Capt. Lyman Banks to Asst. Adjut. Gen. D. W. Taggard, Vicksburg, Miss., 11 November 1864; Capt. William E. Derrigan to Taggard, Vicksburg, Miss., 14 November 1864, box 347, ser. 366, Letters Received Relating to Recruiting, Colored Troops Division, RG 94, NA.

38. General Orders No. 64 (Richard B. Irwin, Asst. Adjut. Gen.), New Orleans, La., 29 August 1863 (reel 2) ser. 390 (M858), RG 94, NA.

39. Lorenzo Thomas to E. D. Townshend, Memphis, Tenn., 8 December 1863, vol. 2, ser. 9, Letters and Telegrams Sent by L. Thomas, RG 94, NA. Jim Downs makes a very strong case for viewing the black involvement with the U.S. Army as having had a devastating effect on the collective health of freedpeople. See Downs, *Sick from Freedom: African-American Illness and Suffering during the Civil War and Reconstruction* (New York: Oxford University Press, 2012).

40. Col. John J. Mudd to Thomas, Carrollton, La., 18 September 1863, box 2, ser. 363, Letters Received by Adjutant General L. Thomas, RG 94, NA.

41. Berlin, Reidy, and Rowland, *Freedom: The Black Military Experience*, 153–57 (quote on 153).

42. Court-Martial of Edward Williams, Vicksburg, Miss., 11 March 1864, case #LL2118, box 679, Court-Martial Case Files, Records of the Office of the Judge Advocate General (Army), RG 153, NA.

43. Court-Martial of Mose Germain, Vicksburg, Miss., 25 January 1864, case #LL1734, box 623, and Court-Martial of Pvt. Augustus Harrison, Vicksburg, Miss., 15 December 1863, case #LL1565, box 598, Court-Martial Case Files, RG 153, NA.

44. Court-Martial of Henry Jones, Vicksburg, Miss., 2 December 1863, case #LL1734, box 623, and Court-Martial of James Brown, Vicksburg, Miss., 4 December 1863, case #LL1565, box 598, Court-Martial Case Files, RG 153, NA.

45. See testimony of the trial in *OR* 26(1):458–79 (quote on 458); Brig. Gen. William Dwight to Brig. Gen. Charles P. Stone, Fort Jackson, La., 15 December 1863 (reel 2), ser. 390 (M858), RG 94, NA. The best examination of this episode is Fred Harvey Harrington, "The Fort Jackson Mutiny," *Journal of Negro History* 27, no. 4 (1942): 420–31. See also Howard C. Westwood, "The Cause and Consequence of a Union Black Soldier's Mutiny and Execution," *Civil War History* 31, no. 3 (1985): 222–36.

46. This point is made particularly well in Steven J. Ramold, *Slaves, Sailors, Citizens: African Americans in the Union Navy* (DeKalb: Northern Illinois University Press, 2002), and Lande, "Trials of Freedom."

47. Special Order No. 13, Milliken's Bend, La., 20 April 1863, box 1, ser. 159, Generals Papers and Books: Gen. Lorenzo Thomas, RG 94, NA; Circular (L. Thomas), Natchez, Miss., 27 October 1863, *OR*, ser. 3, 3:939–40.

48. One of the best overviews of the free labor system in the Mississippi Valley remains Berlin et al., *Freedom: The Wartime Genesis of Free Labor*, 3:621–50, but see also W. E. B. Du Bois, *Black Reconstruction: An Essay toward a History of the Part Which Black Folk Played in the Attempt to Reconstruct Democracy in America, 1860–1880* (New York: Russell and Russell, 1935), 3–128; Lawrence N. Powell, *New Masters: Northern Planters during the Civil War and Reconstruction* (New York: Fordham University Press, 1998); Eric Foner, *Reconstruction: America's Unfinished Revolution, 1863–1877* (New York: Harper and Row, 1988), 1–123; Julie Saville, *The Work of Reconstruction: From Slave to Wage Laborer in South Carolina, 1860–1870* (Cambridge: Cambridge University Press, 1994); Amy Dru Stanley, *From Bondage to Contract: Wage Labor, Marriage, and the Market in the Age of Slave Emancipation* (Cambridge: Cambridge University Press, 1998); and Hahn, *Nation under Our Feet*. On the Treasury plan, see James E. Yeatman, *A Report on the Condition of the Freedmen of Mississippi* (St. Louis: Western Sanitary Commission, 1864), and Report of the Secretary of the Treasury, on the State of the Finances, for the Year Ending June 30, 1863, H.R. Doc., No. 3 (1863), 410–22.

49. *New York Times*, 28 November 1863.

50. Col. Samuel Thomas to Lorenzo Thomas, Vicksburg, Miss., 15 June 1864 (quoted), and W. Burnet to Thomas, Natchez, Miss., 13 August 1864, box 2, ser. 363, RG 94, NA. For Thomas's order, see Berlin et al., *Freedom: The Wartime Genesis of Free Labor*, 3:802–8. For Thomas's update on African American troops stationed in the Mississippi Valley, see

Thomas to Edwin P. Stanton, Vicksburg, Miss., 14 March 1864, vol. 2, ser. 9, RG 94, NA. On Meridian, see Berlin et al., *Freedom: The Wartime Genesis of Free Labor*, 3:642–43.

51. Berlin et al., *Freedom: The Wartime Genesis of Free Labor*, 3:799; Isaac Shoemaker Diary, 12 March 1864, Special Collections, DU.

52. Berlin et al., *Freedom: The Wartime Genesis of Free Labor*, 3:807.

53. *Joint Committee on Reconstruction* (Washington, D.C.: GPO, 1866), pt. 3, p. 1.

CHAPTER FIVE

1. Cong. Globe, 38th Cong., 2nd Sess. 138–41 (1865) (quote on 140). For more on the political machinations behind the Thirteenth Amendment, see Michael Vorenberg, *Final Freedom: The Civil War, the Abolition of Slavery, and the Thirteenth Amendment* (New York: Cambridge University Press, 2001).

2. Marius C. C. Church to Andrew Johnson, New York, N.Y., 16 April 1865, and Sarah H. Hill to Johnson, Norristown, Pa., 17 April 1865, in *The Papers of Andrew Johnson* (Knoxville: University of Tennessee Press, 1967–), 16 vols., 7:564–65, 570. For more on the collective national reaction to Lincoln's death, see Martha E. Hodes, *Mourning Lincoln* (New Haven: Yale University Press, 2015).

3. *Speeches of Andrew Johnson, President of the United States*, ed. Frank Moore (Boston: Little, Brown, 1866), 176–289, esp. 204–5. On Johnson as wartime governor in Tennessee, see Peter Maslowski, *Treason Must Be Made Odious: Military Occupation and Wartime Reconstruction in Nashville, Tennessee, 1862–65* (Millwood: KTO Press, 1978), but also Hans L. Trefousse, *Andrew Johnson: A Biography* (New York: Norton, 1989), 152–75. See also Speech at Nashville, 4 July 1862, in *Papers of Andrew Johnson*, 5:534–41.

4. Proclamation Ordering Elections, 26 January 1864, in *Papers of Andrew Johnson*, 6:594–96; Acceptance of Vice-Presidential Nomination, Nashville, Tenn., 2 July 1864, in *Papers of Andrew Johnson*, 7:7–11 (quote on 10).

5. W. E. B. Du Bois, *Black Reconstruction: An Essay toward a History of the Part Which Black Folk Played in the Attempt to Reconstruct Democracy in America, 1860–1880* (New York: Russell and Russell, 1935), 322. By the early twentieth century, Johnson was seized upon by historians of Reconstruction as a victim of radical overreach and the unjustifiable elevation of African Americans to positions of power in the postwar South. As a result, much of the early literature on Johnson has been rightly dismissed. For the best of the Johnson historiography, see Howard K. Beale, *The Critical Year: A Study of Andrew Johnson and Reconstruction* (New York: F. Ungar, 1930); Eric L. McKitrick, *Andrew Johnson and Reconstruction* (Chicago: University of Chicago Press, 1960); LaWanda Cox and John Cox, *Politics, Principle, and Prejudice, 1865–1866: Dilemma of Reconstruction America* (New York: Macmillan, 1963); Michael Perman, *Reunion without Compromise: The South and Reconstruction, 1865–1868* (Cambridge: Cambridge University Press, 1973); Michael Les Benedict, *The Impeachment and Trial of Andrew Johnson* (New York, Norton, 1973); Hans L. Trefousse, *Impeachment of a President: Andrew Johnson, the Blacks, and Reconstruction* (Knoxville: University of Tennessee Press, 1975); Donald G. Nieman, "Andrew Johnson, the Freedmen's Bureau, and the Problem of Equal Rights, 1865–1866," *Journal of Southern History* 44, no. 3 (1978): 399–420; Eric Foner, *Reconstruction: America's Unfinished Revolution, 1863–1877* (New York: Harper and Row, 1988), 176–227; Trefousse, *Andrew*

Johnson; and Paul H. Bergeron, *Andrew Johnson's Civil War and Reconstruction* (Knoxville: University of Tennessee Press, 2011).

6. Johnson to Abraham Lincoln, Nashville, Tenn., 13 July 1864, in *Papers of Andrew Johnson*, 7:30–31. On the Wade-Davis Bill, see Foner, *Reconstruction*, 60–62. For the debate over the bill, see Cong. Globe, 38th Congress, 1st Sess. 1729–44 (1864). For Lincoln's proclamation explaining his veto, see *The Collected Works of Abraham Lincoln*, 7:433–34, https://quod.lib.umich.edu/cgi/t/text/text-idx?page=browse&c=lincoln (21 February 2017).

7. Speech near Gallatin, Gallatin, Tenn., 19 July 1864, in *Papers of Andrew Johnson*, 7:41–44 (quotes on 41, 43).

8. Cong. Globe, 38th Congress, 1st Sess. 2613 (1864).

9. Cong. Globe, 38th Congress, 1st Sess. 2617 (1864). For the best study on interwar northern politics and the lead-up to the 1864 election, see Adam I. P. Smith, *No Party Now: Politics in the Civil War North* (New York: Oxford University Press, 2006), 85–100, 124–53.

10. *Speeches of Andrew Johnson*, 405–50 (quote on 425–26); Proclamation Concerning Guerrilla Raids, Nashville, Tenn., 9 May 1862, in *Papers of Andrew Johnson*, 5:374–75; Andrew Johnson to Col. Stanley Matthews, Nashville, Tenn., 3 June 1862, in *Papers of Andrew Johnson*, 5:438. For a very good early study of Johnson's administration in Tennessee, see Clifton R. Hall, *Andrew Johnson: Military Governor of Tennessee* (Princeton: Princeton University Press, 1916), esp. 71–138.

11. Speech on Restoration of State Government, 21 January 1864, in *Papers of Andrew Johnson*, 6:574–90 (quotes on 576, 578).

12. Ibid., 6:582–83. For a survey of slavery in wartime Tennessee, see Ira Berlin et al., eds., *Freedom: A Documentary History of Emancipation, 1861–1867: The Wartime Genesis of Free Labor, the Lower South*, ser. 1 (Cambridge: Cambridge University Press, 1990), 3:367–86.

13. Trefousse, *Andrew Johnson*, 197–98, 207, 209.

14. The military reconstruction under Johnson has been best examined by Gregory Downs in *After Appomattox: Military Occupation and the Ends of War* (Cambridge, Mass.: Harvard University Press, 2015), 11–60.

15. For troop deployments, overall numbers, and their stations in Mississippi and elsewhere, see Gregory P. Downs and Scott Nesbit, *Mapping Occupation: Force, Freedom, and the Army in Reconstruction*, http://mappingoccupation.org (21 February 2017).

16. Stephen M. Barbour to Johnson, Philadelphia, Pa., 1 May 1865, in *Papers of Andrew Johnson*, 8:3; North Carolina Blacks to Johnson, Newbern, N.C., 10 May 1865, in *Papers of Andrew Johnson*, 8:57–58.

17. John F. Claiborne to Johnson, Hancock Co., Miss., 1 May 1865, in *Papers of Andrew Johnson*, 8:4. For the best work on the changing constitutional ideas that grew out of the Civil War, see Harold M. Hyman, *A More Perfect Union: The Impact of the Civil War and Reconstruction on the Constitution* (New York: Knopf, 1973); Michael Les Benedict, *Preserving the Constitution: Essays on Politics and the Constitution in the Reconstruction Era* (New York: Fordham University Press, 2006); Mark E. Neely Jr., *Lincoln and the Triumph of the Nation: Constitutional Conflict in the American Civil War* (Chapel Hill: University of North Carolina Press, 2011); and Laura F. Edwards, *A Legal History of the Civil War and Reconstruction: A Nation of Rights* (Cambridge: Cambridge University Press, 2015).

The end of the war and the problems inherent in the Union occupation of the South have been examined in particular detail in Downs, *After Appomattox*, 1–38.

18. Interview with John A. Logan, 31 May 1865, in *Papers of Andrew Johnson*, 8:153–54 (quotes on 154). The ideas of seceding states in suspended animation has been dissected most carefully by Eric McKitrick in *Andrew Johnson and Reconstruction*, 93–119.

19. Interview with Pennsylvania Delegation, 3 May 1865, in *Papers of Andrew Johnson*, 8:21–23 (quote on 21–22). For the best surveys of the politics of Presidential Reconstruction, as well as Johnson's motivations, see McKitrick, *Andrew Johnson and Reconstruction*, 138–40; Cox and Cox, *Politics, Principle, and Prejudice*; Kenneth M. Stampp, *The Era of Reconstruction, 1865–1877* (New York: Knopf, 1965), 50–82; Michael Les Benedict, *A Compromise of Principle: Congressional Republicans and Reconstruction, 1863–1869* (New York: Norton, 1974); Foner, *Reconstruction*, 176–84; and Mark Wahlgren Summers, *The Ordeal of the Reunion: A New History of Reconstruction* (Chapel Hill: University of North Carolina Press, 2014), 58–106.

20. Amnesty Proclamation, 29 May 1865, in *Compilation of the Messages and Papers of the Presidents*, ed. James D. Richardson (Washington, D.C.: GPO, 1897), 6:310–12.

21. Henry P. Fessenden to Johnson, New York, N.Y., 19 May 1865, *Papers of Andrew Johnson*, 8:92–93. The power that Johnson reserved to his office to decide amnesty claims dovetails with the imperial and monarchical undertow that Andrew Heath has examined in postwar politics. See his "'Let the Empire Come': Imperialism and Its Critics in the Reconstruction South," *Civil War History* 60, no. 2 (2014): 152–89.

22. James Bingham to Johnson, Memphis, Tenn., 6 June 1865, in *Papers of Andrew Johnson*, 8:188.

23. Joseph Noxon to Johnson, New York, N.Y., 27 May 1865, in *Papers of Andrew Johnson*, 8:119; Samuel R. Snyder to Johnson, Petersburgh, Ind., 5 June 1865, in *Papers of Andrew Johnson*, 8:184–86 (quotes on 184–85).

24. Thaddeus Stevens to Johnson, Caledonia Iron Works, Pa., 16 May 1865, in *Papers of Andrew Johnson*, 8:80–81; J. George Harris to Johnson, Key West, Fla., 8 June 1865, in *Papers of Andrew Johnson*, 8:201.

25. *Proceedings of the Mississippi State Convention, Held January 7th to 26th, A.D. 1861* (Jackson, Miss.: Power and Caldwater, 1861), 7, 13; *Daily Mississippian*, 27 January 1862; *Journal of the House of Representatives of the State of Mississippi, Called Session at Columbus, February and March, 1865* (Meridian: J. J. Shannon and Co., 1865), 22. On Alcorn's life, see Lillian A. Pereyra, *James Lusk Alcorn: Persistent Whig* (Baton Rouge: Louisiana State University Press, 1966).

26. Alcorn to His Wife, Mound Place, Miss., 16 March 1865, folder 3, box 1, James L. Alcorn and Family Papers, MDAH.

27. Application of James L. Alcorn, roll 31, Case Files for Applications from Former Confederates for Presidential Pardons, 1865–67 (M1003), RG 94, NA.

28. To expedite the deluge of pardons that Johnson was sure would follow his amnesty proclamation, he directed the appointed governors of southern states to vet applications before sending them on to Washington. For this reason, Alcorn's application includes a note of support from William Sharkey, the provisional governor, who assured Johnson that Alcorn would be "a true loyal and peaceable citizen" who would "most gladly return to his allegiance to the Government." For Sharkey's letter, see ibid. For more on the pardon process, see Summers, *Ordeal of the Reunion*, 66.

29. Application of Thomas P. Barton and Application of Alexander M. Clayton, roll 31, Applications for Presidential Pardons.

30. Application of L. Q. C. Lamar, roll 33, Applications for Presidential Pardons. While the history of the Lost Cause has been well documented in studies on Civil War memory, taking these claims seriously in the immediate postwar period lays bare a broader set of issues about the ties of loyalty and citizenship that connected many white southerners to the failed Confederate state. For more on the Lost Cause, see David W. Blight, *Race and Reunion: The Civil War in American Memory* (Cambridge, Mass.: Belknap Press of Harvard University Press, 2001), and W. Scott Poole, *Never Surrender: Confederate Memory and Conservatism in the South Carolina Upcountry* (Athens: University of Georgia Press, 2004).

31. Application of Mary J. Parker and Application of Andiana V. Rogers, roll 34, Applications for Presidential Pardons.

32. Application of John W. C. Watson, roll 35, Applications for Presidential Pardons.

33. A. K. Farrar to Gov. Sharkey, Kingston, Miss., 27 June 1865, folder 4, box 954, ser. 771, Letters and Petitions, MDAH; *Weekly Panola Star*, 4 November 1865.

34. H. E. Moore to Gov. Sharkey, Tippah Co., Miss., 23 September 1865, folder 11, box 956, ser. 771, Letters and Petitions, MDAH; Citizens of Noxubee Co. to Gov. Humphries, Macon, Miss., 31 October 1865, folder 4, box 962, ser. 779, Governor Benjamin Humphries, Correspondence and Papers, 1865–1868 and Undated, MDAH.

35. *New York Times*, 18 June 1865; *Journal of the Proceedings and Debates in the Constitutional Convention of the State of Mississippi, August 1865* (Jackson: E. M. Yerger, 1865), 42, 56–57.

36. *Constitutional Convention of the State of Mississippi, August 1865*, 112; *The Coahomian*, 20 September 1865. For the relationship between women and oaths of loyalty, see Stephanie McCurry, *Confederate Reckoning: Power and Politics in the Civil War South* (Cambridge, Mass.: Harvard University Press, 2010), 85–132.

37. *New York Daily Tribune*, 10 August 1865.

38. *New York Times*, 19 August, 22 November 1865.

39. *Joint Committee on Reconstruction* (Washington, D.C.: GPO, 1866), xi–xii.

40. Ibid., pt. 3, pp. 5–6, 24.

41. Ibid., pt., 3, pp. 116–17, 122, 131.

42. Cong. Globe, 39th Cong., 1st Sess. 39–40 (1866); *New York Tribune*, 6 March 1866.

43. *Atlantic Monthly* 16, no. 98 (December 1865): 745–61 (quote on 758).

44. Johnson to James B. Steedman, Washington, D.C., 26 November 1865, *Papers of Andrew Johnson*, 9:434.

CHAPTER SIX

1. For an excellent history of Wall Street Baptist, see Justin Behrend, *Reconstructing Democracy: Grassroots Black Politics in the Deep South after the Civil War* (Athens: University of Georgia Press, 2015), 42–76, esp. 46–48. For more on black religion in the late antebellum period, see Albert J. Raboteau, *Slave Religion: The "Invisible Institution" in the Antebellum South* (New York: Oxford University Press, 1978); Orville Vernon Burton, *In My Father's House Are Many Mansions: Family and Community in Edgefield, South Carolina* (Chapel Hill: University of North Carolina Press, 1985), 148–90; Margaret Washington Creel, *"A Peculiar People": Slave Religion and Community-Culture among the Gullahs* (New

York: New York University Press, 1988), 276–302; John B. Boles, ed., *Masters and Slaves in the House of the Lord: Race and Religion in the American South, 1740–1870* (Lexington: University Press of Kentucky, 1988); and Erskine Clarke, *Dwelling Place: A Plantation Epic* (New Haven: Yale University Press, 2005), 152–66.

2. Congregants of the Wall St. Baptist Church to Col. Samuel Thomas, Natchez, Miss., 1 July 1865, Letters Received (roll 8), Asst. Comm-MS, BRFAL, NA.

3. Deacons of the Wall St. Baptist Church to Col. Samuel Thomas, Natchez, Miss., 26 July 1865, Letters Received (roll 8), Asst. Comm-MS, BRFAL, NA. On the history of wartime Natchez, see Michael Wayne, *The Reshaping of Plantation Society: The Natchez District, 1860–1880* (Baton Rouge: Louisiana State University Press, 1983), and Behrend, *Reconstructing Democracy.*

4. Battles over property during Reconstruction have been a focus in Roger L. Ransom and Richard Sutch, *One Kind of Freedom: The Economic Consequences of Emancipation* (New York: Cambridge University Press, 1977), 81–105; Edward Magdol, *A Right to the Land: Essays on the Freedmen's Community* (Westport, Conn.: Greenwood, 1977); Eric Foner, *Reconstruction: America's Unfinished Revolution, 1863–1877* (New York: Harper and Row, 1988), 124–75, 346–411; Loren Schweninger, *Black Property Owners in the South, 1790–1915* (Urbana: University of Illinois Press, 1997), 143–84; Julie Saville, *The Work of Reconstruction: From Slave to Wage Laborer in South Carolina, 1860–1870* (Cambridge: Cambridge University Press, 1994), 5–31; Dylan C. Penningroth, *The Claims of Kinfolk: African American Property and Community in the Nineteenth-Century South* (Chapel Hill: University of North Carolina Press, 2003), 131–62; Dylan C. Penningroth, "The Claims of Slaves and Ex-Slaves to Family and Property: A Transatlantic Perspective," *American Historical Review* 112, no. 4 (2007): 1039–69; Steven Hahn et al., eds. *Freedom: A Documentary History of Emancipation, 1861–1867: Land and Labor, 1865,* ser. 3 (Chapel Hill: University of North Carolina Press, 2008), 1:1–70; and Rene Hayden et al., eds., *Freedom: A Documentary History of Emancipation, 1861–1867: Land and Labor, 1866–1867,* ser. 3, vol. 2 (Chapel Hill: University of North Carolina Press, 2013). While this literature has collectively underscored just how important battles over property were to freedpeople and their owners, less has been said about the claims freedpeople made and the connection between black professions of personal loyalty to the Union that buttressed them.

5. While historians are beginning to think in new ways about the broader narrative of Reconstruction, the dominant story told about Presidential Reconstruction remains one of unrealized possibilities. For the best of this work, see W. E. B. Du Bois, *Black Reconstruction: An Essay toward a History of the Part Which Black Folk Played in the Attempt to Reconstruct Democracy in America, 1860–1880* (New York: Russell and Russell, 1935), 248–323; Eric L. McKitrick, *Andrew Johnson and Reconstruction* (Chicago: University of Chicago Press, 1960); William C. Harris, *Presidential Reconstruction in Mississippi* (Baton Rouge: Louisiana State University Press, 1967); Michael Perman, *Reunion without Compromise: The South and Reconstruction, 1865–1868* (Cambridge: Cambridge University Press, 1973); and Foner, *Reconstruction,* 176–227. For a collection that seeks to rethink the reigning paradigms of the Reconstruction period, see Gregory P. Downs and Kate Masur, eds., *The World the Civil War Made* (Chapel Hill: University of North Carolina Press, 2015).

6. Isaac Shoemaker Diary, 3 March 1864, DU. On wartime Vicksburg, see James T. Currie, *Enclave: Vicksburg and Her Plantations, 1863–1870* (Jackson: University Press of

Mississippi, 1980). On the wartime movement and experiences of African Americans, particularly the women and children who found themselves in contraband camps all over the South, see Chandra Manning, *Troubled Refuge: Struggling for Freedom in the Civil War* (New York: Knopf, 2016).

7. Col. R. F. Lowrey to Maj. Gen. J. R. Chalmers, Oxford, Miss., 26 September 1864, folder 12, box 392, ser. 400, Adjutants-General Correspondence, 1861–1864, MDAH. On the rights of property in a time of war, see John Fabian Witt, *Lincoln's Code: The Laws of War in American History* (New York: Free Press, 2012), 197–219. While his work does not venture into the war itself, the importance of slavery as an institution that gave property in southern society its meaning is underscored by Walter Johnson in *Soul by Soul: Life Inside the Antebellum Slave Market* (Cambridge, Mass.: Harvard University Press, 1999).

8. Asst. Adjut. Gen. T. L. Bowers to Maj. Gen. Dana, City Point, Va., 5 February 1865, box 1, entry 2433, Letters Received, Dec. 1864–Aug. 1868, RG 393, U.S. Army Continental Commands, 1821–1920, NA.

9. K. Rayner to Gov. Sharkey, Raleigh, N.C., 21 August 1865, folder 1, box 960, ser. 776, Governor William Lewis Sharkey, Correspondence and Papers, 1865, MDAH. See also Hayen L. Leavel to Gov. Sharkey, Yazoo Co., Miss., September 1865, folder 1, box 956, ser. 771, Letters and Petitions, 1865, MDAH. For Schurz's report, see Senate Exec. Doc. No. 2, 39th Congress, 1st Sess. (1865), 14.

10. For the background to American ideas of emancipation, wedded as they were to events in the Caribbean, see Edward B. Rugemer, *The Problem of Emancipation: The Caribbean Roots of the American Civil War* (Baton Rouge: Louisiana State University Press, 2008), and Edward B. Rugemer, "Slave Rebels and Abolitionists: The Black Atlantic and the Coming of the Civil War," *Journal of the Civil War Era* 2, no. 2 (2012): 179–202. For more on British emancipation, the claims of slaveholders, and the Morant Bay rebellion, see William A. Green, *British Slave Emancipation: The Sugar Colonies and the Great Experiment 1830–1865* (Oxford: Clarendon Press, 1976); Thomas C. Holt, *The Problem of Freedom: Race, Labor, and Politics in Jamaica and Britain, 1832–1938* (Baltimore: Johns Hopkins University Press, 1992), 13–53, 263–309; Gad J. Heuman, *The Killing Time: The Morant Bay Rebellion in Jamaica* (London: Macmillan Caribbean, 1994); and Seymour Drescher, *The Mighty Experiment: Free Labor versus Slavery in British Emancipation* (New York: Oxford University Press, 2004). On the radicalism of American emancipation and the counterfactual question of whether it could have gone even further, see Steven Hahn, "Class and State in Postemancipation Societies: Southern Planters in Comparative Perspective," *American Historical Review* 95, no. 1 (1990): 75–98.

11. On the relationship between Haiti and the American Civil War, see Matthew J. Clavin, *Toussaint Louverture and the American Civil War: The Promise and Peril of a Second Haitian Revolution* (Philadelphia: University of Pennsylvania Press, 2010). On the notion of Haiti as a beacon of emancipated freedom for all Africans in the Caribbean, see Ada Ferrer, "Haiti, Free Soil, and Antislavery in the Revolutionary Atlantic," *American Historical Review* 117, no. 1 (2012): 40–66, and Ada Ferrer, *Freedom's Mirror: Cuba and Haiti in the Age of Revolution* (Cambridge: Cambridge University Press, 2014).

12. Capt. Frederic Speed, Asst. Adjut. Gen. for Dept. of Mississippi, to Brev. Brig. Gen. E. D. Osband, Vicksburg, Miss., 20 May 1865, folder 1, box 960, Sharkey Correspondence, MDAH; Capt. James T. Organ to Maj. Gen. George D. Reynolds, Washington, Miss., 2 June

1865 (A-9482), in Hahn et al., *Freedom: Land and Labor, 1865*, 1:88; Col. Samuel Thomas to. Maj. Gen. O. O. Howard, Vicksburg, Miss., 29 July 1865 (roll 1), Letters Sent, Asst. Comm-MS, BRFAL, NA. On life in the contraband camps, see Manning, *Troubled Refuge*, 31–149.

13. Alex P. McMillan, Citizen, to Col. Thomas, Natchez, Miss., June 1865 (roll 11), Letters Received, Asst. Comm-MS, BRFAL, NA.

14. A. Bunwell to Col. Samuel Thomas, 20 July 1865 (roll 8), Asst. Comm-MS, BRFAL, NA; M. Emanuel to Maj. Gen. Slocum, Vicksburg, Miss., 18 July 1865 (roll 9), Letters Received, Asst. Comm-MS, BRFAL, NA.

15. Lieut. Stuart Eldridge to Col. B. R. Johnston, 26 July 1865 (roll 1], Letters Sent, Asst. Comm-MS, BRFAL, NA. On cotton stealing, see Henry Reynolds to George J. Thomas, Mobile, Ala., 12 July 1865, folder 7, box 1, ser. 1.2, Henry Lee Reynolds Papers, SHC. See also Lieut. Col. R. S. Donaldson to Capt. J. H. Weber, Jackson, Miss., 6 November 1865 (roll 9), Letters Received, Asst. Comm-MS, BRFAL, NA.

16. W. R. Gilreath to Col. Thomas, Natchez, Miss., 2 August 1865 (roll 10), Letters Received, Asst. Comm-MS, BRFAL, NA.

17. Circular No. 9, 4 August 1865 (A-10892), in Hahn et al., *Freedom: Land and Labor, 1865*, 1:152–55.

18. Hahn et al., *Freedom: Land and Labor, 1865*, 1:399n14.

19. Col. Samuel Thomas to Maj. Gen. O. O. Howard, 14 September 1865 (roll 1), Letters Sent, Asst. Comm-MS, BRFAL, NA. On the numbers of bureau officials in Mississippi by the end of 1865, see Report of the Commissioner of the Bureau of Refugees, Freedmen and Abandoned Lands, House Exec. Doc. No. 11, 39th Congress, 1st Sess. (1865), 38.

20. Narrative of Anna Baker, Monroe Co., Miss., in *The American Slave: A Composite Autobiography*, ed. George P. Rawick, Jan Hillegas, and Ken Lawrence (Westport, Conn: Greenwood, 1977), ser. 1, vol. 6, pt. 1, pp. 90–101 (quote on 94–95).

21. Penningroth, *Claims of Kinfolk*, 133. The historiography surrounding postwar apprenticeship has been fruitfully mined in case studies of North Carolina, Maryland, and other regions of the Reconstruction South. In this work, apprenticeship of African American children has served a larger argument about either the problems of labor control or the difficulties freedpeople faced in rebuilding their families after slavery. Its place here serves as a way into understanding more about the political ideas that evolved out of this conflict. For the literature on apprenticeship, see Harris, *Presidential Reconstruction in Mississippi*, 121–40; Barbara J. Fields, *Slavery and Freedom on the Middle Ground: Maryland during the Nineteenth Century* (New Haven: Yale University Press, 1985), 131–66; and Laura F. Edwards, *Gendered Strife and Confusion: The Political Culture of Reconstruction* (Urbana: University of Illinois Press, 1997), 24–65. For the efforts of freed women to protect their rights as parents to their children, see Mary Farmer-Kaiser, *Freedwomen and the Freedmen's Bureau: Race, Gender, and Public Policy in the Age of Emancipation* (New York: Fordham University Press, 2010), 96–140.

22. The best work on the relationship between emancipation and the laws of contract remains Amy Dru Stanley, *From Bondage to Contract: Wage Labor, Marriage, and the Market in the Age of Slave Emancipation* (Cambridge: Cambridge University Press, 1998), and Amy Dru Stanley, "Instead of Waiting for the Thirteenth Amendment: The War Power, Slave Marriage, and Inviolate Human Rights," *American Historical Review* 115, no. 3 (2010): 732–65.

23. Lieut. Col. H. R. Brinkenhoff to Maj. Gen. O. O. Howard, Clinton, Miss., 8 July 1865 (roll 10), Letters Received, Asst. Comm-MS, BRFAL, NA; *Laws of the State of Mississippi, Passed at a Regular Session of the Mississippi Legislature, held in Jackson, October, November, and December, 1865* (Jackson: E. F. Yeager, 1866), 82–93, 165–67.

24. On bureau policy regarding apprentices in Mississippi, see Circular No. 5, 26 July 1865, House Exec. Doc. No. 70, 39th Congress, 1st sess. (1866), 152–53, and General Ord. No. 13, 31 October 1865 (A-9536), in Hahn et al., *Freedom: Land and Labor, 1865*, 1:288–92.

25. Lieut. John L. Critchfield to Lieut. Col. R. S. Donaldson, Canton, Miss., 14 October 1865 (roll 12), Letters Received, Canton Field Office, Sub-Assistant Commissioner Field Office Records (M1907), BRFAL, NA.

26. Indenture of Rosanna Charles, Canton, Miss., 1 October 1865 (roll 12), Miscellaneous Records, Canton Field Office, Sub-Assistant Commissioner Field Office Records (M1907), BRFAL, NA.

27. Bvt. Maj. Jonothan J. Knox to Capt. E. Barnberger, Meridian, Miss., 28 January 1866 (roll 30), Letters Sent, Meridian Field Office, Sub-Assistant Commissioner Field Office Records (M1907), BRFAL, NA. See also Nelson G. Gill to Lt. Bernberger, Holly Springs, Miss., 20 December 1865 (roll 10), Letters Received, Asst. Comm-MS, BRFAL, NA. On the Fitzgerald case, see Chap. Thomas Smith to Capt. E. Barnberger, Jackson, Miss., 11 January 1866 (roll 13), Letters Received, Asst. Comm-MS, BRFAL, NA.

28. Christopher Waldrep, *Roots of Disorder: Race and Criminal Justice in the American South, 1817–80* (Urbana: University of Illinois Press, 1998), 176, table A-2.

29. James W. Davis (Solicitor) to Col. Samuel Thomas, Vicksburg, Miss., 1866 (roll 13), Letters Received, Asst. Comm-MS, BRFAL, NA.

30. The State vs. Lewis Connor (Freedman), Case #13114; The State vs. Eliza Davis, Case #1357; and The State vs. Peter Shaw (Freedman), Case #1340, Noxubee County Circuit Court Docket, Regular Term (October 1866), Noxubee County Courthouse, Macon, Miss.

31. Diane A. Wray et al. vs. Stephen Thickfeld, Esq., Case #3792, Pontotoc County Circuit Court, April Term (1867), Pontotoc County Courthouse, Pontotoc, Miss.; Julia F. Claggett vs. Melinda Williams, Case #189, Bolivar County Chancery Court Papers, Regular Term (November 1869), Bolivar County Old Courthouse, Rosedale, Miss. The argument here echoes in Laura F. Edwards, *A Legal History of the Civil War and Reconstruction: A Nation of Rights* (Cambridge: Cambridge University Press, 2015), esp. 120–45.

32. Gov. Humphries to Maj. Gen. M. F. Force, Jackson, Miss., 3 November 1865, box 1, H-77, entry 2433, Letters Received, Dec. 1864–Aug. 1868, RG 393, U.S. Army Continental Commands, NA; *Natchez Daily Courier*, 6 October 1865.

33. The best work on this subject remains Dan T. Carter, "The Anatomy of Fear: The Christmas Day Insurrection Scare of 1865," *Journal of Southern History* 42, no. 3 (1976): 345–64, and Steven Hahn, "'Extravagant Expectations' of Freedom: Rumour, Political Struggle, and the Christmas Insurrection Scare of 1865 in the American South," *Past and Present* 157 (1997): 122–58.

34. See also Lieut. Col. R. S. Donaldson to Capt. J. H. Weber, Jackson, Miss., 6 November 1865 (roll 9), Letters Received, Asst. Comm-MS, BRFAL, NA.

35. F. Marion Shields to President Andrew Johnson, Noxubee Co., Miss., 25 October 1865, and Gov. Sharkey to Maj. Gen. O. O. Howard, Jackson, Miss., 10 October 1865 (roll 11), Letters Received, Asst. Comm-MS, BRFAL, NA.

36. Maj. Wood to Gov. Humphries, Vicksburg, Miss., 8 January 1866, folder 10, box 962, ser. 779, Governor Benjamin Humphries, Correspondence and Papers, 1865–1868 and Undated, MDAH.

37. Lieut. Col. R. S. Donaldson to Lieut. Stuart Eldridge, Jackson, Miss., 18 December 1865 (roll 9), Letters Received, Asst. Comm-MS, BRFAL, NA.

38. Capt. J. H. Mathews to Eldridge, Pike Co., Miss., 12 January 1866 (roll 15), Letters Received, Asst. Comm-MS, BRFAL, NA.

39. Cong. Globe, 40th Cong., 1st Sess. 38, 203–8 (1867).

40. *Weekly Panola Star*, 12 May 1866.

41. *Vicksburg Daily Herald*, 17 April 1868. On Jones County, see Victoria E. Bynum, *The Free State of Jones: Mississippi's Longest Civil War* (Chapel Hill: University of North Carolina Press, 2001), and Victoria E. Bynum, *The Long Shadow of the Civil War: Southern Dissent and Its Legacies* (Chapel Hill: University of North Carolina Press, 2010). On black political organization during Reconstruction, see Foner, *Reconstruction*, 346–411, and Steven Hahn, *A Nation under Our Feet: Black Political Struggles in the Rural South from Slavery to the Great Migration* (Cambridge, Mass.: Harvard University Press, 2003), 163–215. On Mississippi in particular, see Behrend, *Reconstructing Democracy*.

42. Claim of John W. Austin (no. 3729), Alcorn Co. (1876); Claim of William C. Lewis (on behalf of Ozias Lewis) (no. 13874), Attala Co. (1877); and Claim of John C. Kirk (no. 2743), Bolivar Co. (1871), Southern Claims Commission, Approved Claims, RG 217, Records of the Accounting Officers of the Department of the Treasury, NA. These insights build on the work of Susanna Michelle Lee, *Claiming the Union: Citizenship in the Post–Civil War South* (Cambridge: Cambridge University Press, 2014).

43. Claim of Lorenzo Grant (no. 20631), Pontotoc Co. (1877), Southern Claims Commission, Approved Claims, RG 217, NA.

44. Claim of Henry Banks (no. 14443), Warren Co. (1874), and Claim of Martha Berry (no. 6938), Warren Co. (1871), Southern Claims Commission, Approved Claims, RG 217, NA. On the many dimensions of blacks' claims of loyalty in the commission records, see Lee, *Claiming the Union*, 90–132.

45. A Colored Man, *The Review of the Revolutionary Elements of the Rebellion, and of the Aspect of Reconstruction, With a Plan to Restore Harmony Between the Two Races in the Southern States* (October 1868), 13, 15.

46. Harold M. Hyman, *To Try Men's Souls: Loyalty Tests in American History* (Berkeley: University of California Press, 1960), 263–64.

EPILOGUE

1. *Atlantic Monthly* 18, no. 110 (December 1866): 761–65 (quotes on 761, 764).

2. Cong. Globe, 39th Cong., 1st Sess. 2890–91 (1866).

3. Cong. Globe, 39th Cong., 1st Sess. 2898–99 (1866). On the wording of the Civil Rights Act, see Act of 9 April 1866, ch. 31, *Stat.* 27–30.

4. *New York Tribune*, 21 February 1867. Worries about national reunification and the stability of the republic have been examined by Gregory Downs in "The Mexicanization of American Politics: The United States' Transnational Path from Civil War to Stabilization," *American Historical Review* 117, no. 2 (2012): 387–409.

5. *North American Review* 103, no. 212 (July 1866): 241–50 (quote on 245–46); R. G. Horton, *A Youth's History of the Great Civil War in the United States, from 1861 to 1865* (New York: Van Evrie, Horton and Co., 1867), 309–10.

6. *Atlantic Monthly* 23, no. 135 (January 1869): 124–29 (quote on 125).

7. *Union League Documents* (Morgantown, W.Va., 1904), 17, 19, 22–23, 25.

8. W. F. Simonton to Gov. Powers, Lee Co., Miss., 6 June 1872, folder 2, box 980, ser. 794, Governor Ridgley C. Powers, Correspondence and Papers (1871–1874); C. H. Green to Gov. Ames, Macon, Miss., 22 November 1875, folder 6, box 998; W. M. Connor to Gov. Ames, Macon, Miss., 25 December 1875, folder 10, box 998, ser. 803, Governor Adelbert Ames, Correspondence and Papers (1874–1876), MDAH.

9. For biracial alliances and fusion politics during Reconstruction, see Steven Hahn, *A Nation under Our Feet: Black Political Struggles in the Rural South from Slavery to the Great Migration* (Cambridge, Mass.: Harvard University Press, 2003), 364–411; Annual Report to the Attorney General from the Northern District of Mississippi (1873); J. D. Barton to Col. G. Wells, Lee Co., Miss., 26 February 1873, Source-Chronological File, Northern Mississippi, Jan. 1873–Oct. 1877 (roll 1), Letters Received by the Department of Justice from Mississippi, 1871–1884 (M970), RG 60, General Records of the Dept. of Justice, NA.

10. Thomas R. Knowland to Ames, Warren Co., Miss., 7 October 1875, folder 10, box 997, Ames Correspondence, MDAH; Florence W. Sillers, *History of Bolivar County, Mississippi* (Jackson: Hederman Bros., 1948), 162–63. For the congressional investigation, see *Report of the Select Committee to Inquire into the Mississippi Election of 1875* (Washington, D.C.: GPO, 1876).

index

Citizenship: in creation of Confederacy, 40, 46, 66; early republican ideas about, 4, 9, 13, 14; and gender, 69; historiography on, 5, 179n6; and race, 23–24, 69, 125–26; and secession crisis, 34–35; state versus national definitions of, 15, 16, 25, 29–31; and subjecthood, 17, 19; and suffrage, 20–21, 170; and territorial expansion, 21–23, 24–25. *See also* Obligation; Treason

Claggett, Julia, 159

Claiborne, John, 127–28

Clark, Charles, 1; election of, 58; wartime administration of, 59, 60–61

Clark, J. T. C., 96

Clayton, Alexander, 134

Clayton, John M., 16

Clemens, J. F., 33

Coahoma County, 138

Colonization, American South as, 98–101, 113, 123, 125, 128

Compromise of 1850, 25–26

Confederate Army: desertion from, 80–83, 84; religious observance in, 78–81; religious sacrifice for, 80–82; as "school of citizenship," 66–67, 70–71; socialization in, 76–78. *See also* Courts-martial

Confederate States of America: citizenship in, 65, 68, 70–71; constitution of, 67–68; creation of, 67; historiography of secession, 40, 189n4; historiography of state's formation, 66, 195n3; military mobilization in, 69–70, 71–72; nationalism in, 69. *See also* Citizenship

Confiscation: Confiscation Act (1862), 100–102; slave impressment in Mississippi, 61–62; wartime experience of, 148–49

Connor, Lewis, 158–59

Conscription: in Confederacy, 72–75; in Mississippi, 54

Courts-martial: in Confederacy, 76, 83–84; punishments of African American soldiers in U.S. Army, 110–12; punishments of Confederate soldiers, 83

Cowan, Edgar, 168

Critchfield, John L., 157

Dantzler, Absalom, 42, 44, 45–46

Davis, Eliza, 159

Davis, James, 158

Davis, Jefferson: capture of, 127; and Confederate citizenship, 68; and conscription, 72; decision to accept state troops into Confederate Army, 53; decision to leave Senate, 36–37; views of, 133

Davis, Louis, 103

DeBow, J. D. B., 26

Delay, William, 59

Dillingham, W. A. P., 141

Dodge, Robert, 97

Donaldson, R. S., 160

Douglass, Frederick, 167–68, 170

Dowdell, James, 34

Dred Scott v. Sandford (1857), 29–30

Du Bois, W. E. B., 121

Dwight, William, 112

Dyer, J. M., 45

Eldridge, Stuart, 153

Emancipation: during Civil War, 90–91, 123–24; in early republic, 19; and loyalty, 5; in Mississippi, 7, 38, 102–9, 114–16; and property, 147–52, 154–55, 158–59; views on, 170. *See also* African Americans

Emanuel, Morris, 152–53

Fessenden, Henry, 130

Fitzgerald, Jane, 158

Florida, and secession, 34

Foster, Lafayette S., 92

Fourteenth Amendment, 8, 167–69

Freedmen's Bureau: and apprenticeship, 156–58; relations with African American claimants, 154–55; relations with white claimants, 153–54; white appeals for property, 151–53. *See also* Emancipation

French Revolution, 19

Fugitive Slave Act (1850), 27–28

Furniaful, George, 73